Transformative Visions of Legal Education

Edited by

Anthony Bradney
and
Fiona Cownie

BLACKWELL
Publishers

ISBN 0-631-21137-3

First Published 1998

Published simultaneously as Vol. 25 No. 1 of
Journal of Law and Society ISSN 0263–323X

Blackwell Publishers
108 Cowley Road, Oxford OX4 1JF, UK
and
350 Main Street, Malden, MA 02148, USA.

British Library Cataloguing in Publication Data applied for

Library of Congress Cataloguing in Publication Data applied for

Printed on acid free recycled paper

Typeset by Poole Typesetting (Wessex) Ltd, Bournemouth, Dorset
Printed and bound in Great Britain by Whitstable Litho
Whitstable, Kent

Contents

JOURNAL OF LAW AND SOCIETY
VOLUME 25, NUMBER 1, MARCH 1998
ISSN: 0263–323X, pp. 1–13

Thinking About Law Schools: Rutland Reviewed

WILLIAM TWINING*

Thinking about law schools as institutions requires tools of analysis and the questioning of some common assumptions. This paper applies some of the general ideas in the recent report on Legal Education in Xanadu *to the Faculty of Law at the University of Rutland, with particular reference to institutional goals and functions, clientele, league tables, and who counts as a 'law student'.*

On a recent visit to a respected Commonwealth law school, I asked a group of senior academics: 'What is your staff-student ratio?'[1] They looked a bit abashed. Then one said: 'It is about twenty to one, which is embarrassingly favourable in this country'. I asked how this was calculated. 'Naturally, we divide the total population of LLB students by the number of full-time faculty.' This seemed strange, for the law school aspired to emulate the model of a multi-functional institution that provides a wide range of educational and other services at a variety of levels.[2] About 35 per cent of their teaching was invested in the LLB, another 20 per cent in courses for non-law degrees, and about 45 per cent in 'outreach' programmes, including seminars for judges; continuing legal education for private practitioners,

* *Faculty of Laws, University College London, 4 Endsleigh Gardens, London WC1H 0EG, England*

I wish to thank Tony Bradney, Fiona Cownie, Martin Loughlin, Avrom Sherr, and participants in the Commonwealth Legal Education Association Conference at Kuala Lumpur in September 1997 for helpful comments and suggestions. Responsibility for opinions, errors, heresies is, of course, mine alone.

1 This paper extends the argument in a number of previous writings, especially W. Twining, *Blackstone's Tower: The English Law School* (1994); 'What are Law Schools For?' in W. Twining, *Law in Context: Enlarging a Discipline* (1997) ch. 15; and W. Twining, 'Rethinking Law Schools' (1996) 21 *Law and Social Inquiry* 1007. Although some of the ideas are based on first-hand experience of actual law schools in the United Kingdom, the Commonwealth, and the United States of America, the law schools of Xanadu and Rutland are fictional constructs and any resemblance to any actual institution is incidental.

2 International Legal Center, *Legal Education in a Changing World* (1975) 39, discussed in id. (1994), pp. 51-8.

government lawyers, and local government officials; workshops for law teachers in neighbouring institutions; an access course; a legal literacy programme; and short courses for police, accountants, and social workers. Some, but not all of these activities were included in the school's budget, but in their social organization, their public relations, and their daily discourse only those taking the single-subject honours degree in law counted as their 'students'. Similarly, only full-time salaried teachers counted as 'faculty'.

The steady bureaucratization of universities is bringing to the surface similar disjunctures in such concepts as 'law students' and 'law teachers'. In the United Kingdom, a relatively bureaucratized institution, such as Rutland, may have quite sophisticated notions of 'student load', 'full-time equivalents', and unit costs for accounting purposes, but nuanced or not-so-nuanced deviations in usage in other contexts. For example, in the same institution, the student Law Society is in practice confined to undergraduates; the Alumni Office keeps address lists of graduates, but not holders of diplomas or certificates of attendance; supervising research students has recently been included in 'teaching load', but not involvement in Continuing Professional Development (CPD) or other short courses or a legal awareness programme. Work in the neighbourhood law office is 'voluntary'; seminars for judges and law teachers are unpaid; teaching on the access course is expenses only; external examining attracts a laughable 'honorarium'; but teaching on CPD courses is quite well paid as 'outside work'. The youngest member of staff is typically assigned to 'service teaching' as part of her duties; those whom she teaches count as 'students' for purposes of student load, but they are definitely not 'law students'. As has been noted elsewhere, full-time post-graduates are almost never photographed and are treated as invisible in most other respects until they become alumni.[3] The advent of modularization and distance learning will further muddy the waters. What counts as 'moon-lighting' by full-time staff is ill-defined and generally not regulated in practice, but two extreme cases in the Business School and one in Architecture have recently resulted in litigation. Similar uncertainties apply to the status and duties of part-time staff. 'Who are law students?' and 'What are law teachers?' are questions that deserve attention.

Some conceptual confusions might be quite easily cleared up through rationalization by a trade union, a dean, or other bureaucrats. For purely administrative purposes, it might be sensible to define 'law student' and 'law teacher' differently for different purposes. But most of the difficulties are not semantic; rather they are symptomatic of wider uncertainties about the actual and potential nature and functions of law schools in rapidly changing situations.

From a bureaucratic or managerial point of view, Rutland is only partly 'reconstructed' compared to other institutions. However, its organization is

3 id., p. 72.

a great deal more sophisticated and complex than the increasingly influential 'league tables' of universities and law schools, pioneered by *US News and World Report* in the United States of America and recently adapted in only slightly less crude form by the London *Times*.[4] The United States version is explicitly restricted to full-time JD students and has been severely criticized from a number of points of view.[5] The *Times* tables are relatively new and are in large part based on the findings of the three national assessment exercises dealing with academic audit, teaching, and research. Since we are going to have to live with these comparators, there is a need for a careful appraisal of their assumptions and criteria and the uses that can be made of them.

This symposium recognizes that the time is ripe for a 'rethinking' of law schools. This represents a significant step away from the tradition of talking about legal education mainly in terms of process rather than institutions. A process perspective, however liberal, almost inevitably focuses discussion of legal education onto the early stages of professional formation – as happens with most official committees and reports because of their remit.[6]

Institutional analysis of law schools is no cure-all. First, an institution can be analysed from a variety of standpoints and perspectives: reports on the same law school by a management consultant, a historian, an ethnographer, and a disaffected former student can be unrecognizably different.[7] Second, no institution is an island, although it is often tempting to present it as a 'total institution'.[8] Apart from its history, the 'context' of a university law school typically includes the university of which it is a part, the local environs and community, the national higher and legal education systems, and international legal and academic associations and networks. There are also complex international, historical, political, and ideological dimensions that are not easily captured by rational-bureaucratic analysis. Thirdly, the relationship of individual students and academics to particular institutions is changing. Ironically, just as league tables of academic institutions are becoming more influential, the sense of belonging to a community or team

4 For example, *US News & World Report*, 18 March 1996, at 82–6; *US News & World Report*, 10 March 1997, 76–8; the *Times*, 'Good University Guide', 21 May 1997. Compare 'Those League Tables – what do they mean?' (1995) 29 *The Law Teacher* 213 (editorial discussing an earlier version in the *Times Higher Education Supplement*).

5 Richard Lempert did a brilliant critique of the methodology employed by *US News & World Report* at the Law and Society Conference in Glasgow in July, 1996. It is hoped that a revised version of his paper will be published in due course.

6 Twining, op. cit (1997), n. 1, p. 293.

7 Compare, for example, such different genres as US Law School Visiting Committee reports, official 'house histories' (criticized by A.S. Konefsky and J.H. Schlegel, 'Mirror, Mirror on the Wall: Histories of American Law Schools' (1982) 95 *Harvard Law Rev.* 837); the ethnographic account of Rutland in Twining, op. cit. (1994), n. 1, chs. 4 and 5, and American 'whinge' literature, for example, Scott Turow, *One L* (1977) and Richard D. Kahlenburg, *Broken Contract* (1992). It is reported that a new genre of 'house history', more detached, scholarly and critical, is being planned for several leading United States law schools.

8 Compare E. Goffman, *Asylums* (1961).

is being undermined. For example, most law teachers are specialists, and modern technology facilitates 'networking' in ways that may profoundly alter the balance between an individual's loyalty to her institution and to her specialism.[9]

Despite these caveats, individual law schools are significant units in respect of finance, prestige, culture, student choice, and forward planning. Rethinking law schools as institutions requires some tools of analysis. In *Blackstone's Tower* and some subsequent papers I sketched a series of ideal types as a first step in this direction.[10] I made the case for most English university law schools moving from being essentially undergraduate institutions ambivalently pursuing ambiguous objectives towards a more self-conscious multi-functional model that serves a more varied clientele, while maintaining a balance between educational, scholarly, and social objectives.[11] Subsequently, I used parts of a report on the national system of legal education in Xanadu to develop the approach.[12] The purpose of this paper is to take the process one step further by elaborating some of these ideas and by applying them to the Faculty of Law at the University of Rutland.

As a preliminary, it may be helpful to recap briefly on the general ideas in the Xanadu report. This report is unusual in three ways: first, it looks at the national system of legal education as a whole and at all its recipients. As part of this, it considers the role of law in general culture and intellectual life. Second, it adopts a broad view of legal education, which includes learning about the why, what, and how of legal phenomena, however that learning is acquired. It emphasizes the distinction between informal and formal legal education.[13] It treats the former as the more significant, even though under the latter it includes judicial training, the education and certification of specialists, and what is sometimes patronizingly referred to as 'law for non-lawyers'. Thirdly, the report focuses on institutions as well as processes and includes in those institutions some that are not specialized to law, for example, business schools, secondary schools, institutes of public administration, and non-governmental organizations, such as associations concerned with civil liberties, consumer protection, and the rights of women and children.

9 Twining, op. cit. (1994), n. 1, p. 78.

10 id.

11 Social objectives include service to the local, or a wider community, through legal advice, participating in law reform and pressure group activities, and the critical role of legal academics in serving as a part of the conscience of the legal system and of society. The bureaucratization of universities through such devices as research assessment tends to marginalize their social role.

12 Twining, op. cit (1997), n. 1, pp. 298–301, and op. cit. (1996), n. 1, pp.1012–16.

13 Informal' education in this context includes matters learned from first-hand experience (for example, getting married, being arrested, negotiating a loan, entering into a contract), from newspapers, television, novels, and other popular media, first-hand observation, bar-room conversation, and gossip. Institutionalized apprenticeship, however casual, organized work experience, public lectures, law in schools, moot competitions, and continuing professional development are treated in the report as 'formal'.

Naturally, 'mainstream' or 'traditional' legal education and training is given due attention, but it is considered within the context of a total picture of needs and demands for learning about law by a more varied clientele and at a number of levels. Similarly, a great deal of attention is paid to specialized law schools, but as part of a broader picture of other legal educational provision. As institutions dedicated to the advancement, stimulation, and dissemination of learning about law, they have a key role to play in the national system as a whole. This is particularly the case where, as in Xanadu, the Law Faculty of the University is the national law school or, as in Bangalore, a model law school has been set up specifically to upgrade legal education in the country as a whole.[14]

The Xanadu report begins by articulating some speculative general hypotheses that might apply to any national system of legal education:

> In (almost) all societies
> (i) almost everyone receives some legal education;
> (ii) that process lasts from cradle to grave;
> (iii) the amount of informal legal education (i.e. outside educational programmes) greatly exceeds the amount of formal legal education, even for career lawyers;[15]
> (iv) actual and potential demand for formal legal education almost invariably exceeds the supply;
> (v) most formal legal education is delivered by institutions other than law schools;
> (vi) within most countries, specialized institutions called law schools can be quite varied. For example, they vary within and between countries in respect of: wealth; size; manifest and latent functions; prestige and influence; the age, class and gender of students, faculty and other staff; academic standards; conceptions of scholarship; and even architecture;[16]
> (vii) the culture of law schools is to some extent international within legal traditions or families, but it is also much influenced by local historical, economic, ideological and other factors, including the structure and financing of higher education, distributions of power and authority, and the nature of the legal system and the legal profession.

In respect of the role of university law schools, the report challenged a number of entrenched ideas inherited from the traditional culture of the common law. These include the following widespread assumptions:

> (i) that all university law schools have the same mission and should be judged by identical criteria. Like football clubs, they compete with each other in a single hierarchy of prestige (the football league model);
> (ii) that the core of that mission is primary legal education and that the term 'law student' refers only to someone taking a first degree in law (the primary school image);[17]
> (iii) that the main priority need for legal education is basic education and training for intending and newly qualified private practitioners of law, even in contexts where the absorptive capacity of the legal profession exceeds the supply of new lawyers and most

14 Report of Review Panel on the *National Law School of India University in Bangalore* (1996).
15 Above, n. 13 .
16 See, further, Twining, op. cit (1994), n. 1, pp. 51–2.
17 In so far as much of 'the vocational stage' is concerned with introducing practical skills and knowledge in an elementary way it is also arguably 'primary', even though it represents the second stage of professional formation. Similar considerations apply to conversion courses. The main distinction of substance is between elementary and advanced study.

law graduates start their careers in the public service or non-legal work (the private practitioner image);
(iv) that the supply of entrants to the legal profession can be artificially controlled by manpower planning, the pass rate in the bar examination, apprenticeship requirements, or other restrictive practices (the numbers game);[18]
(v) that providing legal educational services for other clients is beneath the dignity of university law schools and that this is reflected in treating such teaching as 'outside work' and in the derogatory use of such terms as 'service teaching', 'law for non-lawyers', and (mainly in the United States) 'legal studies' and 'pre-law courses' (the professional snob syndrome);
(vi) that law is by its nature one of the cheapest subjects in higher education (the cheap subject fallacy).[19]

RUTLAND REVIEWED

In 1997, the Faculty of Law at Rutland, decided to review the Faculty's strategic plan in the light of the general ideas in the Xanadu report. The immediate context of this review included several developments at national and local levels. The Lord Chancellor's Advisory Committee on Legal Education and Conduct (ACLEC) had produced its first and second reports on legal education, dealing with the academic stage and CPD respectively.[20] Shortly after a new Labour Government took office, the Dearing committee published the first comprehensive report on higher education since the Robbins report of 1963.[21] In the past three years, the University of Rutland had struggled on in a situation of ever-increasing financial stringency. The Faculty of Law had resisted pressures to increase its undergraduate intake, mainly on grounds of the size of its main lecture theatre, but it had slightly expanded its postgraduate programme. During this period the collective efforts of the Faculty had been somewhat frenetically focused on improving their Research Assessment Exercise (RAE) rating, but it had again been disappointed to be graded 3aB in the 1996 exercise; it nevertheless had been rated 'excellent' for teaching since 1993–94. During the same period there were other noteworthy developments: for example: the National Centre for Legal Education at Warwick had been established, Le Brun and Johnstone's *The Quiet (R)evolution* had been published,[22] and the Open University had

18 Twining, op. cit. (1997), n. 1, pp. 249–53.

19 The case against this assumption was made, with only limited success, in Heads of University Law Schools, *Law as an academic discipline* (1983).

20 ACLEC, *First Report on Legal Education and Training* (1996); *Continuing Professional Development for Barristers and Solicitors: A Second Report on Legal Education and Training* (1997).

21 *Higher Education* (the Robbins report) (1963; Cmnd. 2154); *Higher Education in the Learning Society* (the Dearing report) (1997).

22 M. Le Brun and R. Johnstone, *The Quiet (R)evolution* (1994) is a substantial monograph applying modern educational theory to the practice of law teaching. It is discussed in W. Twining, 'Bureaucratic Rationalism and The Quiet (R)evolution' (1997) 8 *Legal Education Rev.* 291.

joined with the College of Law in planning a new distance-learning undergraduate degree in law. This was the backdrop to the 1997 review.

In 1994 it had been reported that:

> Rutland is in process of transition without very clear ideas about how to cope with a rapidly changing situation. In recent years it has started to diversify its teaching and other activities, but with no definite sense of direction. To some extent its practice has outrun its self-image as essentially an undergraduate institution. It has not committed itself wholeheartedly either to being mainly a professional school, involved at all levels in professional formation and development, nor to diversifying its activities along the lines of the I.L.C. model. Almost all non-degree teaching and other outside activities are done on an individual rather than an institutional basis. At undergraduate level, so long as the faculty is too ambivalent and divided to provide a clear lead and messages from the profession are ambiguous, it seems that a narrow and probably deluded set of vocational attitudes is likely to continue to dominate student culture and to condemn the institution to be and to be treated as little more than a mediocre nursery school for the profession.[23]

Not much has changed since that rather depressing judgement. Stimulated in part by the ACLEC report and lowered expectations about opportunities to qualify as a barrister or solicitor, the prospects for gaining credibility for the LLB as providing a liberal education have improved. The RAE result, combined with some changes in personnel, prompted a thoroughgoing review of all the activities of the faculty in a climate which at least recognized that there was a need for change.

THE NATIONAL AND INTERNATIONAL CONTEXT

The goals and priorities of a law school need to be set in the context of its overall mission, the national system of legal education, and specific conditions and trends at local, regional, national, and international levels. Legal Education in Xanadu provides a very general framework for locating a particular institution or programme in the context of a national system of legal education. The review accepted that all of the initial hypotheses could plausibly be applied to England, except that in respect of (vi) there are no reliable figures about the amount of formal legal education that takes place outside law schools in other institutions.[24] The scene in England and Wales has been characterized as diversity in respect of institutions, pluralism in respect of educational ideas and methods, fragmentation of stages of professional formation, relative diffusion of power, rapid expansion in a period of financial stringency, and continuous, but less rapid, change at a variety of levels.[25]

23 Twining, op. cit. (1994), n. 1, pp. 84–5.

24 It is also unclear whether some or all commercial law tutors should count as 'law schools' for this purpose.

25 Twining, op. cit. (1994), n. 1, ch. 2; ACLEC, op. cit. (1996), n. 20, ch. 1.

Rutland is one small part of an extremely complex system. If it is correct that the demand for formal legal education exceeds the supply, this provides Rutland and like places with an opportunity to choose between particular kinds of clientele and by spotting gaps in national provision to establish a 'niche' in respect of one or two areas.[26] However, Rutland is a relatively small law school in a middle-sized university and there are considerable limitations on the scale and range of activities that it can sensibly undertake on its own. Almost all developments will in practice have to be self-financing. The range of activities can be increased somewhat through collaboration with other institutions – for example, through pooling resources to achieve 'critical mass' in respect of CPD, other outreach programmes, or even undergraduate modules.[27]

Given the range of potential demand, it is in theory not necessary for a university law school to be involved in undergraduate legal education at all,[28] but that would almost certainly be too sharp a break with tradition for places like Rutland. It would also probably be financially risky in the present climate. The multi-functional New York International Legal Center (ILC) model does not mandate the abandonment of primary legal education, but merely suggests diversification upwards and outwards. In Rutland's case, a move towards allocating about 60 per cent of its teaching resources to non-undergraduate teaching is the most that can sensibly be expected.

THE XANADU 'FALLACIES'

More interesting are the assumptions underlying orthodox discourse about legal education. Some of these appear to apply more clearly to the United States of America than to England and Wales. The United States is almost unique in the world in not subscribing to the idea that law is inherently a cheap discipline (vi);[29] in England law is officially treated along with politics

26 To think in such terms does not involve a commitment to the kind of commercialization of education satirized in Frank Partkin's *The Mind and Body Shop* (1987) on which see J.H. Schlegel, 'Talkin' Dirty' (1996) 21 *Law and Social Inquiry* 981, at 989, fn. 13. Rather, it suggests that an institution like Rutland should build up special expertise in a few areas and develop a distinctive persona, based on such factors as a clear ethos, traditional and current strengths in the university and the faculty, geographical location, established links, and so on.

27 Such co-operation need not be restricted to other university law schools or departments in the same university nor, for certain purposes, to institutions in the same locality.

28 This situation has almost been achieved at certain points in history by the Inns of Court School of Law and the College of Law. However, both have in practice been involved in primary legal education in respect of Part I of the Bar and Law Society Examinations and, in the case of the College of Law, with conversion courses for non-law graduates. In 1997 the College of Law announced that it was moving into undergraduate legal education in co-operation with the Open University.

29 But see R. Stevens, *Law School* (1983) at 268–9, 282–3.

as having the lowest unit costs. American discourse about legal education seems to be particularly susceptible to the football league model (i); the primary school image (ii); the private practitioner image (iii); and the professional snob syndrome (v). These are facets of a version of the primary professional school in a system in which most university law schools have hardly been involved in specialization or postgraduate studies and only spasmodically in continuing legal education.

In England all of these are matters of almost systematic ambiguity. I have argued that English law schools are in process of moving away from the primary school model (ii), although our practice still outruns our discourse, for example in respect of who count as 'students'. The proclaimed ideology of nearly all undergraduate law degrees is that they are providing a general, even a liberal, education at the academic stage which is a good preparation for many different kinds of career. This suggests a distancing from the private practitioner image (iii). In practice fewer than 60 to 70 per cent try to qualify and many fewer pursue a career in legal practice. The percentage may be declining. However, as at Rutland, student culture has tended to be more vocationally oriented than either the official line or the job market warrants.[30] As in the United States of America, artificial attempts to limit the numbers of people embarking on law degrees or qualifying have usually been rejected; however, our formal apprenticeship systems for barristers and solicitors serve as a bottleneck which both limits numbers and facilitates institutionalized discrimination.[31] It seems that English university law schools are less prone to 'the professional snob' syndrome, but law teachers in both countries are often accused by students and practitioners of intellectual snobbery.[32]

The football league analogy (i) is less straightforward. On the one hand, there are clearly some hierarchies: for example, the dominance of Oxbridge, the 'binary divide' between universities and polytechnics (which has unfortunately been accentuated since its formal abolition), and the recent introduction of external quality assessment in respect of academic audit, research, and teaching. On the other hand, the system of external examining, especially

30 Twining, op. cit. (1994), n. 1, at pp. 73–6, 83–5.

31 D. Halpern, *Entry into the Legal Profession; The Law Student Cohort Study 1 and 2* (1994); M. Shiner and T. Newborn, *Entry into the Legal Profession: Cohort Study 3* (*Law Society Research Study 18*) (1996).

32 Tony Bradney comments: 'Perhaps some in Rutland still worry about charges of intellectual snobbery but others worry about how little law schools have contributed to the intellectual history of either the United Kingdom or the United States and think that intellectual snobbery, which might be seen as pride in the value of matters of intellect, as appropriate to the university as a house of intellect. What they worry about is the fact that law schools have too little to be snobbish about' (letter to the author, 11 September 1997). This raises complex issues about the marginalization of law in general culture (a central theme of *Blackstone's Tower*), the contribution of law to intellectual life (on which see Twining, op. cit. (1997), n. 1, ch. 17), and a tendency among academic lawyers to treat concern with 'skills' or clinical education as anti-intellectual (on which see Twining, id., ch. 9).

during the Council for National Academic Awards (CNAA) era, was intended to sustain a notional 'parity of esteem' about academic standards – how far it does so is a matter of controversy.[33] Largely centralized public funding has a tendency to produce homogenization, yet there has been a genuine diversification of law schools in respect of both function and style. Further, perhaps because we live in a compact country, institutional affiliation is rather less important in career development: there is a good deal of lateral movement, even out of Oxbridge and between institutions that are thought to be approximately equal;[34] and the new systems of peer review purport to assess quality in terms of each institution's own goals and to include post-graduate courses. However, some of the bureaucratic pressures associated with external evaluation have stimulated a moral panic and have threatened to drive universities in the direction of an emerging unregulated transfer system that might set a bad example to footballers. Whether that leads to further homogenization or to other kinds of diversification remains to be seen.

At Rutland most of the Xanadu 'fallacies' have been part of the ways of thought of many students and at least some academics, not all of whom would accept that they are fallacies. At least they have belatedly become the subject of open debate. It is worth looking briefly at Rutland's response to one of them: The Football League Syndrome.

Rutland has a dilemma in respect of league tables. On the one hand, like it or not, the law school will be rated and compared with other university law schools according to externally determined criteria. If it plays the game wholeheartedly, it nevertheless has to accept that the most it can hope for is that, like Coventry City, it will have a continuous and anxious struggle to stay in the Premier League; or, less ambitiously, like Oxford United, it can cruise in the middle reaches of the euphemistically named 'First Division', occasionally hitting the headlines with a good run in the Observer Mooting Competition or public recognition of a rising star who will almost certainly be transferred to a more prestigious club. One cost of such a strategy is to marginalize some things that Rutland does well, but for which it gets no points, such as increasing educational opportunity, serving the local community and legal profession in various ways, and involvement in law reform and pressure group activities.[35] An alternative strategy is to take down the goalposts that others move so frequently and so arbitrarily and to opt out of the competition by presenting itself as a different kind of institution, like a general sports club that contributes to the health, entertainment, and cohesiveness of the local community while registering only occasional successes in a variety of national sporting competitions.

33 The Dearing report recommended a thorough overhaul and strengthening of the external examiner system (rec. 49).

34 P.S. Atiyah and R.S. Summers, *Form and Substance in Anglo-American Law* (1987) at 386–7.

35 See above, n. 11.

Not surprisingly, Rutland decided to compromise on this and other issues. After lengthy debate they managed to reach agreement on a mission statement that was both in harmony with the University's avowed mission 'to advance, stimulate and disseminate learning' and which was broadly in accord with the underlying ideas of *Legal Education in Xanadu.* The following extracts from the executive summary of the report of the Review Committee illustrate one attempt to apply the Xanadu perspective to a particular middle-ranking English law school:

The Football League syndrome : The Law Faculty should:

- maintain a balance between educational, scholarly and social functions;
- continue to aim for excellence in teaching;
- prepare carefully for academic audit;
- aim for a 4B in the next RAE;[36]
- where 'football league' criteria threaten to skew the Faculty's objectives or give a false impression, counteract the effect of that in public relations and recruitment;
- campaign for flexible criteria for national ratings that recognise the diversity of missions and activities of university law schools and that do not penalise or marginalise such policies as liberal admissions or the social and critical functions of law schools;
- review the orientation and balance of the undergraduate programme (see below).

Moving away from the primary school model

The aim of Rutland is to move from being mainly a professionally oriented undergraduate primary school towards becoming a multi-functional institution that contributes to legal education at a number of levels. This will be done over a period of time. In the next 3–5 years the Faculty should:

- increase the postgraduate programme to approximately 30% of student load
- extend the outreach programme to represent approximately 30% of student load
- diversify offerings at undergraduate level (see below)
- in view of Rutland's resources and provision elsewhere, discontinue involvement in the vocational stage for barristers and solicitors, but consider possible contributions to (a) other kinds of vocational training; (b) continuing professional development (see below);

36 The RAE users' guide, *Playing the System* (3rd ed.,1997), includes the following rules of thumb: diagnose what went wrong last time and confront remediable defects; strengthen the research culture of the institution in respect of faculty seminars, research leave, specialist groups, and so on; strengthen the research element in the postgraduate programme; accord parity of esteem to teaching, research, and other institutional activities; do not try to make all members of faculty research-active, but ensure that all faculty are accountable as much for their research plans and performance as they are for their other duties; recruit, encourage, and give real institutional support to outstanding researchers; plan the faculty's research strategy over an eight year (two rounds) cycle, especially in respect of younger colleagues; gear recruitment to the research strategy as well as to the educational programme; build on strengths in three or four areas in which the faculty can hope to build an international or at least a good national reputation; try to harmonize faculty research interests with teaching at all levels.

- aim to make the postgraduate programme and the 'outreach' programme, considered as units, self-financing;[37]
- give priority to an advanced programme of research and teaching in at least two areas, such as Law and Medicine (or Science) and Law and Communications or Law and History;
- adjust the content and organization of postgraduate offerings to fit the needs and situation of local part-time candidates;[38]
- review the Ph.D. programme;[39]
- recognize that involvement in access courses, legal literacy, or law in schools may be best done through teacher training colleges and other institutions rather than through direct provision. The Faculty of Law may have a constructive role to play in helping to design, accrediting, evaluating, or advising or in targeted activities such as 'training trainers';[40]
- offer short courses on teaching civil liberties and other particular topics in schools in collaboration with the Faculty of Education and the Rutland College of Higher Education.

Undergraduate teaching

- maintain and possibly increase total undergraduate numbers;
- reduce the LLB intake, but try to increase the proportion of LLB and joint honours students taking four years over their first degree;
- review LLB admissions criteria to ensure, as far as is feasible, that (a) the target of a minimum of 20% mature students is maintained; (b) those admitted accept the objectives and ethos of the LLB; (c) the criteria are not biased directly or indirectly in respect of gender, class, or ethnic origin;[41]
- reduce the number of required courses in the LLB and tailor the programme to individual needs of overseas students;[42]
- introduce an element of structured choice into the LLB curriculum, including requiring all LLB candidates to do one advanced option and one 'foreign law' option as part of their degree;
- increase involvement in integrated inter-disciplinary programmes and options offered at undergraduate level;[43]

37 Rutland's strategy involves a significant move away from dependency on public funding and the vagaries of government policy. Such semi-privatization creates dilemmas for institutions that are largely dependent on fee-income, but are committed to policies of enhancing educational opportunity. This is an area in which the experience of American universities, especially 'private' institutions, in providing financial support for students is, at the very least, suggestive. This is too large a topic to pursue here.

38 W. Twining, 'Postgraduate Legal Studies' in *Reviewing Legal Education*, ed. P. Birks (1994) 98.

39 For criticism of Rutland's past practice, see id. at pp. 99–100.

40 In *Legal Education in Xanadu* it is stated: 'Police training or judicial seminars may best be done mainly by police and judges respectively ("judges should teach judges how to judge, but legal educators can teach judicial trainers how to teach")'. Whether this applies to England is an open question.

41 A current concern at Rutland is the class bias of A-level performance. See, generally, Twining, op. cit. (1997), n. 1, ch. 13.

42 For example, even if local students are required to take English Land Law, this should not be compulsory for students from other jurisdictions. Of course, overseas students wishing to qualify in England may opt to take such courses for exemption purposes.

43 This is in line with the Dearing report's call for broader degrees, but runs counter to the pressures of RAE criteria and league tables, which may have the effect of discouraging inter-disciplinary co-operation.

- design and implement an attractive and coherent foundation course on 'Introduction to Law' open to the whole university. This should be self-standing, it should serve as a pre-requisite for most/nearly/all other law modules, and it should involve the best teachers;
- increase the range of modular options, including packages of options, offered to the rest of the university;
- develop expertise in presenting legal topics and materials to 'non-lawyers' at all levels.

The 'private practitioner image'
In view of Rutland's move towards the ILC model, it will be necessary to redefine the Law School's relations to the private practice of law. However, the multi-functional ILC model is entirely consistent with strong involvement with the legal profession and vocational training in appropriate areas, judged by resources and needs.

The Faculty should:

- re-emphasise that the LLB aims to provide a liberal education in law with a strong emphasis on transferable intellectual skills that will be relevant to a variety of occupations, including most kinds of private practice of law;[44]
- ensure that LLB students, and some others taking modular degrees, will have the opportunity but will not be required to satisfy the requirements of a 'recognised degree' for purposes of exemption;
- provide Rutland graduates who have not completed all the requirements with an opportunity to take up to two 'add-ons' after graduation in order to qualify for exemption;
- develop, in collaboration with two or three other parts of the university, other institutions and with relevant professional bodies, a continuing professional development programme that meets some identified local needs and concerns and that includes advanced work at a high level of excellence in a few areas that may have national standing;
- recognise that the CPD programme need not be confined to barristers and solicitors in private practice, but could include others involved in legal work or other occupations.

These extracts are merely illustrative of a particular perspective. The full report deals with a number of other topics, including finance, staffing, and faculty governance. Of these finance is crucially important, but the Xanadu perspective suggests that semi-privatized law schools may have more control over their own destinies than they had in the past, especially in areas where demand for formal legal education exceeds the supply. As with similar institutions, consensus was not easily or fully achieved, even within the framework of an apparent agreement about objectives in the mission statement. Rutland is not exactly a radical institution and its internal review represents a relatively quiet evolutionary adjustment to a different model of university law schools in a changing situation. Next time you visit Rutland, look at the photographs in Denning House: maybe they have radically redefined their conception of a law student.

44 On Rutland's shift to an emphasis on intellectual skills, see W. Twining, 'Intellectual Skills at the Academic Stage: Twelve Theses' in *Examining the Law Syllabus: Beyond the Core*, ed. P. Birks (1993) 93–5.

JOURNAL OF LAW AND SOCIETY
VOLUME 25, NUMBER 1, MARCH 1998
ISSN: 0263–323X, pp. 14–32

The Political Economy of Canadian Legal Education

H.W. ARTHURS*

The political economy of Canadian legal education is characterized by conflicts over resources, values, and interests. These conflicts manifest themselves in divergences between faculty and students over issues of law school governance and politics, in the sometimes incompatible demands placed upon law schools by the legal profession and the university, in the intramural politics of class, race, and gender, and in rivalry among competing bodies of legal knowledge. Most importantly, the New Economy is reshaping legal education because the restructuring of Canada's society, economy, and polity is undermining the position and power of both the universities and the profession.

INTRODUCTION AND HISTORICAL BACKGROUND

The central premise of this essay is that legal education is lodged in a political economy whose contending forces shape universities, the legal profession and, of course, the encompassing society, economy, culture, and polity. Hence, legal education is not an autonomous regime capable of defining and redefining itself from within, in response to national reports, the prescriptions of professional bodies, decanal visions or even the initiatives of a reformist professoriate – though all of these make their contribution.

A brief glance at the history of Canadian legal education reinforces the point – or would if there were such a history to be glanced at.[1] Alas, the definitive history of Canadian legal education has yet to be written; nor given the decentralized nature of Canada, is it ever likely to be. Education,

* *Osgoode Hall Law School, York University, 4700 Keele St., Toronto, Canada M3J 1P3*

I should like to express my thanks to Raziel Zisman for his able research assistance.

1 Indeed, there was not much history written about anything legal in Canada until the 1970s and 1980s, other than a few legal-historical works by judges of an antiquarian bent, see, for example, W. Riddell, *The Bar and the Courts of the Province of Upper Canada, or Ontario* (1928).

the administration of justice, and the regulation of professional bodies are matters within the constitutional competence of provinces, not the national government. The centrifugal force of the constitution reinforces, and is reinforced by, Canada's bisystemic and bilingual character, its demography, and its geography. Differing rates of political, economic, professional, and educational development in each province, and the effect of local circumstances and personalities in what were often relatively small and new communities also helped to ensure that each law school followed a somewhat different path of development. Thus, there is no such thing as a history of Canadian legal education, strictly speaking – only a history of legal education in Quebec, Nova Scotia or Manitoba.

On the other hand, certain common themes seem to recur. First, legal education in Canada's provinces comprised a succession of missed opportunities and noble failures.[2] Second, the profession exercised overt control over legal education in some provinces, and acted more subtly in others; but its influence was pretty much dominant until well after the Second World War. Third, during this period, the Canadian legal academic community remained tiny – a few full-time academics in each faculty, less than fifty across the country by 1950, barely one hundred by 1960. And finally, its collective scholarly output was lamentably meagre and mostly pedestrian.[3]

These themes converge in the dramatic and well-documented controversy surrounding Osgoode Hall Law School in Ontario. Founded, after several false starts, in 1889 with the aspiration of becoming 'the Harvard of the North' (another recurring theme: the influence of the United States of America), it soon became the largest common law school in the country. But it was not a distinguished institution: it was ruled with a heavy hand by the Benchers of the Law Society of Upper Canada,[4] operated as a *doppelganger* to a system of articling (apprenticeship), had low admissions standards, was retrograde in its curriculum, and lacked sufficient faculty, classrooms, and library facilities. In 1949, the law school's tiny staff of determined and able full-time academics sought to establish its control over curriculum and teaching methods. These academic pretensions were derided

2 See, for example, B. Baker, 'Legal Education in Upper Canada 1785-1889: The Law Society as Educator' in *Essays in the History of Canadian Law*, ed. D. Flaherty (1983); J. McLaren, 'The History of Legal Education in Common Law Canada' in *Legal Education in Canada*, eds. R. Matas and D. McCawley (1987); W. Pue, 'Common Law Legal Education in Canada's Age of Soap, Light and Water' (1996) 23 *Manitoba Law J.* 654; D. Howes, 'The Origin and Demise of Legal Education in Quebec (Or Hercules Bound)' (1989) 38 *University of New Brunswick Law J.* 127.

3 M. Cohen, 'The Condition of Legal Education in Canada' (1950) 28 *Cdn. Bar Rev.* 267; F. Scott (chair), 'Report of the Committee on Legal Research' (1956) 34 *Cdn. Bar Rev.* 999.

4 Ontario was known as Upper Canada prior to Confederation in 1867; the Law Society continues to use its pre-Confederation name. See C. Moore, *The Law Society of Upper Canada and Ontario's Lawyers, 1797-1997* (1997).

5 B. Bucknell, T. Baldwin, and D. Lakin, ' Pedants, Practitioners and Prophets: Legal

by the conservative governing body; their initiative was rebuffed; and they resigned *en masse* to join the School of Law of the nearby University of Toronto, which did not confer professional credentials. From this vantage point, they relentlessly attacked their former school and its proprietors; by 1958, they had succeeded in breaking the Law Society's monopoly over legal education in the province.[5]

The immediate consequence of this success was a proliferation of university law schools in Ontario, the largest province, and ultimately, in 1968, the Law Society's transfer of Osgoode Hall Law School to a more conventional and congenial setting at York University.[6] These developments were to have critical consequences well beyond Ontario. The fact that Canada's largest and most influential legal profession had significantly modified its claims to dictate legal curriculum and pedagogy constituted a precedent of some importance in other provinces whose professional governing bodies continued to exercise *de facto* or *de jure* control. The proliferation of law schools in Ontario and across Canada, and significant curriculum reform at the reconstructed Osgoode Hall Law School and elsewhere, produced a dramatic swelling of faculty ranks and – for the first time in Canada's history – something like a critical mass of legal academics.

The timing of these events was crucial. The decade from the late 1950s through to the late 1960s was a transformative moment for Canada, for higher education generally, for law, and for legal education and scholarship. During this period, at the height of a prolonged post-war boom fuelled by immigration and foreign investment, Canada rapidly urbanized and shook off the last vestiges of its colonial past. Quebec's 'quiet revolution', Ontario's industrial expansion, the growth of resource-based industries in western Canada, and other projects of social and economic modernization proceeded in tandem with the growth of a welfare state and of state-supported cultural institutions and industries. Universities were part of this project of modernization, and expanded rapidly to provide not only highly skilled personnel for the new economy and state structures, but also the intellectual and institutional underpinnings of an unprecedented attempt to define Canadian, provincial, and community identities.[7] The legal profession also experienced enormous growth and affluence, benefiting from economic expansion, the rise of the interventionist state, and a new sense of the possibilities and responsibilities of legal practice. And finally law itself began

5 B. Bucknell, T. Baldwin, and D. Lakin, 'Pedants, Practitioners and Prophets: Legal Education at Osgoode Hall to 1957' (1968) 6 *Osgoode Hall Law J.* 137; C. Kyer and J. Bickenbach, *The Fiercest Debate: Cecil A. Wright, The Benchers, and Legal Education in Ontario 1923-1957* (1987).

6 H. Arthurs, 'Osgoode Hall Law School of York University' (1967) 17 *University of Toronto Law J.* 194.

7 *To Know Ourselves – Report of the Commission on Canadian Studies* (the Symons report) (1974).

to change: beginning in the 1960s, many Canadian jurisdictions introduced legal aid programmes, established law reform and human rights commissions, reformed the governance of the legal profession, and began to think seriously about civil liberties, welfare rights, and environmental law.

These dramatic transformations in the economic, social, and cultural life of the country, in the role of law and the legal profession, and in Canadian academic institutions, left their mark on law faculties. A new generation of legal academics with graduate degrees, training in the social sciences, and activist ambitions soon outnumbered the small cadre of black-letter scholars and part-time practitioners which had dominated most law schools. New pedagogies, curriculums, and research priorities were introduced. Law professors began to busy themselves inside and outside academe with a wide range of both critical and constructive projects of research and reform. Their new status and influence were symbolized by a coincidence which would have been unthinkable a few years earlier: in 1973 the Prime Minister, Minister of Justice, and Chief Justice of Canada were all former law professors.

These developments seemed to presage a revolution in Canadian legal education and scholarship. However, as things turned out, that revolution was less ambitious and successful than might have been predicted. This was the conclusion, at least, of *Law* and *Learning*, a comprehensive 1983 report on Canadian legal research and education.[8] That report, and its accompanying research studies, concluded that in the heady atmosphere of the 1960s, law schools had launched themselves on the project of 'offering a legal education that is humane and professional, rather than narrowly vocational' by combining three elements: 'learning legal rules . . . ; learning legal skills; [and] developing a humane perspective on law, and a deeper understanding of law as a social phenomenon and an intellectual discipline'.[9] However, the fact that these elements were '. . . arranged in no fixed proportion or sequence . . . within an eclectic, optional curriculum' resulted in serious under-achievement:

> The basic problem of legal education is that it espouses a broad range of goals and has opted for no specific structure to achieve any of them. As a result, professional formation – undoubtedly the primary objective of Canadian law schools – is neither as effectively professional nor as broad and humane as it aspires to be. Scholarly or intellectual legal study is diluted and marginalized by the predominance of professional concerns.[10]

8 Consultative Group on Research and Education in Law, *Law and Learning* (1983). The study was co-sponsored by the Social Sciences and Humanities Research Council of Canada, the Committee of Canadian Law Deans, and the Association of Canadian Law Teachers. I was chair of the Consultative Group and principal author of its report.

9 id., p. 47.

10 id., p. 153.

To overcome this problem, the report recommended a strategy of 'genuine pluralism' in law schools, based on a 'clear and explicit statement' of objectives:

> Law faculties should substitute for their present eclectic curriculums a series of clearly defined alternatives based on intellectual insights, social goals, pedagogic strategies, or professional specialties . . . Among the alternatives offered should be clearly defined scholarly programs leading to a first degree in law . . .[11]

This latter recommendation, for a specifically scholarly education in law, reflects the central conviction of *Law and Learning*:

> . . . [Scholarly] studies cannot be expected to develop while they are a peripheral interest of students and faculty members who are chiefly preoccupied with preparation for professional practice. As long as the scholarly study of law does not develop, the quantity and quality of legal scholarship are unlikely to improve significantly . . . The intellectual training and career circumstances of legal researchers have not helped to give shape and direction to legal research . . .[12]

Given the strategic priority attached to the intellectual dimension of legal education, the report made a number of recommendations designed to ensure the better preparation of legal intellectuals, and to improve the quality, quantity, and diversity of legal scholarship. These changes, it was hoped, would not only protect the minority of students with specific intellectual goals and career objectives but would also, in the end, benefit the majority who were intending practitioners.

The post-history of *Law and Learning* is instructive. It was received with modest enthusiasm in Canada, although rather more abroad.[13] No law faculty actually privileged or protected students with intellectual interests. And while the Canadian law teachers now produce more fundamental and interdisciplinary research, and while graduate programmes in law have expanded and research centres have proliferated, it is by no means clear that *Law and Learning* was the proximate cause of such changes. At most, the report identified, legitimated, reinforced, and accelerated changes which were largely attributable to the transformation of Canadian society especially through the 1960s. However, as that transformation ran its course and as counter-influences developed, the momentum of reform in legal education slowed, and its future direction became contested.

This brings us to a crucial weakness of *Law and Learning*, a weakness it shares with most reports on legal education. It recorded and analysed the recent history of Canadian legal education with reasonable accuracy. It offered a plausible critique of existing structures and strategies. But it did not adequately investigate the political economy which had produced those

11 id., p. 154.
12 id., pp. 153-4.
13 J. Schlegel, 'Law and Learning' (1984) *Stanford Law Rev.* 1517.

structures and strategies, and consequently did not accurately anticipate future developments.[14] This essay is an attempt – fifteen years on – to address issues which *Law and Learning* left largely unexamined.

GOVERNANCE AND POLITICS: FACULTY AND STUDENTS

Prior to the 1960s, as noted, legal education was dominated by the profession in at least three senses. It was largely education *by* the profession: given the small number of full-time legal academics, much (sometimes most) instruction was offered by practising lawyers. To some extent, it was education *in* the profession: in all provinces, articling remained a strong component of the process of professional formation; in several – notoriously Ontario – only graduates of the profession's own law school could be admitted to practise; and almost everywhere, the profession played a formal or informal role in the governance of the local law school. And with some honourable exceptions, it was largely education *for* the profession: even the most spectacular upheaval of the period, the Osgoode Hall crisis of 1949, was prompted by a dispute over whether academics or the Bar knew best how to educate future practitioners.

Thus, until the 1960s, there was little occasion to be concerned about the internal governance of legal education. But occasion soon arose. In law schools, as elsewhere in the university and in society generally, the 1960s were a moment of upheaval. Traditional values and the institutions through which they were conveyed were under attack. By the end of the decade, the profession's role in society, its recruitment policies, its culture and governance had become matters of vigorous debate, especially in the law schools which were – how odd it now seems! – mapped as commanding heights whose seizure would transform the legal system and all of its emanations, if not society in general. One characteristic passion of the period, especially in Canada, was the democratization of universities and their faculties, initially by giving the professoriate the dominant voice in academic decision making, and subsequently by extending participation rights to students, even in such important matters as curriculum and faculty appointments.[15] Closely linked to this development was the release of students from institutionalized constraints such as structured curricula and inflexible, authoritarian forms of pedagogy and academic evaluation. These reforms appealed not only to students, but also to young faculty members who believed that students would use their new-found freedom wisely, in ways which supported their own reformist aspirations.

14 H. Glasbeek and R. Hasson, 'Some Reflections on Legal Education' (1987) 50 *Modern Law Rev.* 777 had prophesied as much.

15 *University Governance in Canada* (the Duff-Berdahl report) (1966).

Those aspirations were in part procedural, in the sense that young professors wished to operate free of professional requirements,[16] the professional ethos of law faculties, or the authority of deans and senior professors. However, the aspirations were substantive as well. The professoriate sought to undermine the very basis of professional monopoly and power: its distinctive forms of knowledge. Despite occasional flirtations with philosophy and political science as early as the nineteenth century,[17] Canadian legal education and scholarship had never really experienced the equivalent of the American realist revolution. This is hardly surprising, given the paucity of revolutionaries and their precarious perch in professionally-dominated law schools. The new, self-confident academics saw themselves as agents of change. They wanted to use the social sciences to overthrow the profession's intellectual orthodoxy, the positivist school of black-letter law, and to redefine the mission of law schools. That mission, they contended, was not merely to replicate the profession, but to transform it; and not merely to transform it but to develop new empirical and critical perspectives on law, the legal system, and the profession; and not merely to develop these new perspectives but to share them with present and future policy makers, scholars, administrators, and informed citizens in all walks of life. The movement to democratize the governance of law schools, then, was part of a larger project of transforming law as an intellectual discipline, as a profession, and as a technique of social ordering.

However, these two motivations – democratization for its own sake, and as part of a larger transformative strategy – diverged. This divergence largely shaped law school politics of the period. Students – even many who considered themselves politically and intellectually radical – tended to see themselves as legal practitioners, albeit with new ideals and in the service of a new clientele. Consequently, they wanted law schools to equip them with the skills and knowledge necessary to achieve their professional objectives. Some law schools were able to accommodate this demand by establishing legal clinics, which combined skills training and social activism with a strong intellectual component. However, such programmes did not satisfy the new legal *intelligentsia* which wanted to reconceptualize law in both a systemic

16 While each provincial Law Society is free to determine which students qualify for admission as a result of having completed an 'approved' LLB course, the requirements of the Law Society of Upper Canada have national salience because so many students ultimately gravitate to Ontario. Its requirements are minimal: law schools must offer three years of full-time instruction comprising seven compulsory courses (real and personal property, contracts, torts, criminal law, civil procedure, constitutional law) and twenty-five additional courses which must be offered 'regularly' to students 'on a required or an optional basis' in the discretion of the 'academic planning authority' of each law school. Law schools must have at least five full-time staff; their recommended maximum teaching load is six hours per week; and library facilities must be 'adequate'.

17 R.St.J. Macdonald, 'Maximilien Bibaud, 1823-1887: The Pioneer Teacher of International Law in Canada' (1988) 11 *Dalhousie Law J.* 721; D. Stanley, ' Richard Chapman Weldon 1849-1925 – Fact, Fiction and Enigma' (1989) 12 *Dalhousie Law J.* 539.

and substantive sense, a daunting task – as *Law and Learning* suggested – for which most of its members were not well prepared.

Within the political economy of law schools, this conflict took the form of contestations over the allocation of resources. Faculty time and energy devoted to research was not devoted to teaching, community education or public advocacy – activities which students tended to value highly. When the first, admittedly meagre, fruits of critical scholarship began to ripen in the classroom, as sociology, history, and politics displaced legal doctrine, as more and more faculty members introduced new interdisciplinary offerings, students made their displeasure clear. They voted against these innovations in faculty council debates, ignored them when selecting optional courses, and if enrolled, passively resisted them by not taking them seriously. Likewise, students often favoured the appointment of new faculty recruits with apparent promise as teachers and mentors rather than those who displayed the most impressive intellectual credentials.

In sum, students tended to be a political drag on the intellectual revolution in Canadian law faculties. While eager to gain the democratic right to decide things for themselves, they were not much inclined to exercise this right to explore the foundations and frontiers of law. And to anticipate a point which will be made later, when the idealism of the 1960s was ultimately replaced by neo-conservatism and market discipline in the 1980s and 1990s, students began to reconceptualize themselves as consumers, with consumers' motivations and consumers' rights.

THE POLITICS OF BORDERLANDS: THE PROFESSION AND THE UNIVERSITY

Legal education is not *terra nullius* – territory unclaimed by any legitimate power. On the contrary: as *Law and Learning* insisted, it is located in the borderlands between two powerful suzerains, the higher education sector and the legal profession. Each of these, to be sure, is less a single state than a congeries of interests, ideologies, and institutions. None the less, when either asserts its claims, legal education becomes contested terrain.

If the profession – the governing body, the major law firms, the bar association, the alumni – becomes convinced that law schools should concern themselves with technical competence, moral tutelage, or the deployment of their graduates elsewhere than in private practice, law schools are likely to respond by increasing the number, length or content of 'core' courses (deemed, with no good reason save history, indispensable for the practice of law) and of specialized or advanced courses with obvious professional salience or a skills-training component, by reducing theoretical and interdisciplinary seminars and support for social activism, and by introducing counselling programmes designed to shift law graduates to other career options.

If, on the other hand, universities – the education ministry, senior academic administrators, the Senate – insist that law professors conform to university- or system-wide expectations of scholarly productivity, meet high standards of pedagogic competence, and perform their fair share of university service, a different set of institutional adjustments will likely occur. These may include rewards and incentives for faculty members who win grants and publish prolifically, better support for research centres, greater investment in teaching technology, pedagogic training, and the systematic assessment of teaching, or more law professors 'volunteering' for university committees.

Of course, pressures from the profession and the university only rarely arrive in the form of explicit prescriptions or even clearly articulated requests. What the profession wants from law schools it can generally secure by subtle signals: after all, most students and some faculty members identify with the profession's aspirations and interests, self-image, and world-view. If a governing body ruminates on the increase of malpractice claims involving young practitioners, if it becomes common knowledge that litigators are undertaking more alternative dispute resolution, if the Attorney-General announces a reform of family property legislation, it is entirely predictable that someone will propose or demand that law schools should alter their curricula or teaching methods accordingly. Indeed, members of the faculty with relevant interest or expertise will themselves frequently initiate proposals for change which they justify on the basis of a new public or professional 'need', reinforced by the suggestion that if the law school does not rise to the occasion, it is likely to face professional intervention. Far from resisting such initiatives as unworthy of an educational institution, students tend to support them, imagining that in doing so they are improving their own marketability and professional competence.

Similarly, law schools seldom receive explicit instructions from university authorities. Rather, they wish to appear to be responsive to general university policies. The reason is simple: if they fail to adhere to standards for promotion and tenure, their new recruits will not pass muster; if they fail to recruit international students, their budgets may be cut; but if they can respond to policies in a distinctive 'professional' mode, they can continue to do pretty much as they please. However, margins for deviation may be diminishing. Pressed to ensure greater accountability to government and 'consumers', universities are subjecting all units – including law schools – to periodic quality reviews, requiring them to produce standard data to support large-scale academic planning processes, and helping them to meet the criteria which drive such exercises.[18] And here again influences are often

18 *Maclean's Magazine*, which ranks the undergraduate programmes of Canadian universities, introduced a 'league table' of law schools in 1997.

more subtle. As many law professors come to share credentials, intellectual interests, and socializing experiences with other academics, they are likely to seek to reproduce prevailing teaching techniques, intellectual and political agendas, and academic cultures within law faculties.

Legal education, then, remains subject to influences emanating both from the profession and from the university. Although these influences seldom take the form of explicit directions, law schools respond to them in part to avoid negative consequences, in part to gain institutional advantages, but in part because internal constituencies align themselves opportunistically with or against the profession or the university. Thus, the internal political dynamic of Canadian law schools is often destabilized by the competing visions of legal education of its 'suzerains'.

Of course, destabilization is not inevitable: some versions of the academic enterprise are more acceptable to the profession than others; some universities are willing, even eager, that their law schools should be held in high repute by the Bar, an affluent and influential sector of the community; some law schools manage to achieve at least the appearance of a balance between the divergent perspectives and their respective adherents. But in the end, the two visions are different: at any given moment, they do not project equal power and influence, and whichever is ascendant in a particular law school will shape its teaching programme and intellectual ethos.

THE POLITICS OF CLASS, RACE, AND GENDER

In the proto-revolutionary atmosphere of the 1960s, Canadian law schools became – were forced to become – aware of two linked paradoxes: although the legal profession's claim to its monopoly rested in part on its defence of equality before the law, the profession itself was not itself an exemplar of egalitarian virtue; and although within the profession, academic voices were amongst the loudest advocates of the egalitarian principle, the academy had also failed to ensure equal access to legal education – and legal practice – regardless of race, gender or class.

Responses were not long in coming. Articles began to document and denounce the Bar's failures and those of legal academe as well.[19] Law schools established community clinics to take up the challenge of delivering legal services to the disadvantaged, and of training lawyers for careers as their advocates.[20] Courses on the rights of the poor, consumers, women, and racial

19 See, for example, H. Arthurs, L. Taman, J. Williams, 'The Toronto Legal Profession: An Exploratory Survey' (1971) 21 *University of Toronto Law J.* 498; L. Dranoff, 'Women as Lawyers in Toronto' (1972) 10 *Osgoode Hall Law J.* 177.

20 N. Gold, 'Legal Education, Law and Justice: The Clinical Experience' (1979) 44 *Saskatoon Law Rev.* 97; M.J. Mossman, 'Community Legal Clinics in Ontario' (1983) 3 *Windsor Yearbook of Access to Justice* 375.

minorities effloresced modestly (or not so modestly, in the view of conservative lawyers).[21] One new law school made an explicit and controversial commitment to popular and democratic education in law.[22] Mandated by an unexpectedly liberal Law Society report,[23] Ontario law faculties began to admit mature students, including many individuals who had been prevented by socio-economic disadvantages from pursuing normal pre-law studies. New federal funding assisted law schools in seeking out and admitting aboriginal students, especially graduates of a 'head start' programme at the University of Saskatchewan, and to educate common-law Francophone students outside Quebec in their own language.[24]

However, the great changes in the population of Canadian law faculties – and thus ultimately of the profession – were less the result of internal programmatic initiatives than of demography and a general increase in higher education participation rates. Post-war immigration to Canada gradually produced greater ethnic diversity first in undergraduate programmes, then in law schools, and ultimately in the profession.[25] Women, who were on the way to comprising more than half of the undergraduate population in arts faculties, began to appear in increasing numbers in law schools. By 1993 they comprised 48 per cent of the population of Canadian law schools and 27 per cent of the legal profession. With some time delays, and after some controversy, women began to take their place in the legal academy: by 1993, 28 per cent of Canadian law teachers were women, and as of 1996-97, eight of the twenty-one serving deans of Canadian law schools were women.[26]

This is by no means to say that by the 1990s, the democratization of entry into law schools was complete, or that the egalitarian principle had been fully accepted and implemented by the legal profession. As recent research attests, barriers to women and to racial and ethno-religious groups still remain in many professional settings.[27] And race and class apparently continue to stunt the ambitions and prejudice the life chances of poor people

21 H. Arthurs, 'Progress and Professionalism: The Canadian Legal Profession in Transition' in *Law and Social Change*, ed. J. Ziegel (1972).

22 R. Bureau and C. Jobin, '*Les Sciences Juridiques à l'Université du Québec à Montréal*: Fifteen Years Later' (1987) 11 *Dalhousie Law J.* 295.

23 *Report of the Special Committee on Legal Education* (the MacKinnon report) (1972).

24 R. Thompson, 'The University of Saskatchewan Native Law Centre' (1988) 11 *Dalhousie Law J.* 712. M. Bastarache, 'Teaching the Common Law in the French Language' (1983) 7 *Dalhousie Law J.* 348.

25 D. Stager with H. Arthurs, *Lawyers in Canada* (1990) at 143; J. Hagan, M. Huxter, P. Parker, 'Class Structure and Legal Practice: Inequality and Mobility Among Toronto Lawyers' (1988) 22 *Law and Society Rev.* 9.

26 *Touchstones for Change: Equality, Diversity and Accountability* (the Wilson report) (1993).

27 J. Hagan and F. Kay, 'Changing Opportunities for Partnership for Men and Women Lawyers During the Transformation of the Modern Law Firm' (1994) 32 *Osgoode Hall Law J.* 413.

and blacks who remain under-represented in tertiary education generally, and likely even more so in law schools and the legal profession.[28]

Moreover, the innate egalitarianism and moral fervour of Canadian law schools should not be overstated: to a large extent reformist and egalitarian initiatives were fuelled by the highly publicized American civil rights revolution of the 1950s and 1960s. In particular, the American experience inspired the adoption in 1982 of the Canadian Charter of Rights and Freedoms, and the Charter in turn transformed legal discourse and juridified politics.[29] Law schools have responded predictably: courses on constitutional law shifted their focus from federalism to Charter rights; new courses on civil and personal liberties proliferated; Charter themes appeared prominently in courses such as criminal law and administrative law; and legal journals sometimes seem concerned with little else.[30] More to the point for present purposes, the definition and implementation of equality rights has become a central theme in the political economy of law faculties. Faculty members and students from equality-seeking groups and their sympathetic colleagues – women, gays, blacks, first nations, the disabled – have not only demanded access to legal education and to law teaching jobs; they have sought protection of their dignity and sensibilities within law schools through institutional guarantees and administrative structures; they have claimed recognition of their distinctive perspectives on law in the form of special courses and scholarly initiatives; and they have done all of this using not merely the conventional polite and impolite tactics of academic politics, but if needs be, the occasional threat of litigation as well.[31]

Much remains to be done; some institutions have changed less than others; but noticeable progress has been achieved mostly by means of strategies which were less formal and legally-based (and hopefully less vulnerable to

28 B. Mazer and M. Peeris, *Access to Legal Education in Canada: Databook 1990; Report of the Special Committee of the Law Society of Upper Canada on Equity in Legal Education and Practice* (1991); A. Timoll, *Black Access to the Legal Profession: The Timoll Report to the Black Law Students Association and the Attorney General for Ontario* (1996). However, the Wilson report, op. cit., n. 26, indicates that visible minority students in a sampling of law schools comprise 12 per cent of the graduating class as opposed to 6 per cent of Canada's overall population; for aboriginal students, the figures are 2 per cent as opposed to 2.3 per cent.

29 See, for example, D. Beatty, *Talking Heads and the Supremes: The Canadian Production of Constitutional Review* (1990); M. Mandel, *The Charter of Rights and the Legalization of Politics in Canada* (1994); A. Hutchinson, *Waiting for Coraf: A Critique of Law and Rights* (1995).

30 In the first edition of P.W. Hogg, *Constitutional Law of Canada* (1977), the leading Canadian text, section III covering materials on civil liberties took up 7 per cent; by the time of the fourth edition (1996), section III, covering materials on civil liberties and Charter issues, accounts for 41 per cent.

31 The broad sweep of these claims is captured in R. Devlin, 'Towards An/Other Legal Education: Some Critical and Tentative Proposals to Confront the Racism of Modern Legal Education' (1989) 38 *University of New Brunswick Law J.* 89; see also Wilson, op. cit., n. 27.

reversal) than those adopted in the United States of America. On the other hand, progress has not been cost-free: law schools have faced choices – explicit and tacit, real and imagined – between egalitarianism and meritocracy; the ensuing controversies have sometimes ruptured faculty-student and collegial relations; and sometimes the compromises adopted have been inauthentic, unsuccessful or morally untenable. And the cost of progress is likely to go up: choices are harder and harder to make in a law school economy of dwindling resources and in a labour market characterized by intense competition for scarce academic and professional jobs

THE POLITICS OF KNOWLEDGE

Reference has already been made to the early, not wholly successful, attempts at interdisciplinary scholarship and teaching in Canadian law schools in the 1960s, to the role of *Law and Learning* in helping to consolidate and legitimate this development in the early 1980s, and to the subsequent momentum which has developed. In the early stages, interdisciplinarity consisted largely of attempts to provide a brief historical, sociological, economic or political background context for the discussion of conventional legal issues; over time, law professors actually tried their hand at historiography, empirical research or philosophy, though not always confidently or competently; and recently, law professors with advanced degrees in the humanities and social sciences have begun to produce interdisciplinary work of a higher standard.

The 'normalization' of law within the constellation of university disciplines obviously enriches the intellectual experience and contribution of Canadian law professors. However, it is also the source of considerable conflict. Law professors who prefer to continue to teach and write in the classic black-letter tradition sometimes resent and disparage their more adventurous colleagues; deans who feel pressure to staff 'core' courses or to respond to professional expectations of conventional scholarship, sometimes fail to support interdisciplinary initiatives; scholars in other disciplines do not always appreciate encroachments by their neighbours; and interdisciplinary scholars alienated by unsympathetic students, colleagues or administrators – and by the intrinsic difficulty of their task[32] – sometimes become disillusioned and resentful. Nor does a shared commitment to interdisciplinarity necessarily create bonds amongst colleagues. In law, as in other disciplines, adherents of positivist social science, critical studies, econometrics, feminist, gay, and black studies, and postmodernism are often at war with each other and amongst themselves.[33]

But most importantly, interdisciplinarity represents – and to some extent

32 L. Salter and A. Hearn, *Outside the Lines – Issues in Interdisciplinary Research* (1997).
33 R. Macdonald, 'Office Politics' (1990) 40 *University of Toronto Law J.* 419.

is intended to represent – a challenge to the very foundation of the Bar's wealth and power: professional knowledge. True, by allocating resources to teaching and research in specific fields previously ignored by practitioners, law schools helped to 'invent' new fields of professional practice, such as labour law, immigration and refugee law, family law, and civil liberties. But the academy's epistemic divergence from the Bar has itself engendered misunderstanding and mistrust, not least because interdisciplinary research has helped to diminish the influence and market value of conventional professional knowledge in automobile accident litigation, tax and regulatory regimes, patterns of judicial recruitment, and elsewhere.

Thus, the academy's role in rearranging the market for legal services has exacerbated resentment caused by the growing asymmetry between what lawyers and academics know about law and perceive as the essential elements of legal education and legal practise. Since divergences in professional knowledge have also become an important factor in the specialization, diversification, and stratification of the Bar – deepening existing fault lines of gender, class, and ethnicity, and confounding attempts to maintain professional solidarity and the institutions of professional governance[34] – the academy's development and dissemination of 'new knowledge' is rightly perceived by the Bar as a divisive and threatening influence.

However, once again, Canadian law faculties should not be awarded undue credit for intellectual innovation: much – not all – of what has transpired in legal-intellectual circles is derived from, or in reaction to, familiar developments in the United States of America. As will be suggested below, American influence pervades Canadian social, political, and, especially, economic life. But law represents a special case even as compared with other policy disciplines which have similarly experienced 'globalization of the mind'.[35] The sheer size, virtuosity, variety, reputation, generosity, productivity, and power of the great American law schools has made them a 'finishing school' for a high proportion of Canadian law teachers, especially those from English-speaking provinces, and American academic literature – in particular, specialized and interdisciplinary publications – comprises a large part of the literature available to Canadian scholars.[36]

The dominance of Canadian law schools by American legal-academic culture, American social science, and American intellectual and political agendas more generally has by no means been entirely negative. Canada has borrowed (and sometimes improved upon) American legislation in areas such as collective bargaining, securities regulation, human rights,

34 H. Arthurs, 'A Lot of Knowledge is a Dangerous Thing: Will the Legal Profession Survive the Knowledge Explosion?' (1995) 18 *Dalhousie Law J.* 295 .

35 H. Arthurs, 'Globalization of the Mind: Canadian Elites and the Restructuring of Legal Fields' (1998) *Cdn. J. of Law and Society* (forthcoming).

36 The *Canadian Journal of Law and Society* first appeared in 1986, twenty years after its United States counterpart, and there is still no Canadian equivalent of the *Journal of Legal Education*, published by the Association of American Law Schools, or of most of the specialist scholarly publications in law and adjacent disciplines which appear in the United States.

environmental protection, and freedom of information. Emancipatory movements in Canada, which tend to draw strong support in law faculties, were often inspired by, and linked to, American movements. And Canadian scholars were able to exert increasing influence on law reform bodies, the Supreme Court and the practising Bar thanks in part to the reassuring example provided by their American counterparts. But all that said, the United States of America has a different history, different political institutions and values, different economic and social problems, a different sense of its own destiny as a hegemonic power. If Canadian legal scholarship is excessively influenced by American sources and strategies, if Canadian academics, practitioners, judges, and students act as carriers of American ideas and discourse, what is distinctive about Canadian institutions may be diminished, and Canada's integration into a continental legal regime, dominated by the United States of America, may become irreversible.

LAW SCHOOLS IN CANADA'S NEW POLITICAL ECONOMY

Most western, industrialized countries have been experiencing the combined effects of globalization, technological change, and the retreat from the welfare state. Canada is no exception. However, its encounters with the 'new economy' have been exacerbated by certain low-intensity but long-standing Canadian crises: America's physical proximity, massive direct investment, and increasing cultural hegemony; the resulting paucity of home-based entrepreneurs and investors, relative to Canada's size and GNP; the modesty of its social democratic programmes, even at their height; and the centrifugal effects of Quebec nationalism, western regional alienation, and their respective constitutional perspectives and politics.[37] Both of legal education's two powerful suzerains – the legal profession and the higher education sector – are being transformed by these developments.

Higher education first. Almost all Canadian universities are public institutions. However, government grants have been moving down an increasingly steep gradient; students are having to pay higher fees (though still very modest compared to American private universities); and greater reliance on corporate donations, contracts, and 'partnerships' is being encouraged, even required, as a matter of government policy.[38] These developments are the direct result of the neo-conservative agenda of reducing taxes, public expenditure, and the size of government, which seems to prevail

37 I have canvassed some of these ideas in a series of articles: 'Labour Law without the State?' (1996) 46 *University of Toronto Law J.* 1; '"Mechanical Arts and Merchandise": Canadian Public Administration in the New Economy' (1997) 42 *McGill Law J.* 29; Arthurs, op. cit., n. 35.

38 Between 1981-82 and 1995-96, the share of university revenues attributable to government grants declined from 72.6 per cent to 61.1 per cent; student fees rose from 9.6 per cent to 16.8 per cent: donations and bequests rose from 4.6 per cent to 7.9 per cent; and sales of services and products also rose from 7.1 per cent to 8.7 per cent. Centre for Education Statistics, *Statistics Canada*, reported in K. Unland, 'Inflation Outpaces University Revenues' *Globe and Mail*, 6 August 1997, A6.

in greater or lesser degree in most Canadian governments, regardless of their ostensible ideology. Potentially more dangerous to universities, though not yet dominant, is an anti-élite, anti-intellectual populism which is likely to express itself in demands to reduce funding for 'academic' activities in general and for research in particular, in the abolition of tenure and research leaves, in increased teaching loads, in enhanced transparency and attacks on traditional institutional autonomy, and in the ruthless translation of students into empowered 'customers' or 'consumers' of higher education, with economic and possibly legal power to force institutions to respond to their wishes. Universities are responding as best they can, but the predictable results of these pressures are already beginning to become clear.

Within their universities, law faculties find themselves in a somewhat ambiguous position. Because they were not yet firmly established during the expansionary period of the 1960s, law schools tended to receive inadequate per capita grants for teaching. Because they have only begun fairly recently to take scholarship seriously – especially interdisciplinary scholarship – they generally do not attract large research grants. On the other hand, law schools have been experiencing rapidly rising unit costs: pedagogic innovations such as clinical legal education and student research assignments are labour intensive; new, specialized periodicals subscriptions strain library budgets; computing costs rise exponentially as new research technologies and administrative systems are brought on stream. And finally, because they tend to be small faculties, still often regarded as marginal by larger and better-established parts of the university, law schools have limited capacity to influence the increasingly strident debates over internal resource allocation.

On the other hand, law schools do have certain advantages. Despite a decline from the peak application years of the 1970s, most of them have so far been able to sustain both the size and quality of their enrolments. Because of their connection with the profession, they have been able to attract at least some financial support, though this may dwindle as the profession itself experiences serious dislocations. In response to policies which promote privatization and self-advancement, law faculties and the legal professoriate are sometimes able to find remunerative work – professional training for practitioners in the one case, consulting and private practice in the other. And because they have always been run 'on the cheap', law schools are able to adjust to their declining fortunes somewhat more easily than historically privileged faculties.

The future of the legal profession is more complicated, but no more optimistic. The globalization of production and financial markets, the advent of hemispheric free trade and the enlarged technical capacity for remote control of corporate functions appear to have intensified the consolidation of authority at the head offices of American-based transnational corporations.[39] This consolidation in turn has resulted in narrower mandates

39 H. Arthurs, 'The Hollowing out of Corporate Canada?' in *Navigating through Globalizations: The Challenge to Institutions*, eds. J. Jenson and B. Santos (tentative title, forthcoming, 1998).

and diminished autonomy for their Canadian subsidiaries, in some cases the end of the Canadian company as a separate legal entity, increased resort to global rather than local capital markets, and the removal of various high value-added service functions from Canadian regional offices to the head offices of the parent firm. And of course, because service providers who support the work of Canadian subsidiaries are likely to feel the knock-on effects, Canada's leading metropolitan law firms may well be confronting the loss of their most important corporate clientele. Nor are they likely to recoup this loss by seeking business abroad, given the paucity of Canadian-based transnational companies on whose coat-tails to ride. Nor can they easily shift to an increased emphasis on regulatory law, given the considerable deregulation wrought by neo-conservative governments, or to litigation, given the notorious reluctance of sensible businesses to litigate and the inability of ordinary citizens to do so, phenomena which are verified by the exponential growth of alternative dispute resolution – itself an expanding area of practice, but not one which lies within the legal profession's monopoly. If they wish to continue to serve their present clientele in an increasingly globalized and deregulated economy, the most optimistic option for Canada's élite law firms is to seek integration either into foreign-based transnational law firms or into multi-disciplinary practices built around a small number of large consulting and accounting firms.

Prospects for other lawyers are equally daunting. Niche law firms and mid-sized partnerships will continue to provide legal services to small and middling businesses, no doubt, but the destiny of such businesses is to be absorbed into larger companies represented by other law firms. Collections and conveyancing – the staple services provided by solo practitioners and small law firms to working- and middle-class individuals – may well pass into the hands of computerized, franchised 'storefront' providers, as seems to be happening in the United States of America, or be made superfluous by legal reforms which enable people to do for themselves.[40] And legal practices based on criminal law, family law, and immigration and refugee law have been badly eroded by radical cuts in legal aid funding.

Moreover, these developments coincide with a particularly unpropitious historical moment. Lawyers, like other professionals and persons in authority, are being stripped of formal prerogatives and of the deference and respect they traditionally enjoyed; they are being held to higher levels of expertise, accountability, and cost effectiveness; and they are therefore being forced to make greater investments in their own training, in technical systems for delivering and monitoring client services and in insurance and professional regulatory machinery. At the same time, and for many of the same reasons, divisive tendencies have undermined formal and informal

40 These developments are traced in somewhat more detail in H. Arthurs, 'Lawyering in Canada in the 21st Century' (1996) 15 *Windsor Yearbook of Access to Justice* 202.

processes of professional governance and made it difficult to rally professional constituencies to any common cause or culture.[41] And finally, given the extent of stratification within the legal profession, in large measure along socio-economic and ethnic lines, it is all too likely than that the negative consequences of all of these developments will – as always – come to rest first and most heavily on those who are most vulnerable, women lawyers and those from disadvantaged communities.[42]

If this is any thing like an accurate account of the near-future of the Canadian legal profession, it is clear that its political economy will change rapidly. The prestigious corporate firms will be unable to sustain their incomes, recruitment patterns, quality of practice, influence within the profession, and perhaps their very existence as independent entities. The medium sized firms and many specialists in the private and public sectors will be hard hit, though they may possibly find the means to adapt to the new situation. And the yeomanry of the profession – solo practitioners and small firms – will find themselves reduced to employment in the dark satanic mills of mass-production, franchised legal service providers, or be driven out of practice altogether.

The consequences for legal education are fairly predictable. Legal professions may well attempt to limit entry, by means licit and illicit; governments may decide to save money by closing law schools or reducing their intake; universities are likely to lack either the will or the resources to resist; some legal academics may become redundant; some law graduates may face unemployment or underemployment. But even if none of this were to actually happen, the new economy provides a hostile environment for both law professors and their students. Quite understandably, students have become very nervous about their future job prospects. Most try to make themselves more marketable by using their recently acquired power as 'consumers' to insist on courses, syllabuses, and pedagogies which, in their perception, reinforce their survival skills. As a corollary they are increasingly impatient, as a group, with 'humane professionalism', the ethos of Canadian law schools since the 1960s, and they increasingly exercise their right to avoid 'purely academic' offerings.[43] And this brings them into direct conflict with their already beleaguered professors, who confront heavier work loads, more rigorous performance measures, declining financial prospects – and now, it seems likely, intellectual frustration.

How will law schools respond to this crisis of shrinking resources? Essentially they have only three options: to charge their students more; to seek new sources of revenue, especially from the profession; and to reduce

41 H. Arthurs, 'The Dead Parrot: Does Professional Self-Regulation Exhibit Vital Signs?' (1995) *University of Alberta Law Rev.* 800.

42 See Hagan et al., op. cit., n. 25; J. Hagan and F. Kay, *Gender in Practice: A Study of Lawyers' Lives* (1995).

43 *Law and Learning*, op. cit., n. 8, at pp. 47 ff.

and impoverish their programmes. None of these is particularly attractive. Increased charges to students will threaten accessibility to legal education and practice, and reverse the trend to democratization of the profession. If the profession itself is suffering economically, it will be difficult for law schools to secure donations from law firms, or to enrol lawyers in profit-generating programmes such as continuing legal education. And if law schools are forced to reduce their programmes, the first casualties are likely to be those perceived to be costly or peripheral to their educational mission or both: small interdisciplinary courses, graduate studies and research – the very initiatives mandated by *Law and Learning*.

CONCLUSION

The purpose of this essay has been less to persuade readers of impending doom – though doom may indeed impend – than to open up new and broader perspectives on legal education. Canadian law schools are addressing multiple crises and contestations. These have their origins not in the usual contrariness of university communities, nor in the recent and ongoing revolution of legal pedagogy and research, nor even in the ambiguous relations of legal academe with the practising bar. For the most part, they are outcroppings of the larger and deeper crises of Canada's troubled political economy. Thus, Canadian law professors confront an awful choice. Since they cannot do much about the real source of their discontents, should they focus scarce talents and energies on sustaining law schools as long as possible, by all expedient means including pandering to students and the profession, until better times arrive? Or should they commit their critical skills and intellectual talents to efforts to alter the larger political economy, despite the absence of institutions, processes and constructive strategies through which legal academics and other citizens can work for a brighter future?

JOURNAL OF LAW AND SOCIETY
VOLUME 25, NUMBER 1, MARCH 1998
ISSN: 0263–323X, pp. 33–50

'Failed Sociologists' in the Market Place: Law Schools in Australia

CHRISTINE PARKER* AND ANDREW GOLDSMITH**

This paper traces the stunted evolution of Australian law faculties from 'trade schools' to liberal law schools. Higher education funding cuts and increased accountability to a government that is throwing the universities onto the competition of the market now combine with the traditional influence of a conservative profession to put Australian law schools in a precarious position. We argue that Australian law schools should transform themselves by embracing the contradictory position they inhabit, and using it to develop a broader concept of the legal knowledge they pass on and the legal practice for which they prepare their students.

INTRODUCTION

In the late 1990s Australian law schools occupy a precarious position between profession, state, and market. Publicly-funded for much of their history, they are currently in the grip of diminishing grants while simultaneously being subjected to heightened regulatory demands. Increased student contributions to the cost of education (contributions which line government, not faculty or even university, coffers) are matched by a rise in student consumer consciousness. Law schools, already in an ideological and professional bind over their allegiances between academy and profession, seem fixed in reactive mode (perhaps understandably) rather than engaged in trying to re-negotiate the terms on which legal education is offered. For the most part they continue to demonstrate a commitment to producing graduates geared for practice in a profession which, to date, has lent modest support to legal educational objectives in the face of external challenges. In this essay we will review the current situation, and suggest that Australian law schools must explore a different model of legal education, based upon a transformative notion of legal knowledge and legal practice, if they are to overcome their current malaise.

* *Law Faculty, University of New South Wales, Sydney NSW 2052, Australia*
** *Legal Studies, School of Cultural Studies, GPO Box 2100, Adelaide 5001, Australia*

The Australian legal profession enjoyed a degree of self-regulation and market control unrivalled among the professions between 1900 and 1970.[1] Its autonomy was made perfect in its strategic control of professional university education affording it a monopoly on the definition of legal knowledge and expertise as well as on the supply of legal practitioners.[2] From their beginnings Australian law schools readily submitted to professional control and influence. Six university law faculties opened between 1857 and 1936, one in each state capital. These schools competed with apprenticeship to become the major mode of entry to the profession,[3] and 'were generally viewed as adjuncts to the legal profession, rather than truly academic institutions dedicated to liberal educational aims'.[4] Until the 1960s there were few full-time academic staff members and teaching was a part-time activity of practitioners. 'Trade school' mentality flourished, aided by the fact that profession-dominated councils of legal education and professional admission boards enabled a high degree of influence over the content of the LLB. The degrees granted by the universities were accepted as a qualification to practise in their own right (apart from the completion of a period of articles of clerkship). The substance of the law degree was therefore firmly under the guardianship of the judiciary and private practising profession. The recent history of Australian law schools can be partially understood as a story of separation from the practising profession, escape from the trade school mentality, and concomitant entanglement with the state, the market, and the university.

The opportunity for academic lawyers to differentiate themselves from the practising profession was provided by the state's expansive higher education policies of the 1960s and, even more so, the 1980s. The first major state intervention into legal education was the federal government's 1964 Martin report which found that an over-self-regulated profession was not producing the 'volume and form' of lawyers necessary for national economic growth including the needs of corporate practice and the rapidly expanding welfare state.[5] The Martin report recommended that the state ought to culturally re-engineer the profession through a publicly-funded expansion of places and of subjects studied in the law schools. At the same time a general federal

1 See J. Disney, P. Redmond, J. Basten, and S. Ross, *Lawyers* (1986) 27–46.

2 M. Larson, *The Rise of Professionalism* (1977) 48.

3 In the most populous state of New South Wales (NSW) apprenticeship remained the major mode of entry to the profession until 1968: D. Weisbrot, *Australian Lawyers* (1990) 72.

4 M. Chesterman and D. Weisbrot, 'Legal Scholarship in Australia' (1987) 50 *Modern Law Rev.* 709, at 711; See also N. Stephen, 'Once and Future Law Schools' (1992) 1 *Griffith Law Rev. 10.*

5 *Report on the Future of Tertiary Education in Australia to the Australian Universities Commission* (1964) (the Martin report). See J. Lancaster, *The Modernisation of Legal Education: A Critique of the Martin, Bowen and Pearce Reports* (1993) 23.

government expansion of the higher education sector was already beginning.[6] Between 1960 and 1975 the number of law schools doubled from the original six to twelve with 'second-wave' law schools being established with federal funds at the Australian National University (1961), Monash University (1964), the University of New South Wales (1971), and Macquarie University, Queensland Institute of Technology, and New South Wales Institute of Technology (all 1975).[7] The number of undergraduate law students expanded from 4,075 in 1965 to 8,000 in 1975 to over 11,000 by 1981.[8]

These developments placed the law schools firmly within the university and created the conditions for the development of a law school culture different to and critical of practising lawyers and legal institutions. Yet, as Lancaster argues, while the Martin report and later, the New South Wales Bowen report, sought to expand and systematize legal education to produce lawyers to meet 'community needs', in fact they both concentrated purely on producing lawyers to serve national economic development.[9] This continued to leave legal education open to the influence of a narrow vocationalism. There were an 'absence of recommendations addressing the civic dimensions of law', a failure most notably illustrated in the Bowen report's refusal to address the implications for legal education of government research revealing the massive problems the poor faced in gaining the services of lawyers.[10] The contradictions of government and university policy regarding legal education have become more evident as time has passed.

The Pearce report, a discipline assessment of legal education released in 1987, criticized Australian law schools for neglecting the 'critical and theoretical' dimensions of law required for a flourishing intellectual academic legal culture and an understanding of what role law and lawyers should play in society.[11] However it too contradicted itself by seeing the legal curriculum as predicated solely upon satisfying professional admission requirements.[12] The critical and theoretical dimensions of legal education would have to remain conditioned by the higher demands of a vocationalism defined by the practising profession and business consumers of legal services.

The Pearce report was released shortly before a further expansion of Australian higher education. Total enrolments in higher education grew by

6 In 1959 the development of the Australian Universities Commission heralded the beginning of the federal government's dominance of higher education policy (prior to that it had been primarily a state issue), and a concomitant rise in funding: Lancaster, id., p. 31.

7 id., p. 33.

8 C. Parker, 'An Oversupply of Law Graduates? Putting the Statistics in Context' (1993) 4 *Legal Education Rev*. 255, at 262.

9 *Legal Education in NSW: Report of the Committee of Inquiry* (1975) (the Bowen report).

10 Lancaster, op. cit., n. 5, p. 40. See also M. Cass and R. Sackville, *Legal Needs of the Poor: Commission of Inquiry into Poverty: Law and Poverty Series* (1975).

11 D. Pearce, E. Campbell, D. Harding, and Commonwealth Tertiary Education Commission, *Australian Law Schools: A Discipline Assessment for the CTEC* (1987) (the Pearce report).

12 Lancaster, op. cit., n. 5, p. 53.

42.1 per cent in the five years between 1987 and 1992 from 393,734 to 559,365:[13] '[T]he rate of growth in student load in law exceeded the rate of growth in all other fields of study by a margin of more than ten percent.'[14] More generous government funding policies meant that universities could decide for themselves which new schools or departments to open without having to seek special-purpose capital funding from the government. By 1995 there were twenty-six law schools and almost 20,000 undergraduate students.[15] By the start of 1997 there were twenty-nine law schools and 20,558 LLB (or full-time equivalent) students.[16] Enrolments in coursework masters programmes also rose sharply from 708 in 1988 to 2,220 in 1996 as LLMs began to become a prerequisite for promotion within the profession.[17]

Much of the growth in higher education in general was achieved by the abolition of the binary system of Australian higher education in 1988 so that Colleges of Advanced Education and Institutes of Technology became universities. Fewer and larger institutions were developed by encouraging mergers and expansions in course offerings and student places. The opening of law schools became a very attractive option for newer universities because they were relatively cheap and prestigious and would also bring good students who would frequently enrol in combined degrees thus benefiting other faculties of the university. As one commentator noted at the time:

> The central message of the *Pearce Report* on Australian Law Schools was that legal education in Australia is being run on the cheap, and this is a Bad Thing. The moral for Vice Chancellors, University Councils and Governments, however, is that legal education in Australia can be run on the cheap, and this is an Absolutely Splendid Thing.[18]

It was not just the new universities that fed the jump in law student numbers in the 1980s and 1990s. It was also the expansion of older law schools under pressure to increase funding by increasing student load. The new policy of funding by *equivalent full-time student units* (EFTSU) gave universities an incentive to increase places in the courses which were cheapest to teach. The law schools were a prime target for such expansion.[19] Although the profession originally welcomed the growth, by the early 1990s a panic about law school numbers set in and the professional élite worried that

13 Pearce, op. cit., n. 11.

14 C. McInnis and S. Marginson, *Australian Law Schools After the 1987 Pearce Report* (1994) 15. See also E. Clark and M. Tsamenyi, 'Legal Education in the Twenty-First Century: A Time of Challenge' in *What Are Law Schools For?*, ed. P. Birks (1996) 17, at 20; Parker, op. cit., n. 8.

15 C. Roper, *Career Intentions of Australian Law Students* (1995) 1.

16 Centre for Legal Education, *Australasian Legal Education Yearbook 1996* (1996) 25.

17 McInnis and Marginson op. cit. n. 14, p. 14; Centre for Legal Education, id., p. 57.

18 D. Weisbrot, 'Recent Statistical Trends in Legal Education' (1990–1991) 2 *Legal Education Rev.* 219, at 219.

19 See McInnis and Marginson op. cit. n. 14, pp. 16–17.

supply of law graduates would soon exceed demand.[20] Some attempts were even made by the profession to force the law schools to limit their intakes of students.[21] But the genie was out of the bottle. University legal education had become at least partially independent of the profession and captive to the higher demands of an education policy which made the expansion of law very attractive to the universities.

THE EMERGENCE OF THE LIBERAL LAW SCHOOL[22]

The burgeoning growth of legal education from the 1960s onwards created the critical mass necessary for law school lawyers to differentiate themselves from the profession and begin to develop their own agenda. If expansive government higher education policy provided an opportunity for law schools to increase in number and grow in significance, the 1987 Pearce report, despite its inconsistencies, played a crucial role in articulating what their distinctive values might be. Bypassing the older law schools located in the sandstone universities (Sydney, Melbourne, Adelaide, Queensland, and Western Australia), the Pearce report gave its stamp of approval to the second-wave law schools. Monash in Melbourne and the University of New South Wales in Sydney became the standard bearers to which other law schools should aspire. It was the committee's emphasis upon the importance of good teaching and the need for curricular and scholarly integration of theoretical and practical concerns which shaped their evaluation.

Academic lawyers in the late 1980s had begun to value teaching as an activity in its own right, a fact reflected in the commencement of the annual Australasian Law Teaching Workshops and the development of a distinctive Australian scholarship on legal education.[23] The most striking example of this has undoubtedly been the emergence of the *Legal Education Review*, a refereed journal now in its eighth year. This provided further momentum to those law teachers in the newer law faculties who had reacted against the trade school orientation of older faculties and had begun to see the study of law as 'based on liberal, scholarly values traditionally associated with university education generally'.[24] It was reflected in the fact that almost all

20 Parker, op. cit., n. 8; C. Sampford and C. Parker, 'The Key to Legal Education: Quality not Quantity' (1993) 67 *Law Institute J.* 798.

21 For example, in Queensland in 1993 the Attorney-General called a summit of representatives from the law schools, the profession, and government to discuss the problem.

22 On the notion of the liberal law degree, see the discussion in A. Goldsmith, 'Standing at the Crossroads: Law Schools, Universities, Markets and the Future of Legal Scholarship' in *Law Schools: Global Challenges, Local Issues*, ed. F. Cownie (1997).

23 See, particularly, R. Johnstone and M. LeBrun, *The Quiet Revolution* (1992), and also C. Sampford and D. Wood, 'Theoretical Dimensions of Legal Education – A Response to the Pearce Report' (1988) 62 *Australian Law J.* 32.

24 Chesterman and Weisbrot, op. cit., n. 4, p. 715.

students now do their law degree as a joint degree or as a second degree, rather than purely as a professional training course and in an increase in electives that allow students to not only choose courses that delve into the law in more detail but also examine legal institutions in social and theoretical context.[25]

Surprising some, given the make-up of the committee, the Pearce report gave substantial impetus to curricular developments in the area of theoretical and critical perspectives. This stance was confounded to a degree by their highly oppositional stand to Macquarie Law School, Australia's most radically critical and theory-conscious law school. Yet the report has been very influential upon subsequent curricular planning among the large number of new law schools to spring up since its appearance, as well as upon curriculum reform at older law schools. In their recent review of the impact of Pearce, McInnis and Marginson found that most law schools now attached 'considerable importance' to the critical examination of legal issues in their social context, while noting that the expression and emphasis of such issues varies.[26]

The significance of these changes can be measured partly by reference to the reactions engendered among elements of the practising profession. While some among the practising profession welcomed the faculty's increasing role as 'social conscience' of the profession, it also inevitably caused tension.[27] Chesterman and Weisbrot quote the critical reaction of R. Meagher, a former president of the New South Wales Bar Association, to the development of law school culture in 1983:

> In the whole of Australia . . . there are only one or two academic teachers of any real value in real property, in contracts or in torts, yet there are about seventeen [sic] law schools. There are, to be sure, multitudes of academic homunculi who scribble and prattle relentlessly about such non-subjects as criminology, bail, poverty, consumerism, computers and racism. These may be dismissed from calculation: they possess neither practical skills nor legal learning. They are failed sociologists.[28]

The Bar even attempted to exercise its control over the 'failed sociologists' of the University of New South Wales law school by threatening to discredit the Law, Lawyers and Society course as satisfying the Board's requirement for the study of legal ethics (a threat that was turned around by some effective lobbying and the urging of the Chief Justice).[29]

The emergence of the 'failed sociologist' legal academic who could stand largely independent of the profession and the trade school mentality was a

25 J. Goldring and S. Vignaendra's study of first year law students in NSW, Victoria and the ACT found that 71 per cent were doing combined degree courses: *A Social Profile of New Law Students in the ACT, New South Wales and Victoria* (1997).

26 McInnis and Marginson, op. cit., n. 14, p. 157.

27 See Chesterman and Weisbrot, op. cit, n. 4.

28 Quoted in id., p. 716.

29 id., p. 719.

massive achievement.[30] For some indeed, the move away from concerns with professional practice had been too severe, and there was a danger of legal education losing touch with core legal concerns, including the social responsibilities of lawyers.[31] The fear of over-correction aside, it seemed clear enough by the late 1980s that the 'failed sociologists' of the law faculty helped create the climate for social movements of law graduates that have assisted in transforming the legal profession through a variety of specific contributions – community legal centres, clinical legal education, feminist legal scholarship, and new and innovative law faculties (for example, Wollongong, Newcastle, Griffith, LaTrobe, Flinders).[32] The social conscience role of the law school was never a part of state higher education policy nor was it addressed at all by Pearce. Indeed ethical training of lawyers was notably absent as an issue in the Pearce report. However it was a natural outcome of greater law school differentiation from the practising profession, and the consequent space to reflect on the practice of law from a critical and theoretical perspective. We believe that this was a significant achievement.

Autonomy and diversification was not achieved at the expense of matters of practice altogether. Aside from legal academics being involved in the establishment of community legal centres, the establishment of clinical legal education at Monash and the University of New South Wales in the 1970s mirrored some of the changes in United States law schools in the late 1960s.[33] The social conscience aspect of clinical education cannot detract altogether from the broad appeal of clinical experience to students otherwise starved in their faculties of experiential opportunities in law. Since the establishment of clinics at Monash and University of New South Wales, there have been relatively few new clinics established (given concerns about relative cost). But there has been a stronger shift towards skills teaching in the classroom, a move prompted in part by the Pearce recommendations, as well as some recent moves into externships (for example, Sydney and Griffith law schools both organize external placements for students as a clinical elective).

THE STUNTING OF THE AUSTRALIAN LAW DEGREE

The second generation universities continued to challenge the hegemony of the 'sandstone' university model of legal education throughout the 1980s,

30 See M. Thornton, *Portia Lost in the Groves of Academe Wondering What to do About Legal Education* (1991).

31 See, for example, J. Goldring, 'Babies and Bathwater: Tradition or Progress in Legal Scholarship and Legal Education' (1987) 17 *Western Australian Law Rev.* 216.

32 See C. Bois (ed.), *New Foundations in Legal Education* (forthcoming) for a discussion of the contribution of the new law schools to Australian legal education.

33 For an account of the Monash model, see S. Campbell, 'A Blueprint for Clinical Legal Education' (1991) 9 *J. of Professional Legal Education* 121, while on the history of Monash's Springvale Legal Service, see K. Greenwood, *It Seemed Like a Good Idea at the Time: A History of Springvale Legal Service* (1994).

yet by the end of the decade, there was the real prospect of an end to this movement. The Pearce legitimation of many of these shifts had caused much introspection and reform in the sandstone law schools themselves. At Melbourne and Sydney law schools (two of the sandstone universities), teaching took on a new prominence and priority, and there were moves to make the curricula more theoretical and critical. However, by the late 1980s, the new climate of economic rationalism sweeping the Australian federal Labor government threatened the newly found, publicly-funded diversity in legal education. Changes in attitude by (initially) the federal Labor government meant that the funding of higher education did not grow in step with its overall expansion during the late 1980s and early 1990s. This came on the heels of a slower pattern of decline in real terms since 1980.[34]

Labor's introduction in 1990 of the Higher Education Contribution Scheme, a form of tax on users of higher education, did nothing to stem the drop in per capita funding. University planners and policy makers began to consider their options. In 1998, it is now clear that some of the more established Australian law schools are moving to the offering of a limited number of full-fee paying places for domestic students to improve funds. In the absence of a *Gestalt* switch in government policy, law schools face an even more uncertain future in the market-place. It remains true that demand for law is strong, but for those schools which choose not to enrol, or are unable to attract, full-fee-paying local or indeed overseas students, the options are diminishing in number, and are for the most part, rather unpalatable.

It is by now a familiar irony in Australian universities that the same governments who are cutting provision to universities are simultaneously insisting on 'quality' criteria, putting increased bureaucratic obligations on teachers and asserting that students should become more demanding in relation to what the universities are providing.[35] Autonomy and funding are down, yet accountability and 'consumer' expectations are up. There is something almost biblical about the economic rationalist assumptions concerning the relationship between cost and quality in university education. The parable appears to go, 'Provide a few loaves and fishes, and the market or someone other than the government will provide the rest. But woe betide the preparers of the food if the government is unhappy with the diet provided.' The simple arithmetic involved seems lost on government policy makers – if you divide fewer resources by more students, you get a fraction rather than a whole. To assume that the shortfall can be made up by the market is to risk rewarding those faculties that are already advantaged and punishing disadvantage. Because those advantages are historically based and unevenly distributed,

34 McInnis and Marginson, op. cit., n. 14, p. 17.

35 Senator Amanda Vanstone, Minister for Education Employment Training and Youth Affairs has recently announced that her department would establish a 'hot-line' to enable students to complain (to the government department which has imposed funding cuts in the first place) about the quality of their teachers, courses, and so on.

not all universities will be able to benefit equitably from such changes. On a bad day, it can all look a bit Darwinian; on a better day, the prospects can still seem rather Dickensian.

Law schools are not assisted in this climate by their historical funding position. Since the beginning, the universities' funding formula for their law faculties has been based on the traditional approach – lecturing to large lecture halls. Therefore public funding of law faculties has generally been at or near the lowest rates in the universities. The funding of a professionally oriented degree at lower rates than arts degrees seems strange, yet has been a long-standing feature of university funding in Australia. With rising costs, including a recent pay rise (unfunded by the government), decline in teaching standards is a real possibility. The accessibility and degree of preparation of teaching staff are two obvious potential issues raised by larger classes and more teaching obligations.

The full impact of these policy changes is only just beginning to bite. In those law schools not cross-subsidized by full-fee students, staff:student ratios can only get worse. Law has always had a much higher student:staff ratio than other disciplines (23.0 compared with 12.1 in all fields in 1974; 21.4 compared with 12.5 in all fields in 1982). In 1996, Australian law schools had nearly 25,000 students enrolled (undergraduate, postgraduate, full- and part-time), and employed just over 1,000 legal academics.[36] While we are aware of no systematic data relating to law academic workloads, general assessments of Australian academic perceptions of changes in their working conditions suggest a feeling of greatly increased pressure and stress among many of them due to increased demands of both quality and quantity.

Law libraries have not been spared in public funding cuts to universities. In an era of proliferation of the printed as well as electronic word, there is an ill-fit indeed between the availability of research materials and the state of university library budgets. For some years, law libraries have been pruning their collections, resulting particularly in reductions in holdings of materials from other jurisdictions, including materials in foreign languages. To the extent that Australia's law libraries retain access to overseas publications, it is increasingly electronically based, through use of full-text information services via the Internet and on CD-ROM. Law librarians are generally bleak about the future:

> The issue of declining budgets and how to manage our collections and services in the light of them has been with us for some time. The prospects for the immediate future look even bleaker however. 1995 and 1996 saw continued increase in the cost of subscriptions and continued decrease, in real terms, of law library budgets. It is likely that these statistics will show further but perhaps even more marked effect upon law libraries after the foreshadowed larger cuts in 1997 and 1998.[37]

36 Centre for Legal Education, op. cit., n. 16.
37 N. Pengelley, 'University Law Libraries' in id., p. 90.

The present capacity of electronic forms to replace hard-copy materials removed by subscription termination appears very limited. Many items exist only or primarily in hard copy. There is likely to be a significant impact upon original and innovative scholarship unless there are substantial adjustments in availability and approach, not to mention a revolution in the research habits of some established and highly productive scholars long accustomed to traditional forms of information storage.

Despite improved access policies, expansion of student numbers has had surprisingly little effect upon access equity, aside from gender. The former Labor government policy called for a 'clever country' through higher numbers in universities and higher education generally. While there are more law students, their socio-economic profile has remained very narrow. In a recent study, Goldring and Vignaendra[38] compared the socio-economic profile of law students from the eastern states in 1976, 1986, and 1996. They found that the proportion of students from government, catholic, and (private) independent schools remained the same, suggesting no increase in access to students from lower socio-economic backgrounds. Newer law schools as well as those located outside capital cities attracted slightly higher proportions of students from government schools and also older students.[39] However Goldring and Vignaendra concluded that:

> . . . while the newer and regional law schools had been absorbing respondents from lower socio-economic backgrounds, the metropolitan and older law schools had been absorbing a lesser proportion of this group than previously . . .[40]

Thus the emergence of new law schools had merely stemmed the tide of increasing *lack* of access to legal education.

The most significant change in student profile in Goldring and Vignaendra's study was the increase in proportion of female students so that now over one-half of law students are female.[41] However this has not translated into the widespread introduction of materials that raise gender awareness into the core curriculum.[42] Law and gender subjects are still generally at the margins of Australian law schools' elective programmes while women entering the private profession are still finding it very difficult to attain the same status and pay as men.[43]

Very modest gains have also been made in increasing the participation of

38 Goldring and Vignaendra, op. cit., n. 25.

39 Older students were found to be more likely to come from a lower socio-economic status.

40 Goldring and Vignaendra op. cit. n. 25, p. 12.

41 According to the latest figures, the national average is 53 per cent female, 47 per cent male, with one law school, Southern Cross, having almost 65 per cent women. See Centre for Legal Education, op. cit., n. 16, pp. 29–30.

42 See Australian Law Reform Commission, *Equality Before the Law: Women's Equality, Report No. 69 Part II* (1994) 140–3.

43 See Keys Young, *Gender Bias and the Law: Women Working in the Legal Profession in NSW: Research on Gender Bias and Women Working in the Legal System* (1995); M. Thornton, *Dissonance and Distrust: Women in the Legal Profession* (1996).

indigenous Australians in legal education. Up to 1990 there had only ever been twenty-one Aboriginal or Islander graduates of Australian law schools.[44] From the mid-1980s a number of universities have introduced discretionary admission and pre-law programs for indigenous Australians that appear to be improving their participation and success rates.[45] In 1997 there are approximately 150 indigenous law students in Australia, but if they were present in numbers proportionate to their representation in the community there would be 666.[46] At the University of New South Wales Law faculty there is extensive support for indigenous students in the form of a preparatory pre-law programme and a full-time tutor for indigenous students throughout the degree. Numbers have grown from 0.81 per cent of the student population in 1984 to 2.09 per cent in 1994, yet even there, only 60 per cent of commencing indigenous students manage to progress through the whole degree.[47] Clearly much still needs to be done to ensure successful access to legal education for indigenous students and others from low socio-economic backgrounds.

WHERE IS THE AUSTRALIAN LAW DEGREE HEADED?

In the short to medium term, the state of public funding for law schools is likely only to get worse. Naturally enough, those law schools with relative prestige and a pragmatic approach to worries about access equity will be inclined to move in the direction of full-fee-paying positions for local students. For the most part, this will merely allow some of the sandstone universities (plus a few second generation schools) to further entrench their relative resource advantages. They will then be more on a par with Bond University which, for nearly a decade as a private fee-charging institution, has been able to offer smaller classes and more personal attention to its students.

Sydney and University of New South Wales law schools are likely examples of this trend. In the past, both schools have made commitments to small-group teaching. Now, by admitting full-fee-paying local students, they will be better positioned to service this commitment. Presumably, this will influence working as well as study conditions, as these law schools will be able to maintain better library facilities and to offer their staff better teaching hours, leave entitlements, and research support. While student

44 D. Lavery, 'The Participation of Indigenous Australians in Legal Education' (1993) 4 *Legal Education Rev.* 177, at 179. One law faculty (UNSW) had provided over half of these graduates.

45 See id.; C. Penfold, 'Aboriginal Lawyers' (1997) 22 *Alternative Law J.* 148; C. Penfold, 'Indigenous Students' Perceptions of What Contributes to Successful Law Studies' (forthcoming) *Legal Education Rev.*

46 K. Dolman 'Indigenous Lawyers: Success or Sacrifice?' (1997) 4(4) *Indigenous Law Bull.* 4.

47 Penfold, op. cit. (forthcoming), n. 45.

demand for law places shows no signs of abatement, ensuring continued demand for law places even at the less market-oriented or well-established schools, the qualitative disparities of the learning experiences of the students are likely to be considerable. A re-introduction of the binary system by the back door, or an even more stratified scheme of law school ranking, seems a real prospect.

In such a climate, a radical change in access policies is difficult to foresee. The past twenty years of special admissions to law schools must be considered mere tinkering given the marginal changes effected to the law student body over this period. Despite recent discussion about the need to move away from reliance upon a single numerical score (the *tertiary entrance result* (TER)) as the principal criterion for university entrance, as long as 'capacity to pay' remains central to higher education policy, any changes are unlikely to improve access for economically disadvantaged students.[48]

Practical legal training (PLT) has largely replaced articles of clerkship in Australia.[49] More than simply integrating skills into LLB subjects, or meeting the pre-requisite subjects for admission purposes (the 'Priestley 11'[50]), there is a discernible move by a growing number of Australian law schools to offer a complete professional legal education within the LLB structure, or at least within the confines of the university. The current advantage of meeting all the requirements of professional admission within the LLB is the relative convenience and cost to students. In effect, they are able to complete all their requirements for the usual cost of a law degree, without the need to pay upfront fees for and attend a practical legal training course of up to thirty-nine weeks, usually at another institution, after graduation.

For some time, a number of these courses have been run by or under the auspices of the profession, but growth in law graduate numbers and concerns about cost have resulted in a movement towards professional divestiture of this function. One effect of the competitive market for law students has been initiatives by some of the newer or less prestigious schools to take over PLT. The law school at Newcastle University was the first to offer an integrated degree of this kind, followed more recently by the University of Technology Sydney (UTS). The Australian National University, and now Bond University and UTS offer 'stand-alone' PLT programmes. In South Australia, both Adelaide and Flinders law schools are about to enter the PLT field, as the 'stand-alone' programme at the University of South Australia comes to an end.

This move is too new and incomplete to measure in terms of its consequences

48 See, for example, Higher Education Supplement of *The Australian*, 7 August 1997, reporting a recent speech by Education Minister, Amanda Vanstone.

49 See Centre for Legal Education, op. cit., n. 16, pp. 144–5.

50 The Priestley 11 are the eleven subjects agreed upon by all state professional admission authorities as sufficient for admission to the national profession. Consultative Committee of State and Territorial Admitting Authorities, *Uniform Admission Requirements: Discussion Paper and Recommendations* (1992).

for other models of legal education. For the cynic, it might be confirmation of the law schools' overweening concern for the needs of the profession. It can equally be seen as an initiative to increase equitable access to PLT that would otherwise cost a small fortune to buy from the practising profession.[51] However, it should not necessarily be assumed that law academics will embrace this shift, if experience in Australia and the United States of America with clinical legal education is any guide.

While the liberal law degree model lives at least in the rhetoric of Australian law school handbooks and course descriptions, current admission and curriculum policies arguably remain ambivalent in many instances. For example, the move by Flinders to admit law students to the 'straight' LLB (rather than insist upon the generally more favoured combined degree) and Monash's abandonment of its previous policy of accepting students only into joint degrees (a policy never adopted by its principal competitor, Melbourne), suggests some rather market-sensitive (and essentially conservative) decisions on matters of education policy.

While these moves might be defended as matters of financial prudence or even necessity, they signal the growing significance of consumer preferences for the shape of Australian legal education. When the reasons for the current popularity of law degrees are acknowledged (in particular, the relative employability of law graduates), and as students assume more of the costs of legal education, one can easily predict the likely growth of student preference for highly skills-oriented, minimalist forms of legal education. The fact that a growing proportion of students will be unable or elect not to enter private or public legal practice is likely to prove of little consequence, as anecdotal as well as survey evidence suggests that students want the capacity to be able to practise, even if it is never exercised.[52] Professional admission as part of the LLB is likely to magnify the pragmatic tendencies already familiar to those who teach the present generation of law students, but which are increasingly apparent and significant in the current law school climate. Without a clear commitment by law schools, backed by resources, to the aims of the liberal law degree, its significance seems likely to fade further.

In a student/consumer-driven market the profession still has significant control over what is taught in the university. The introduction of the Priestley 11, the eleven subjects that all legal professional associations recognize as necessary for admission, is a vivid example. In some states, especially Queensland, the eleven represented a refreshing change from the conservative profession's previously lengthy list of subjects that had to be studied. But in New South Wales it added considerably to what had to be taught. Law schools like the University of New South Wales found themselves having to make subjects such as Business Associations that were previously electives

51 This is the reason that Flinders law school has entered the field.

52 Roper, op. cit., n. 15.

a compulsory part of the core degree. As the Australian Law Reform Commission has noted, the prescription of these eleven subjects as necessary for admission to the profession throughout Australia:

> appear[s] to be in direct conflict with the movement in legal education over the last decade towards diversity and the inclusion of critical and theoretical dimensions in legal education.[53]

The development of the Priestley 11 was driven by the agenda of nationalization of the Australian profession and abolition of state differences in admission and ethical rules. Nationalization is directly caused by internationalization of markets by GATT and GATS and large solicitors' firms' desire to capitalize on the international market, especially in Asia, for Australians. Thus law schools are not immune from the power of the most powerful sectors of a newly nationalized and newly competitive legal profession, especially where the most powerful sectors of the profession are closely allied with big business.

Australian law schools now exist between the demands and opportunities of the profession, state, and market. While it is tempting to place much of the blame at the feet of the economic rationalists, we must also recognize our own contributions. Law-school traditions and the entrenched expectations of the practising profession in Australia and elsewhere lend a timelessness to the current dilemmas discussed in this paper. As Martin Levine has noted:

> There is no consensus on what the law school should emphasize: debates abound among proponents of practical training, natural law, free-enterprise economics, radical and feminist criticism, varieties of communitarianism, and many other views. And legal doctrine, challenged though it is, is still taught everywhere – and not only in the law schools, but also through independent student study of 'black-letter' texts and through bar review courses. Summer clerkships for students, rotations for American associates, and pupillage for barristers, still provide apprenticeships. Thus the legal education which existed before the rise of university law schools still endures.[54]

We link the recurrent despondency to our law school's fundamental ambivalence about the function of the university law degree and tension between vocationalism and the responsibilities of scholarship and higher learning. This ambiguity is encouraged by the current market in which it benefits us to appear to be all things to all people. The sociology of the professions tell us that a profession needs a defined 'jurisdiction' – a conception of the knowledge in which they have expertise – to maintain their autonomy.[55] Perhaps it is the lack of this jurisdiction that has made Australian law schools particularly vulnerable in their current circumstances. In the following section we suggest that Australian law schools should maintain a distinctive vision in the face of difficult circumstances by embracing the contradictory position they inhabit and the tensions within the knowledge they are asked to pass on.

53 Australian Law Reform Commission, op. cit., n. 42.

54 M. Levine, *Legal Education* (1993) xvi.

55 A. Abbott, *The System of Professions: An Essay on the Expert Division of Labour* (1988).

> [W]hat justifies the existence of a law school [is] the study of the types of legal problems which arise in daily life, and the methods of resolving them satisfactorily, with the least amount of injustice and suffering. Law schools are set up not for the sake of the law or lawyers but ultimately to help human beings to solve legally the problems and predicaments encountered in the pursuit of conflicting social ends.[56]

Australian law schools should reconstitute themselves by embracing and entrenching:

- A broad conception of the legal knowledge which we are responsible for passing on, a knowledge based upon a variety of disciplines from the humanities, social sciences and elsewhere, that allow law students to study the diverse meanings and consequences of law as a social and human variable in everyday life

and:

- An expanded conception of the field of legal practice for which we prepare our students so as to integrate a critical and ethically oriented understanding of how lawyers and others carry law and legal institutions into the communities in which they live and work.[57]

These prescriptions are intended to de-emphasize formal approaches to legal reasoning, and obsessive focus upon black-letter law. It is to advocate 'taking legal practice seriously', but to see as part of practice the values and techniques of self-examination and critique, to see practice as grounded in social responsibilities beyond the immediate paying client, and to look beyond the traditions of private professionalism in the practice of law-school graduates. It seems to us, on pragmatic as well as traditional grounds, that the law school will never entirely escape (nor should it abandon) the focal concerns of the practising profession. But the liberal law degree should not be bounded by those concerns; its future must lie in the pursuit of a *transformative*, rather than *replicative*, view of legal education.

It is not enough to talk about the liberal law degree. A truly liberal, indeed liberated, law degree would not be defined for the most part, if at all, by anything resembling the Priestley 11. Legal knowledge is too wide in its reach and significance to be so limited. The 'failed sociologist' model of the law-school lawyer is important because it brings the perspectives of other disciplines to bear in the study of law. Alongside the 'law and' scholarship of the liberal legal scholar there must exist a critical examination of the nature and limitations of legal practice in its diversity of forms.[58] In our

56 S. Hook, 'Commentary' in *The Law School of Tomorrow*, ed. R. Hutchins (1968) 41.

57 The second author has made this argument in A. Goldsmith, 'Heroes or Technicians: The Moral Capacities of Tomorrow's Lawyers' (1996–7) 14 *J. of Professional Legal Education* 1.

58 The second author has argued the importance of integrating these perspectives in A. Goldsmith 'An Unruly Conjunction? Social Theory and Legal Action in Clinical Legal Education' (1993) 43 *J. of Legal Education* 415.

vision of the transformative law school, 'failed sociologists' with a whole-hearted disdain for all practice matters would be ill-placed unless their positions were based upon an engagement with, rather than dismissal of, such matters.

Law schools must also remain critical of current orthodoxies in professional life, so that graduates who choose to enter professional fields are able to make their own judgements about their professional involvements and commitments including, if necessary, the ability to propose and pursue specific reforms in their spheres of operation and influence. In order to do this meaningfully, law schools must ensure that the special interests involved in law, the different strategic and tactical possibilities within legal practice, and the social consequences of different legal interventions, are rendered transparent and comprehensible to their students. Training in abstract reasoning and legal case analysis is not sufficient to achieve this grasp of context, nor is practical skills training defensible without the provision of opportunity for deep critique of the different applications of particular skills. Professional training without breadth of education and the incorporation of critique, including acceptance of the validity of scepticism towards current professional conventions, is purely *replicative*.[59]

The current market pressure for Australian law schools to provide skills training, clinical legal education, and PLT in the law degree provide an opportunity to implement this broader conception of legal knowledge in which theory, critique, and practice merge. The critical and theoretical excellence of scholar-teachers must not become segregated from the skills-based professional training that law students want in their degrees. John Langbein writes of the boom in clinical legal education in the United States of America that 'the law schools are offering Stratosphere 101 in the classroom and Xeroxing 101 in the clinic'.[60] Australian law schools have an opportunity to avoid this divide by incorporating theory and practice into the clinic and into the curriculum. The earlier (and, for many years, the only) models of clinical legal education, Kingsford (UNSW) and Springvale (Monash), were not about skills in isolation. At Kingsford the students are required to attend lectures and daily meetings that link the practice of law to the theory they are taught in the law school. Thus skills training is not mindless Xeroxing. It is an opportunity for the sociology of everyday practice to inform the critical and theoretical dimensions of the curriculum and therefore to have its impact on the students' development as reflective practitioners. That sort of 'clinical' education has the added advantage of being as attractive to students who will never practise law as to those who will.

It also underlines the importance of the fact that we cannot expect our students to become civic-minded reflective practitioners by stuffing their heads full of theoretical and critical perspectives if we never give them a chance to put their head knowledge into action. Studies in the United States

59 See Goldsmith, op. cit., n. 57, pp. 9–10.

60 J. Langbein, 'Scholarly and Professional Objectives in Legal Education: American Trends and English Comparisons' in Birks, op. cit., n. 14, at p. 7.

of America have shown that it is those students who actually take part in a legal service office or a politically active student group who maintain their idealism through law school and are most likely to act on it in their jobs.[61] Clinical legal education in a clinic that has its own *raison d'être* and mission as community legal centre (or something else) gives our students a much greater chance of taking a social justice orientation away with them than preaching at their minds in the classroom, and then segregating them into a sterile clinic or skills simulation session where they are not required to reflect for their skills education.

Australian law schools need also to abandon the idea that their obligations as legal educators are limited to students who wish to qualify for professional admission. The idea that law schools are there simply to train students for professional careers as barristers or solicitors is palpably wrong. It is increasingly the case that many law graduates will pursue other careers either through choice or necessity.[62] The liberal law degree should offer more than a set of fairly predictable generic skills for those who do not become practising lawyers, and should reflect the reality of practice for those that do. All graduates should take with them from their law school education an understanding of how the law operates in the community, and how their practice might affect it.

A focus upon mundane practice is strangely lacking from most legal education courses, arising at best obliquely in discussions of the role and responsibilities of lawyers. Professional legal education would benefit from turning to what Gordon and Simon call the 'sociology of everyday practice settings'.[63] In the context of a law school that has broadened its concept of the legal practice for which it is preparing students, this will mean more than the sociology of private lawyering: it will embrace the world of the in-house corporate lawyer with significant management responsibilities, the accountant or business consultant with some knowledge of the law, the community worker, and the bureaucrat. In all of these common careers for law graduates, an understanding of the law on the books and critical reflection upon the law in action are appropriate.

Many of our law students will aspire to commercial practice in the large solicitors' firms. Many more will end up as in-house corporate lawyers or managers. A transformative legal education would not just teach the doctrines of company law and securities regulation with a half-semester elective in trade practices. We could be teaching them the regulatory context

61 See R. Granfield, *Making Elite Lawyers: Visions of Law at Harvard and Beyond*, (1992); R. Stover, *Making It and Breaking It: The Fate of Public Interest Commitment During Law School* (1989).

62 A 1994 survey of Australian law students showed that only 55 per cent of first-year respondents intended to be admitted within two years of graduation and only 36 per cent planned to work in the private legal profession: Roper, op. cit., n. 15.

63 R. Gordon and W. Simon, "The Redemption of Professionalism?" in R. Nelson, D. Trubek, and R. Solomon (eds.), *Lawyers' Ideals/Lawyers' Practices* (1992) 230, at 238.

of these interventions into the market-place, the practice of preventive law, the way that legal norms are likely to interact with management and market norms, and the skills and techniques that are necessary to ensure that occupational health and safety, affirmative action, and consumer protection are taken seriously within large public and private organizations. In this way we might work with and not against the flow of business imperatives without giving up our prophetic role.

We might recognize that students within the law school intend to be lawyers and social activists, politicians, and welfare workers. For example, some will want to serve indigenous communities and to do so they will need to deal simultaneously with issues like 'discrimination, land rights, criminal justice, stolen generations, family law, high interest credit, housing and social security' on a legal, political, and personal level and, at the same time, they might need an understanding of customary law and how it can fit into Australian legal institutions.[64] Preparing these students for practice will take much more than our traditional trade-school approach. It will involve the broad sort of legal knowledge that we have discussed above.

CONCLUSION

For law schools to acknowledge the importance of this other sphere of legal education, and to reflect it in their admission policies and range of courses offered, is for them to start the process of acknowledging more directly their potential contribution to the community at large, not simply those members of a (largely) skewed socio-economic group who qualify for admission to, and wish to pursue, the professional degree. The model law school we have in mind is one championed by Twining in several of his writings, and would constitute a multi-function law centre, geared to training of a variety of law-related careers, as well as to scholarly and community-based work grounded in the realities of the poor as well as the rich of the community.[65] By putting into practice a model of pedagogical and scholarly *inclusivity*, such a law school would encourage dialogue and discussion about law and legal practice throughout the community at large, not just the 'usual suspects' in our present law schools. The knowledge produced, and the practices endorsed, would not be replicative in nature in many, if not most, instances but, rather, support a re-configuration of how law serves social interests and the interests that it indeed serves. In this sense, law schools would support a transformative model of legal education, linked to a variety of models of legal practice. One might predict that such a law school would have an even larger market than the one Australian law schools currently enjoy.

64 Dolman, op. cit., n. 46, p. 6.

65 William Twining has recently advocated what is known as the International Legal Center (ILC) model in 'What are Law Schools For?' (1995) 46 *Northern Ireland Q.* 291, at 297.

JOURNAL OF LAW AND SOCIETY
VOLUME 25, NUMBER 1, MARCH 1998
ISSN: 0263–323X, pp. 51–70

Privatizing the Universities

JANE KELSEY*

For most of the twentieth century, privatization of state universities seemed inconceivable. By 1997 government reviews of tertiary education in the United Kingdom, Australia, and New Zealand were all exploring variations on a market-driven theme. Similar policy agendas were being promoted through international agencies like the World Bank and the Organization for Economic Co-operation and Development (OECD). This article examines the convergence of tertiary education restructuring and the extent to which that reflects, and serves to embed, an ascendant neo-liberal hegemony. Taking the extreme example of New Zealand, it assesses the implications of a global competitive model of tertiary education for law schools in the common law world.

THE PRIVATIZATION RATIONALE

For most of the twentieth century, privatization of state universities seemed inconceivable. As we move towards the new millennium, some would still argue that state universities are not being privatized.[1] In the sense of selling off physical assets or enterprises, that is largely, though not wholly, true. The process of shifting from a state-centred to a market-driven system of university education – which is what the term 'privatization' describes – has been more subtle, incremental, and *ad hoc*. While the operational details and extent of this shift have varied across countries, the justifications have coalesced around three common themes.

The first involves a standard application of new institutional economics and new public management theory to the universities. Universities are deemed, like all enterprises 'owned' and run by the state, to be unaccountable, inefficient, and unresponsive to consumer demand. The solution is to expose to them to the rigours of the market, require them to do more for less, and reorganize on private-sector lines. To achieve this, the concept of education

* *Department of Law, University of Auckland, Auckland, New Zealand*

1 For example, New Zealand's Minister of Education Wyatt Creech, in *New Zealand Herald*, 27 August 1997.

must also be privatized. Tertiary education must be redefined as primarily a private good, a commodity to be bought and sold in an artificially constructed education market driven by the forces of supply and demand. Greater dependence on private financing and competition are expected to stimulate efficiency, innovation, and responsiveness. Education is reduced to training and information transfer, and measured through accreditation of standardized outputs. The burden of funding tuition shifts progressively from the state to the student, and at times the employer, as beneficiary.

Logically, research must also be separately funded, preferably from a contestable pool, with research productivity again measured by outputs that can be quantified. Traditional responsibilities of universities – the creation and expansion of knowledge, research, and publication; repositories and transmitters of historical, cultural, and social knowledge; critic and conscience of society; and advising and servicing the state, professions, and communities – are reconceived as 'spillovers'.[2] They are left under- or unfunded and marginalized.

A second common argument is that the traditional model of the university can no longer meet contemporary economic and social needs.[3] This argument describes access to education as a universal right and a legitimate expectation for all. A society's well-being depends on educating its people, especially women and the disadvantaged, and on providing appropriate educational opportunities throughout their lives. Although this right is widely recognized, the educational deficits between rich and poor countries, and between the peoples within each country, continue to grow. Alongside these equity concerns, the nature of work has also changed; it now requires a more educated and technically-skilled workforce with ongoing opportunities to upgrade and retrain. In wealthier countries this has prompted a massive increase in tertiary participation (a trend called 'massification'), placing unprecedented pressure on a system which historically served a privileged minority. A tertiary education system for the future must therefore serve the needs of age-groups, across many locations, who have diverse interests, backgrounds, and qualifications, and varying constraints on their time. This will require greater flexibility, diversity, and equity of access than traditional universities provide. Barriers to be dismantled include the distinction between academic and vocational qualifications, the hierarchical ranking of universities ahead of other education providers, and the monopoly of the universities on granting degrees. By implication, the institutional structure, academic culture, and employment practices of traditional universities must also change.

A third justification draws on the ubiquitous demand for fiscal restraint. Per capita spending on tertiary education is far higher than primary or secondary and caters for a small and privileged group. Yet the social returns

2 A term used by the report of the Ministerial Consultative Group, New Zealand Ministry of Education, *Funding Growth in Tertiary Education and Training* (1994) 155.

3 J. Delors, *Learning: The Treasure Within, Report to UNESCO of the International Commission on Education for the Twenty-first Century* (1996) especially chs. 6 and 8.

from education are greater at the primary and secondary level, than at tertiary. Barriers to access mean the taxpaying poor subsidize university attendance by the rich, who secure ongoing economic and status gains. Available funds should thus be redirected to mass education for the poor.[4]

Many of these arguments pose a dilemma for those who have expressed similar criticisms of the status quo, but who reject the market-driven solutions which are currently proposed. These critics claim that most universities are the traditional preserve of an élite. Ideologically, universities and academics have performed an important hegemonic role for capitalism, patriarchy, and colonialism. The rhetoric of the collective and self-governing academic community has, in many instances, entrenched a self-perpetuating hierarchy of ageing white men, with minimal accountability and little enthusiasm for innovative or critical ideas. At the same time, however, universities have been the, often willing, captives of the rhetoric of academic freedom and defenders of the institutional autonomy on which that depends. Universities have created the space for the development, articulation, and transfer of critical ideas. Privatization threatens these footholds and, with it, the ability in the short and longer term to force a genuine contest of ideas. If this occurs simultaneously across different countries, the global intellectual environment will stagnate and redundant or dysfunctional theories, policies, and laws will be allowed to prevail.

THE INTERNATIONAL DIMENSION

Seemingly unconnected changes to tertiary education policies across many countries display a remarkable congruity.[5] This reflects a coherent policy agenda which is promoted through interlocking networks of international actors and agencies, which cross-fertilize with the officials, politicians, entrepreneurs, and commentators who influence policy at the national level.

A large amount of the international research which criticizes public provision of education has been funded by the World Bank and is reflected in their structural adjustment programmes.[6] Many of their arguments are assertions of 'self-evident truths'. Critics have challenged their underlying assumptions and the scant empirical evidence offered in support, and the imposition of findings from research carried out in the United States of America on countries of the South. The critics also claim that policy outcomes have made problems of scarcity, inequality of access, and international disparity even worse.[7]

4 For example, World Bank, *Priorities and Strategies for Education. A World Bank Sector Review* (1995) 10, endorsed by the UNESCO study, id., p. 167.

5 As discussed, for example, in the OECD Education Committee's draft *Thematic Review of the First Years of Tertiary Education – Comparative Report* (1997).

6 See, for example, World Bank, op. cit., n. 4.

7 See, for example, C. Colclough, 'Who Should Learn to Pay? An Assessment of Neo-liberal Approaches to Education Policy' in *States or Markets? Neo-liberalism and the Development Policy Debate*, eds. C. Colclough and J. Manor (1991) 201.

Four main mechanisms have been promoted by the Bank, often as conditionalities for loans:

(i) *user-charges* covering all living expenses, and some or all tuition fees, are intended to increase pressure for efficiencies, with a limited number of scholarships provided for children of the poor;
(ii) *student loans* are designed to shift the costs onto direct beneficiaries, who are expected to make rational choices and anticipate their future incomes;
(iii) *private provision* is predicted to increase competition, force down costs, and supplement supply; and
(iv) any savings generated are to be *redistributed* to more socially profitable education at junior levels.

As Christopher Colclough notes:

> user charges, student loans and the encouragement of private schooling primarily represent a cost-shifting rather than a cost-reducing strategy. Additional resources for education could be raised by those means assuming no countervailing reductions in existing expenditures on education.[8]

However, fiscal restraints imposed by the Bank mean that additional investment has not occurred.

Few would question the priority placed on literacy and mass education. But sovereign states also require their own quality pool of knowledge and expertise. Severe cuts to spending on university infrastructure and salaries have provoked an exodus of many poor countries' best academics and post-graduate students. The residual student body reflects an ability to pay rather than an ability to learn. The fragile storehouse of indigenous knowledge is almost destroyed, along with the major source of independent critique. Local research by independent academics is minimal. If local universities become unable to educate the next generation, those who will run the country's government and economy in future years are likely to be trained in overseas, primarily United States, universities or seconded from international financial institutions and governments, as part of aid packages or loan conditionalities. Fortuitously for their sponsors, many will bring with them a commitment to neo-liberal ideas.

This structured coherence is not confined to the South. The Organization for Economic Co-operation and Development (OECD) is a prime advocate of neo-liberal restructuring in the 'developed' world and its country reports express strong support for market-driven tertiary education regimes.[9] In 1997 the OECD completed a comparative study of tertiary education in ten member-countries. The draft comparative report drew heavily on the arguments of equity and massification, underpinned by fiscal constraint; the more-market

8 id., p. 210.
9 See, for example, *OECD Economic Surveys. New Zealand, 1996* (1996) 74–80 and 121–5.

approach was promoted as pragmatic and practical, rather than ideological. The report notes:

> a particular problem of 'steering' demand . . . the needs and interests of the clients, the students, and the stakeholders should frame the debate while governments hold the ring and make strategic interventions. This requires that policy making be in a new key: flexible, open, and finely tuned to those needs and interests and centred on the student.[10]

The report observed a growing convergence of policy directions, although experiences, contexts, priorities, and needs differed widely. In all countries, the agenda for reform and policy development in tertiary education was 'extensive and volatile'.[11]

THE GLOBAL MARKET-PLACE

Applied consistently the broad privatization agenda creates the conditions for a deregulated international education market which, once established, will be extremely difficult to re-regulate or contain. That objective has been significantly advanced through the Uruguay Round of the General Agreement on Tariffs and Trade (GATT). The General Agreement on Trade in Services (GATS) seeks to prevent discrimination between domestic and foreign providers of all services which a member offers to include.[12]

Education is defined as a service. Examples of trade in education services include direct foreign investment in private institutions; establishing joint ventures and independent enterprises offshore; export of education consultancy services; distance learning through technology transfer, satellite feeds and specialist software; harmonization and mutual recognition of professional qualifications and standards; and enhanced mobility for education service providers.

The academic community has long embraced internationalization through study, research, and teaching abroad. A 1994 report considered it 'especially encouraging to find a deep conviction among faculty that higher education is, in fact, an international enterprise and that the academic profession is becoming a global community'. It went on to identify a series of vital questions with which universities and the academy need to engage:

> What will be the consequences of the new electronic, international age, and how will the professoriate adapt? How will a newly connected 'network of scholars' affect campus policy making? Will we, for example, see common procedures in evaluation of scholarship? Will procedures regarding credits and courses and student evaluation begin to converge? In the days ahead, we anticipate that in all of these matters national boundaries will become less consequential to intellectual work.[13]

10 OECD, op. cit., n. 5, p. 103.

11 id., p. 108.

12 See, further, J. Kelsey, 'The Globalisation of Tertiary Education. Implications of the GATS' in *Cultural Politics and the University in Aotearoa/New Zealand*, ed. M. Peters (1997) 66.

13 E. Boyer, P. Altbach, and M. Whitelaw, *The Academic Profession. An International Perspective*, (1994) 17 and 20.

At the same time, the study reported an overwhelming feeling of 'professional obligation to apply their knowledge to the problems of society, building a bridge between theory and practice'. At heart, '[c]olleges and universities are deeply embedded in the societies they service.'[14]

This assumes a balance between engagement in the international education arena and the contribution of universities and academics to the communities in which they live and serve. However, once education has been subsumed within the free trade paradigm, it stops being a means to convey unique identities and cultural values, an arena of much-needed contest and critique, and an activity valued for itself. It is transformed into a tradeable commodity to be bought and sold on world markets like any other good or service.

'Free trade' in education services means there is no boundary at which internationalization ends so that the local can be protected. As with other free trade agreements, GATS requires liberalization and deregulation at the domestic level with the ultimate goal of removing all restrictions. A consultancy report prepared for the New Zealand government listed the following preconditions for free trade in education services:

- liberalisation of the foreign direct investment regime;
- liberalisation of immigration policies for students and service personnel;
- deregulation of the framework governing universities' commercial activities;
- a more market-responsive administration and decentralised control;
- increased discretion to universities to charge fees;
- ability to raise venture capital through loans and equity;
- market-driven funding systems to encourage rationalisation of courses;
- greater flexibility in payments to staff in areas of scarcity and demand, including replacement of national or enterprise awards with individual employment contracts;
- incentive-based salary structures to encourage efficient use of resources, increase competitiveness and improve productivity; and
- competitive neutrality between the public and private sector in areas like taxation, depreciation, dividend on investment, and capital charge on the use of state resources and assets.[15]

In other words, the system of state-run universities would have to be privatized.

Most countries recognize that national control over their education system is essential to protect cultural and social, as well as economic, values and goals. Some have greater economic and human capacity and willingness to retain that control. During the Uruguay Round, the United States of America, for example, offered to open only adult education to international competition. By contrast, the aggressively pro-market New Zealand government guaranteed market access and national treatment to all its private primary, secondary, and tertiary education services. This limitation

14 id., pp. 17–18.

15 *Report on the Export of Educational Services*, prepared for the Marketing Development Board by Hugo Consulting Group (1987) (unpublished).

to private education was meaningful only so long as the substantive distinction between public and private was maintained.

The Uruguay Round was merely the first step in a one-way process of liberalization and deregulation. The GATS policy of 'standstill' and 'rollback' means signatories cannot impose new restrictions on services which are bound, and are expected to extend coverage and reduce existing restrictions in future negotiations. Such agreements are being extended all the time. The 'bottom-up' nature of the GATS initially meant services were covered only if expressly included. The OECD Multilateral Agreement on Investment (MAI), scheduled to be signed in April 1998, would supersede the GATS and prohibit a signatory from discriminating against foreign investors in services like education, unless the right to do so was expressly reserved.[16]

Logically, the GATS envisages a global education industry dominated by transnational education corporations (TECs). The TECs would disseminate one dominant value-structure and perspective, using one pedagogy. Branches, serviced mainly by a small mobile staff moving freely between countries, would compete with each other for the education market. Local enterprises would be left to service niche markets and marginal consumers. Profit-driven transnational corporations (TNCs) are already entering the international education market. With international agreements pending to liberalize both information technology and investment regimes, TNCs which control satellite communication could come to dominate global education as they currently dominate the world's media.[17]

Globalization of education therefore adds a new dimension to the internationalization of old. The results may be positive, as well as negative. The advent of new technologies offers genuine opportunities to break down the monopoly of knowledge held by rich countries and expand the pool of knowledge available to the world. However, this assumes a benign motivation on the part of those who control the knowledge and the technology, which is not an intrinsic feature of free trade and TECs. Most bilateral and multilateral investment agreements seek to prohibit requirements for technology transfer.

Trade in education services also offers an important new source of revenue for internationally competitive universities at a time of fiscal restraint. Yet increased dependence on education export earnings creates a high level of exposure to shifts in international education markets. Equally, host countries which permit a high penetration of foreign education providers leave themselves vulnerable to the changing investment strategies and commercial fortunes of the TECs.

Globalization may create new synergies and potential for collaboration. But

16 OECD Negotiating Group on the MAI, *Multilateral Agreement on Investment. Consolidated Text and Commentary*, DAFFE/MAI/NM(97)2, 6 October 1997 (1997).

17 WTO Information Technology Agreement, approved by the December 1996 meeting of the World Trade Organisation in Singapore; OECD MAI, id.

it also erodes local institutional autonomy and academic freedom to determine the substance and style of what universities do. Domestic and international competition bring inevitable pressures to reduce costs, risking a race to the bottom, and to respond to consumer demand by pandering to latest trends. Pressure for greater portability, mutual recognition, and harmonization of qualifications similarly erodes the ability of institutions, and professions, to maintain local content and control. Nor is there any security for the traditional public good role.

Some university systems may survive, even thrive, in this environment. The United States of America with its well-endowed private universities, the United Kingdom with its historical pre-eminence, and Japan with its profound cultural protectionism may hold their own and even profit from this modern variation on cultural imperialism. The education systems of poor and small countries will be most vulnerable.

CONSOLIDATING GLOBAL NEO-LIBERALISM

Underpinning the privatization and internationalization agenda lies a deep ideological belief in the virtue and infallibility of global markets and a corresponding intolerance of alternative views. Universities provide a repository of historical knowledge, a source of critique, and a breeding ground for competing ideas which challenge the portrayal of neo-liberalism as immutable and indisputable orthodoxy. As such, they present an obvious target for radical market-oriented restructuring.

The international literature on 'structural adjustment' recognizes the high degree of ideological hegemony which is required for the long-term survival of global neo-liberalism. In a seminal study published in 1992, Stephen Haggard and Robert Kaufman identified two stages of structural adjustment programmes with significant differences in the political logic of each. The *initiation* phase, they suggest, is best secured through relatively autonomous, free-floating, technocratic 'change teams', and requires a more activist and capable state than classical liberal theory contemplated. The state needs to be strengthened before the government can reduce its role in the economy and extend market forces. This means creating new bureaucratic structures or significantly reorganizing existing ones to operate outside routine decision-making channels:

> [R]eform initiatives are more likely where and when political institutions insulate politicians and their technocratic allies from particular interest group constraints, at least in the short run.[18]

Some argue that *consolidation*, the second stage, follows naturally from the successful initiation of change. Initiation requires strong leadership,

18 S. Haggard and R. Kaufman, 'Institution and Economic Adjustment' in *The Politics of Economic Adjustment*, eds. S. Haggard and R. Kaufman (1992) 19.

unconstrained by the need for social consensus. Once those changes have been made, social consensus and ideological convergence inevitably emerge.[19] Others believe that consolidation requires considerably more sophistication, skill, and engagement with social reality. There is a need for:

> stabilising expectations around a new set of incentives and convincing economic agents that they cannot be reversed at the discretion of individual decision makers. Consolidation is most likely where governments have constructed relatively stable coalitions of political support that encompass major private sector beneficiaries, and have secured at least the acquiescence of the major political forces competing within the political system. Without such tacit or explicit alliances between politicians, technocratic elites, and those gaining from the policy change, reform attempts will necessarily falter.[20]

Alongside this comes a wider need for 'social learning'; the:

> evolution of a broader ideational consensus among leaders, interest groups, party elites and attentive publics that sets some boundaries on the range of economic debate. Such a consensus does not imply stasis or the absence of conflict; distributive struggles will always arise over policy. Nonetheless, it is possible that the long-term sustainability of policy choices will depend on a convergence of thinking about fundamental means-ends relationships in the economy. If so, then the formation of elite preferences, ideas, and ideology, as well as the evolution of public opinion, are potential important explanatory variables.[21]

This involves a consensus of the élite. Universities are the training grounds for that élite. In a market-driven system, student assumptions of what the market demands will increasingly dictate what courses and perspectives universities provide. Likewise, research funding dependent on private commercial sources, or grants from competitive public pools where government designates the priorities, are likely to support market-friendly projects and hypotheses and unlikely to favour critique. The resulting ideological closure will foster and protect the 'consensus', and limit the range of ideas in circulation on which the 'evolution of public opinion' largely depends.

The ideological impact of market forces is complemented by more subtle influences – in particular, new discourses of governance. The terms 'restructuring' or 'structural adjustment' imply a neutral corrective. Fundamental changes to social regulation are portrayed as mere shifts of technique which are devoid of culture, context or power. Citizens are reduced to customers who buy from competing providers those services which were once their entitlements. In the process, responsibility for social well-being becomes individualized, privatized, neutralized. In much official discourse, the concepts of a society whose members have reciprocal obligations and of communities with contending histories, cultures, identities, and relations of power all but disappear.

19 J. Williamson and S. Haggard, 'The Political Conditions for Economic Reform' in *The Political Economy of Policy Reform*, ed. J. Williamson (1994) 527, 574.

20 Haggard and Kaufman, op. cit., n. 18, pp. 19–20.

21 id., p. 36.

The open texts of constitutional law, political philosophy, and administrative theory are displaced by the quasi-scientism of new institutional economics, new management theory, and classical contract law. Such quasi-scientism presents as:

> an organized, specialised, professionalized knowledge susceptible of being produced ad infinitum in apparently context-blind settings, according to formalized and replicable methodologies . . . . It thinks of itself as making only cognitive claims (the truth).[22]

Representing one cultural perception of the nature of world to the exclusion of other perceptions, it is capable of powerful and drastic interventions in society. Yet 'the specific normative claim of science is to purport to make no normative claims.'[23] The artisans of neo-liberal governance perpetuate this quasi-scientism, driven by the belief 'that there exist fundamental economic tests or yardsticks according to which policy decisions can and should be made'.[24] The term 'epistemic communities' has been coined to describe the privileged set of professionals who share these normative and causal beliefs and common policy enterprise, secure in the conviction that their principled approach is supported by scientific tests of validity.[25] They are portrayed, or portray themselves, as a qualitatively different breed, immune from the failings which public choice and agency theories attribute to other government officials and intellectuals. Because of their inherent objectivity, there is no room to question the nature and source of their ideas, their mandate to impose their ideological and policy agenda, or their disdain for democratic procedures and constitutional conventions that get in their way. John Toye has described this intellectual closure as 'the realm of the Empowering Myth'. Constant 'consensus-mongering' implicitly disqualifies any unorthodox economic views, and tends to conflate 'what economists believe with what is economic truth':

> We ought to question what other people believe, not believe it because they believe it. That, at least, is how we got where we are now. Truth is always provisional, and it is the product of criticism just as much as the attempt to promote 'economic correctness'.

This fetish with the economically correct seeks to 'freeze or concretize ideas, losing sight of the fact that they are always in flux, always embedded in critical debate. The learning process disappears.'[26]

Managerialism, backed by theories of agency, transaction cost, and public choice, complements the commitment to economic correctness. The 'ism' indicates that this is an ideology, not just an administrative technique, which

22 B. de Sousa Santos, *Toward a New Common Sense. Law, Science and Politics in the Paradigmatic Transition* (1995) 440–1.

23 id.

24 J. Toye, 'Comment' in Williamson, op. cit., n. 19, p. 36.

25 P. Haas, 'Introduction: epistemic communities and international policy coordination' (1992) 46 *International Organization* 1.

26 Toye, op. cit., n. 24, pp. 39–40.

changes the nature and function of the enterprise.[27] The university becomes a surrogate commercial business whose product is sold to customers at the competitive market price. The traditional relationship of trust between government and universities is replaced by that of purchaser/provider and shareholder/management. The bottom line of the budget becomes the determinant of success. The whole becomes disaggregated into component parts which are designed to maximize allocative efficiency, localize incentives, and increase transparency – irrespective of the increased transaction and opportunity costs and distortions to the optimal activity of the whole. Teaching becomes a commercial transaction assessed through one-dimensional performance appraisal. Research, also commodified, and detached from teaching, is assessed in similar ways. The public good and entrepôt functions disappear.

The academy ceases to be a collective whose value depends upon intellectual reputations, integration of its activities, and the maintenance of a vibrant intellectual community. Its members, once motivated by a sense of public service and intellectual mission, are deemed by agency theory untrustworthy to serve the interests of the state as principal and discredited by public-choice theorists as vested interests out to capture the institution for their own ends. Removed from the decision-making process, academics become mere wage labourers selling their services for a price, subject to strict employment contracts, performance appraisals, and managerial oversight. Labour market deregulation reinforces this deprofessionalization, as national awards are replaced by enterprise or individual contracts with performance incentives and differential pay scales reflecting market demand. Terms such as 'standards of excellence', 'competitive', 'dynamic', 'internationally renowned', 'premier' have enter the lexicon through which universities market themselves; academics re-conceive their qualifications, functions, and promotional prospects accordingly.[28]

Alongside the closure of economic debate and the strictures of managerialism comes the neo-liberal variant on legal liberalism known as law-and-economics. Centred on the revival of classical contract law and property rights, the familiar, but damaged, fiction of law as inherently objective, rational, private, individualized, and value-free must be restored. This truth value then excludes any other legitimate source or form of law, and precludes any analysis of its historical and contextual role. The exception is the relationship of law to the deregulated economy. That nexus is treated as natural and symbiotic.

The reassertion of classical contract law, with the accompanying diminution of state regulation, is cast as one more technical realignment, a represen-

27 M. Trow, 'Managerialism and the Academic Profession: The Case of England' (1994) 7(2) *Higher Education Policy* 11.

28 N. Fairclough, 'Critical Discourse Analysis and the Marketisation of Public Discourse: the Universities' (1993) 4 *Discourse and Society* 133.

tation which insulates the strategic role played by law in the redistribution of power. Theories, intellectuals, and institutions that promote social engineering through law are inherently discredited and present logical targets for restructuring. This strikes, in particular, at the project of socio-legal scholars to analyse law in its social, economic, cultural, and political context.

THE NEW ZEALAND PROTOTYPE

Changes proposed for New Zealand come closest to the global free market ideal. These proposals form an integral part of the broader neo-liberal experiment which began in New Zealand in 1984 and is widely viewed as the most radical in the OECD, if not the world.[29]

The rationale for tertiary education restructuring in New Zealand has been relentlessly ideological, with justifications of fiscal restraint and 'massification' belatedly grafted on. In the Treasury's 1987 post-election briefing it advocated the separation of university functions into: teaching, to be funded by declining government subsidy and increasing student fees; research, funded by competitive tendering for state funds and private contracts; and entrepôt or storehouse functions, which would not be explicitly funded at all.[30] The Treasury acknowledged that traditional critic and conscience functions of universities would effectively disappear:

> Historically universities may have acted as a key source of free information and discussion on political and other sensitive issues. In the information age this is no longer the case and the very multiplicity of information sources is itself a form of protection – as modern totalitarian states have found.[31]

Almost simultaneously, a report from the Business Roundtable, a highly influential business lobby group, proposed turning state universities into profit-driven State Education Corporations (SEC) run by government appointed boards of directors. These SECs would be fully self-funding, operate in a competitively neutral commercial environment, and be driven by consumer sovereignty. Existing staff would reapply for their jobs and be appointed for fixed terms. A subsequent officials' paper in 1992 confirmed the underlying premise that:

> academics must demonstrate their utility to society by placing themselves in an open market and accordingly compete for students who will provide the bulk of core funding through tuition fees. If academic research has a value it can stand up to the rigours of competition for limited funds.[32]

29 J. Kelsey, *Economic Fundamentalism. The New Zealand Experiment: A World Model for Structural Adjustment?* (1996).

30 New Zealand Treasury, *Government Management. Briefing Papers to the Incoming Government, 1987* (1987) vol. 1, ch. 6 and vol. 2.

31 id., vol. 2, p. 178.

32 M. Robinson, 'Governance of Tertiary Institutions', New Zealand State Services Commission paper to the Taskforce on Capital Charging of Tertiary Institutions, 18 August 1992 (unpublished).

There was no place in this agenda for the nation-building function of universities; no virtue in an educated population of graduates and academics committed to the society which invested in them; no inherent value in education and knowledge if it was not highly rewarded in the current commercial market; no purpose in academic contributions to research, policy, legislation, and public debate; no need for expert analysis and public critique which was free from party-political and commercial vested interest; no obligation to comply with the Crown's Treaty of Waitangi obligations to indigenous Maori. All these would be sacrificed to the forces of supply and demand in the global education market.

Changes to tertiary education over the following decade were dramatic. Government allocated funding on the basis of student enrolments, progressively reducing the per capita tuition subsidy and leaving universities to charge their own fees. Students were supported by an income-contingent student loan scheme at near-commercial rates and student allowances which were subject to a rigorous means test. Compared to other areas of economic and social policy, however, progress towards the Treasury's vision was slow. Funding for private tertiary enterprises remained limited and full competitive neutrality between public and private providers was some way off. State tertiary education remained heavily subsidized, with government committed to a limit on student contributions of 25 per cent of tuition fees. Enterprise agreements still covered most permanent academic and general staff, and at all sites unions were recognized. Universities remained governed by majority-elected councils, including staff and students. After intense and effective pressure, section 162(4) of the Education Act 1989 explicitly recognized institutional autonomy, academic freedom, and the academics' critic and conscience role.

Each time the officials and ministers attempted to advance their agenda, the flaws in market-driven model and specific proposals were exposed, and the proposals diluted, deferred or withdrawn.[33] By 1997 the stand-off had reached a critical point. Frustrated at the lack of progress made by officials, the centre-right coalition government formed in late 1996 announced a comprehensive review of tertiary education to be undertaken by officials, led by the Treasury and the Ministry of Education. A Green Paper was released for discussion and submissions in September 1997. The goals it set for tertiary education in the next twenty years reflected the government's stated education strategy, namely:

> to ensure that New Zealand has a tertiary sector that will:
>
> - promote provider responsiveness to the education and training needs of students
> - improve the efficiency of delivery
> - improve access to educational opportunities, particularly for those who are currently under-represented

33 See, further, R. Butterworth and N. Tarling, *A Shakeup Anyway: Government and the Universities in New Zealand in a Decade of Reform* (1994).

- improve the quality and value of educational outcomes
- provide greater incentives for and assure the effective management of tertiary education institutions.[34]

The Green Paper talked solely in terms of providers, funders, owners, and consumers in a competitive, international education market, and focused on tuition funding, research funding, regulatory mechanisms, and governance and accountability. Other critical areas, such as student allowances and proposed changes to the education qualification framework, would be dealt with separately.[35] The paper offered a familiar recitation of the failures of the existing system couched in the terminology discussed above.

The theoretical assumptions of state failure and market solutions remained unchanged from the 1987 Treasury briefing – a document which leading public management analyst Allen Schick described in a 1996 report commissioned by the Treasury and State Services Commission thus:

> Although (the Treasury briefing) alleges serious deficiencies in New Zealand government, it deduces these from the logic of institutional economics, not from the systematic study of public organisations. The evidence offered of government failure is slim. . . . The brief has an undertone of 'everybody knows government is inefficient, so there is no need to prove the point'.[36]

Even the OECD's largely sympathetic 1997 report on New Zealand tertiary education questioned the lack of empirical support for the market-driven model:

> Do the 'market forces' function effectively? If not, what steps can government take to put in place the conditions (or remove the obstacles to) their effective operation? Such evidence as was made available to us is weak or non-generalisable on these points and requires considerable caution in its use. [37]

Officials responsible for the Green Paper subsequently conceded there had been no research *qua* research, aside from four reports commissioned from consultants on specific issues with a very tight turnaround.[38]

There was no opportunity to question the prevailing market paradigm; the Green Paper simply offered choices on the way it should be applied. Again, the government ignored OECD criticisms that the rapid succession of contentious changes had generated more opposition than in any other country, and that greater efforts were required to broaden and strengthen

34 New Zealand Ministry of Education, *Education 1997–1999 Government Strategy* (1997).

35 New Zealand Ministry of Education, *A Future Qualifications Policy for New Zealand: A Plan for the National Qualifications Framework* (1997).

36 A. Schick, *The Spirit of Reform: Managing the New Zealand State Sector in a Time of Change*, A report prepared for the State Services Commission and the Treasury, New Zealand, August 1996, (the Schick report) 18.

37 OECD Education Committee, *Thematic Review of the First Years of Tertiary Education: New Zealand* (1997) 12.

38 Personal communication in a meeting between Ministry of Education officials and Association of University Staff, 25 September 1997.

dialogue.[39] Options were further circumscribed by the primary objective of increasing participation within a capped tertiary education budget.

The government's, or at least officials', preferences had already been disclosed in the Treasury and Ministry of Education 1996 post-election briefings, and a leaked draft of the Green Paper which was much less discreet.[40] The preferred solution for tuition funding was a learning-account or voucher entitling each permanent resident or citizen to a set value of tertiary education. As participation increased the fiscal cap would see per capita value of entitlements fall, with no guaranteed floor. Students could redeem their entitlement for individual courses at any approved provider of an accredited qualification across the entire 'tertiary education sector', whether industry trainers, polytechnics or universities, or publicly, privately or foreign owned. Individual institutions would continue to set fees according to their assessment of the market price, given supply, demand, and their competitive positioning.

Research funds could be allocated either through competition, based on a research quantum or competitive tendering, or through an enrolment-related formula. The latter option was contingent on proof of the relationship between teaching and research, which even then might see the requirement for research-informed teaching restricted to postgraduate degrees. Further research funds would continue to be available through the competitive tendering processes of the Foundation of Research Science and Technology where government set the amount available and the priorities.

The controversial New Zealand Qualifications Authority would accredit qualifications, programmes, and providers with reference to a new minimum quality threshold, potentially extending its jurisdiction to presently autonomous accreditation of university degrees. Use of the term 'university' would be protected, in recognition that New Zealand needed to maintain internationally accepted notions of a university.[41] However, the desire to encourage greater competition would require some trade-offs. The Green Paper raised, then rejected, the possibility that a subsequent review of the statutory characteristics of a university 'could include relaxing the requirement that a university should act as a critic and conscience of society'.[42] Ominously, however, the existing characteristics were considered to be only 'broadly' appropriate.

Governance proposals would see university councils replaced by small governing bodies wholly, or predominantly, appointed by the responsible Minister. These bodies would be required to 'determine strategic direction,

39 OECD, op. cit., n. 37, p. 22.

40 New Zealand Ministry of Education, *Briefing for the Incoming Government* (1996) 7–12 and 89–108; New Zealand Treasury, *Briefing to the Incoming Government 1996* (1996) 48–50 and 115.

41 New Zealand Ministry of Education, *A Future Tertiary Education Policy for New Zealand: Tertiary Education Review. Green Paper* (1997) 42.

42 id., p. 82.

and set financially responsible policies that best contribute to the Government's tertiary eduction strategy and goals and its ownership objectives.'[43] The Minister and governing body would negotiate an annual Statement of Intent setting out financial and non-financial performance requirements.

In organizational terms, the preference was to convert universities into Crown companies which would be required to run as efficient and successful businesses. Alternatively, their current status as statutory corporations could be substantially revised to reflect the new regime. Under either form, profit-making would not be the primary objective of universities; however, they would be required to operate 'in a financially responsible manner' so as to 'meet their educational objectives and maintain financial viability.'[44] Competitive neutrality between public and private providers would see universities meet the costs of capital as part of their normal operating expenses – which under the Crown company model was referred to as a fixed dividend regime – with the right to raise debt against those assets.[45]

IMPLICATIONS FOR NEW ZEALAND LAW SCHOOLS

The Green Paper proposals generated a mass of critique. Only selected points are dealt with here. Some affect all aspects of universities; some effect the law schools particularly.

The Dearing report in the United Kingdom observed:

> Higher education is fundamental to the social, economic and cultural health of the nation. It will contribute not only through the intellectual development of students and by equipping them for work, but also by adding to the world's store of knowledge and understanding, fostering culture for its own sake, and promoting the values that characterise higher education: respect for evidence; respect for individuals and their views; and the search for truth. Equally, part of its task will be to accept a duty of care for the wellbeing of our democratic civilisation, based on respect for the individual and respect by the individual for the conventions and laws which provide the basis of a civilised society.[46]

In New Zealand, the objective of creating knowledge completely disappeared and the longer-term costs to a vibrant and functioning democracy have been utterly ignored. As storehouses of knowledge, universities are not simply museums for information. The national community of the present and the future requires a repository of knowledge, history, and culture which will endure. That same community requires research, teaching, and publications to move social thinking forward; the kind of thinking which the market

43 id., p. 55; see, also, n. 34.

44 id., p. 65–6.

45 id., p. 63, n. 31.

46 National Committee of Inquiry into Higher Education, *Higher Education in the Learning Society* (1997) (the Dearing report), summary report, introduction, at para. 8.

may not reward. Specific communities whom the market fails, perhaps because they are small, unvalued or lack economic power, have a right to the education, knowledge, expertise, research, and recognition which universities provide as public goods. If that pool of knowledge and expertise is lost it cannot easily be restored once trends change or the market approach has proved to fail.

The real assets of universities are not their land, bricks, and mortar, which the Crown claims to own, but their international reputation and their academics' minds. These risk being devalued or lost under a market regime. As government funds are spread more thinly, universities will be forced to rely on further cost-cutting efficiencies and higher student fees. Instability and unpredictability of tuition and research funding will make planning extremely difficult. Investment in physical plant, technology, and libraries will be high risk and costly and the infrastructure on which quality universities depend will become hard to maintain. Similar concerns apply to 'human' capital. Insecurity, depressed employment conditions, greater use of short-term contracts, preference for generalists over specialists, and minimal investment in research and training will make New Zealand universities even less attractive to high-quality academics when compared with overseas universities and local professions.

This effect will be compounded by moves to managerialism within the universities which have already seen the devolution of decision making to faculty-based cost centres. As responsibility for cost-cutting is moved to the periphery, shifts in curriculum, teaching, assessment, and employment practices will become more *ad hoc* and less visible. Increased internal competition for university and private resources is expected to make cross-subsidisation unsustainable, and cross-disciplinary initiatives will become increasingly problematic. Market-friendly sectors of the universities will thrive, while the non-commercial wither and die. Without conscious moves to neutralize these effects, the uni-versity will be replaced by an internally competitive multi-versity.

The combination of significant increases in participation and capped budgets also suggests reduced entry standards, larger classes, lower-quality teachers, and cheaper teaching techniques. Maintaining quality through competition is unrealistic in a market of New Zealand's size. Elite institutions and law schools may respond by capping numbers and branding themselves at the top-end of the market – thereby bidding up their price with serious consequences for equity. A two-tier system of legal education may well emerge. At the lower end, non-university providers will seek accreditation to offer minimum-quality degrees, backed by little if any research-informed teaching, low qualified staff, and few support resources, such as libraries. Proposed deregulation of the legal profession, including removal of the conveyancing monopoly, will encourage niche market programmes for non-lawyers wishing to take up those opportunities. Ethical and professional standards and the quality of legal services will become even more difficult to control, leaving poor or uninformed consumers highly vulnerable.

Removing requirements for research-based teaching at undergraduate levels would mean serious funding cuts for most law schools which predominantly focus on the core undergraduate professional degrees. The current approach to competitive tendering favours long-term collaborative research programmes and is ill-suited to the individual, library-based mode of most legal research, while the existing government-determined priorities include no explicit category for law. Internal cross-subsidies within the universities are very difficult under this kind of scheme.

A research quantum approach could offer significant rewards for high-performing law schools. A lot would depend on the criteria – in a small country, local research is vital, but publishing opportunities for such work in internationally refereed journals are few. There is a risk, however, that this may deliver inadequate funding to support research-based teaching in the less successful law schools. It would also distort the kind of research undertaken and forums in which it is published. Reliance on private contracts can have a similar diversionary effect, placing commercially rewarding research ahead of interest, expertise or public need.

Market-minded law students, as customers, can be expected to demand a greater say over content, ideology, and pedagogy. Socio-legal scholars and courses, which are already scarce on the ground within very traditional law schools, would be under particular threat. So would initiatives directed to increase understanding and prominence of Maori and gender perspectives in curriculum and teaching. Growing participation by full fee-paying and subsidized foreign students will compound the pressure to limit or simplify local content, as will the entry of international providers, the expansion of transnational legal education, and demands for mutual recognition and harmonization of legal qualifications.

New Zealand universities already suffer severe geographical and intellectual isolation. The reciprocal obligations which link local academics to the international academic community expect a significant contribution to international journals, as writers, editors, and referees; as speakers and participants in international forums; as sources of information for visiting academics, politicians, policy-makers or journalists; as commentators for foreign media. It is the quality and visibility of such contributions on which an institution's international reputation largely depends. Funding to support international interaction and exchange, including sabbatical leave, will certainly reduce and may disappear. If departments, qualifications or even institutions are to be born or die according to short-term consumer demand, and staff and research projects fluctuate accordingly, international credibility and reputation will be difficult to maintain. Benchmarking with international universities of high repute will become increasingly unsustainable, as will attraction of overseas students, entry by New Zealand graduates into overseas programmes, and the portability of New Zealand degrees.

Finally, the reconceptualization of legal education as a private good within a commercial market has left no place for public good, public service or critic and conscience roles which law schools have traditionally fulfilled. National legal systems depend on the research and ideas generated within local law schools, without which the development of law would either stagnate or be forced to rely on imported, often inappropriate, arguments and analyses. Legislators and policy-makers depend on legal academics to provide independent expertise as members, researchers, and witnesses for advisory bodies, public inquiries and select committees. Without that, government decision-making becomes a closed shop for officials and those lobbyists and private interests with the resources to produce research, influence public and government debate, and participate in official forums. Academics also provide a free, independent, and diverse source of expertise for the news media, and foster public understanding and constructive debate. Funding, time, and the need for market approval would place this role in jeopardy.

RESPONDING TO THE CHALLENGE

The New Zealand model is at the extreme of the privatization spectrum. The Dearing report, released in July 1997, sought to reposition higher education in the United Kingdom as an international, high technology, competitive enterprise which retained the traditional functions of social integration, intellectual enrichment, and advancing democracy. The rationale of increased participation and fiscal restraint were most prominent, with ideology playing a much less visible role. Despite its comparatively benign tenor, however, Dearing's recommendations of funding to follow the student, an income-contingent deferred contribution scheme, and a centralized qualifications framework to deliver 'learning for life' clearly endorses a more-market line.

In Australia, the seven-person West committee, drawn from academia, education, science and technology, and business, was appointed in 1997 to review and report on tertiary education. Its terms of reference were relatively open and set in an international context. But it also reflected a strongly market-driven theme, building on a series of reviews commissioned by the former Labor government which saw the introduction of full fees for foreign and some postgraduate students, the higher education contribution scheme (HECS) of deferred student loans, and conversion of polytechnics into universities.[47] Severe cuts to universities' income in the new Liberal Government's budget in 1996 suggest that fiscal restraints are likely to remain.

47 *Higher Education: A Policy Discussion Paper* (1987); *Industry Training in Australia: the need for change* (1988); *The National Competition Policy Review* (1993) (the Hilmer report); *Report of the Industry Commission on the Growth and Revenue Implications of National Competition Policy* (1995); *Review of the Management of Higher Education* (1995).

Despite variations of detail and degree, this is clearly a global agenda. Pressures on domestic education policy from international education entrepreneurs can be expected to intensify in future years. The more their rights of entry are advanced and locked in through mechanisms like the GATS and MAI, the more difficult they will be to constrain. If that occurs, the scope for independent legal scholarship will be severely damaged and its critical dimension seriously undermined.

In responding to these trends, it is not enough simply to defend the status quo. Many of the arguments for restructuring have validity. The challenge is to acknowledge current deficiencies and address them in a constructive way. Trow has described the prevailing strategy of universities as appeasement based on 'soft' managerialism – it recognizes the problems of complacency, conservatism, inefficiency, indifference to industry needs, and inequity, but also values universities' norms and traditions, which in turn depend on their continued relative autonomy. This is exemplified in the Dearing committee's compromise. He goes on to suggest that initiatives to improve efficiency, backed by periodic critical reviews, are the best line of defence. While this objective is laudable, it is misleading to assume that global developments can be locally controlled, that national policy decisions are rational or that managerialism can be rendered benign. Effective strategies must recognize the inter-connected global, national, and institutional aspects of privatization agenda and identify where the tensions and contradictions with national tradition, politics, and commitments lie.

JOURNAL OF LAW AND SOCIETY
VOLUME 25, NUMBER 1, MARCH 1998
ISSN: 0263–323X, pp. 71–84

Law as a Parasitic Discipline

ANTHONY BRADNEY*

British university law schools are undergoing a radical change in the nature of legal research and scholarship. They were once dominated by pure doctrinal analysis but the new generation of legal scholars are either abandoning doctrinal work or infusing it with techniques and approaches drawn from the humanities and the social sciences. This essay argues that this change will lead to a greater ability to provide law students with a truly liberal education and will also enable the law school to take a much greater part in the intellectual debates to be found elsewhere in the university.

INTRODUCTION

The academic doctrinal project which has dominated United Kingdom university law schools for most of their history, the attempt to explain law solely through the internal evidence offered by judgements and statutes, is now entering its final death throes.[1] There are few serious scholars of law under forty who are now attempting such work on any significant scale except as a student exercise for a doctoral dissertation. This is not to say that doctrinal work is no longer done. Case-notes are still written.[2] Books using doctrinal technique are produced for students and practising lawyers. But such works are not a sustained attempt to reveal the underpinning of principle which Lord Goff identified as the task and goal of the academic lawyer working in the doctrinal mode.[3] Such books as are written purely in

* *Faculty of Law, University of Leicester, University Road, Leicester LE1 7RH, England*

1 For a contrary view, see G. Jones, '"Traditional" Legal Scholarship: a Personal View' in *What Are Law Schools For?*, ed. P. Birks (1996) 14.

2 Indeed I am preparing one on *Fitzpatrick* v. *Sterling Housing Association* at the same time as writing this article.

3 R. Goff, 'The Search for Principle' (1983) *Proceeedings of the British Academy* 169, at 171. This is an amplification of Dicey's remark that '[b]y adequate study and careful thought whole departments of law can . . . be reduced to order and exhibited under the form of a few principles which sum up the effect of a hundred cases . . .'. A. Dicey, *Can English Law be taught at the Universities?* (1883) 20.

the doctrinal mode vary greatly in size depending on the knowledge of the author and the proposed market for the book. They are all alike, however, in being simply the cumulation of explications of individual legal rules. In scholarly writing doctrinal work is now used not on its own but as part of a broader attempt to understand law. It is used alongside a range of other methods taken from disciplines in the humanities and social sciences. Monographs and serious articles may in part be doctrinal (though more and more frequently they are not doctrinal at all) but the work does not depend on doctrinal theory for its theoretical underpinning.

The abandonment of the doctrinal project should not be seen as a sudden volte-face in the intellectual allegiance of the law school. It represents a new stage in an evolutionary process. In practice in the past doctrinal work has usually involved the overt use of non-doctrinal material. In seeking to understand and explain even the narrowest of legal rules doctrinal scholars have constantly felt it necessary to ask questions which, because they were political, ethical or sociological, could not be answered by their own chosen method. Thus, for example, in one of his books on contract law Smith states that '[f]or a thorough understanding of the subject, there is no substitute for the study of the cases'.[4] In the first chapter he then proceeds to discuss what is 'practical', whether the majority of promises are made under seal or not, 'the way in which contracts are in fact made', what would be 'excessively inconvenient' in an auction and so on and so forth.[5] Doubtless he is correct to raise these matters and consideration of them is necessary for an understanding of contract law. Equally plainly, none of them can be understood by reference solely to case-law. A thorough analysis of any one of these issues is only possible through the use of appropriate methods drawn from the social sciences. Anything else is mere anecdote, hearsay, and assertion. In such instances an author's avowal of the doctrinal method has been a justification for treating non-doctrinal matters without recourse to the appropriate material available from elsewhere in the academy or an excuse for using such material in a cursory or ill-informed manner. Equally, doctrinal work has always been infused with intellectual presumptions and assumptions that have dominated the doctrinal argument even though the doctrinal method has concealed their existence.[6] Doctrinal method has never had the purity its partisans ascribed to it. The realization of this, and the realization that, within the academy, it is unacceptable to deal with any material or with any question with anything less than full attention, is what has characterized the new method of working. This has resulted in either the abandonment of doctrinal method, on the ground that it is incapable of

4 J. Smith, *The Law of Contract* (1989) v.

5 id., pp. 3–5 and p. 8.

6 See, for example, D. Kennedy, 'Form and substance in Private Law Ajudication' (1976) 89 *Harvard Law Rev.* 1685.

a producing satisfactory answers to any intellectually compelling questions, or, as frequently, infusing doctrinal method with other techniques.

A number of writers have already noted the new spirit which is beginning to dominate United Kingdom law schools. In his inaugural lecture at Cambridge University Hepple argued that law students need to study, among other things, 'social sciences, philosophy, ethics, history' and have 'the ability to comprehend the evidence and methods of social sciences'.[7] Thomas has recently asked if there is 'the emergence of a new paradigm: that of socio-legal studies' in university law schools.[8] Cotterell has argued that:

> [a]ll the centuries of purely doctrinal writing on law have produced less valuable knowledge about what law is, as a social phenomenon, and what it does than the relatively few decades of work in sophisticated modern empirical socio-legal studies . . .[9]

This new spirit does not mean the subjugation of law to sociology. Rather, it represents the realisation that law can become a site or focus for many disciplines within the academy and thus the emergence of socio-legal studies.[10]

This essay will consider the implications this new spirit has for the university law school. As law becomes not a discipline unique and self-contained within itself but parasitic in large part on work started elsewhere in the university, what will be the changes for staff and students not just in the university law school but in the wider university community? The disciplinary effects of doctrinal teaching and research have often been the subject of consideration in the past. This essay will argue that the personal effect on the intellectual and emotional growth of students and the institutional effect on the relationship between the law school and the rest of the university are also important.

THE WIDER ACADEMIC CONTEXT

University law schools do not exist in academic isolation. Estimating what law schools will or can become must take account of the possibility of wider changes to higher education. Official and unofficial reports on higher education in general and legal education in particular are usually largely a

7 B. Hepple, 'The Renewal of the Liberal Law Degree' (1996) *Cambridge Law J.* 470, at 485 and 481.

8 P.A. Thomas, 'Introduction' in *Socio-Legal Studies*, ed. P.A. Thomas (1997) 19.

9 R. Cotterell, *Law's Community* (1995) 296.

10 Socio-legal studies has been defined in many different ways. In this essay the term is taken to indicate the use of ideas 'from other disciplines primarily but not exclusively from within the social science and humanities fields'. S. Wheeler, 'Company Law' in Thomas, op. cit., n. 8, at p. 285.

failure.[11] Nevertheless, such reports do have some influence and, particularly where they are in accord with existing currents in academic thought, can suggest which roads are more likely to be travelled down. In this respect both the recent Dearing report on higher education and the Lord Chancellor's Advisory Committee on Legal Education and Conduct (ACLEC) report on legal education must be included in the analysis.[12]

Central to the arguments in this essay is the consideration that ACLEC and Dearing have given to the purpose and function of the law school and higher education; to what the law school is expected to do for the student. ACLEC's position in this respect is much clearer than that in Dearing. ACLEC's view of the purpose of legal education in universities is that 'the [law] degree course should stand as an independent liberal education in the discipline of law, not tied to any specific vocation'.[13] Whilst ACLEC's report is alive to the employment prospects of graduates in law and contains proposals for integrating academic and vocational education, the priority given to liberal education is plain. Other educational aims, seen as being valid in their own right, then follow from that.[14] ACLEC's view is in accord with the majority opinion amongst academics in university law schools who largely subscribe to a belief in the importance of legal studies providing a liberal education.[15]

On the question of the function and purpose of higher education little in Dearing is new. The report encapsulates debates that have a history of at least a century. Such novelty as there is lies in the fact that Dearing seeks

11 Some fail wholly. It is difficult to see any effect on academic legal education that resulted from Lady Marre's report *A Time for Change* (1988). The Jarratt report on universities produced for the Committee of Vice-Chancellors and Principals (CVCP), *Report of the Steering Committee for Efficiency studies in Universities* (1988), produced much comment but little action. Even those that are thought of as being a success are not wholly implemented. Despite Ormrod's recommendations no Institute of Profesional Legal Studies was set up and the universities and colleges of higher education did not take sole responsibility for vocational legal training (*Report of the Committee on Legal Education* (1971; Cmnd 4595) ch. 9, recs. 40 and 23). There were also other recommendations that were not implemented. The Robbins report on higher education, *Higher Education* (1963; Cmnd. 2154) took it is axiomatic that 'courses of higher education should be available for all those who are qualified by ability and attainment to pursue them and wish to do so' (para. 31). This has yet to happen.

12 National Committee of Inquiry into Higher Education, *Higher Education in the learning society* (1997) (the Dearing report); ACLEC, *First Report on Legal Education and Training* (1996). The Government's White Paper on further and higher education had not been published at the time of writing this essay.

13 ACLEC, id., para 4.6.

14 ACLEC's proposal is part of an historical process which has gradually seen English university law schools distance themselves from the legal professions and the legal professions propose decreasing degrees of control over the content of law degrees. (See A. Bradney and F. Cownie, 'Working on the Chain Gang?' (1996) 2 *Contemporary Issues in Law* 15, at 24–6).

15 J. MacFarlane, M. Jeeves, and A. Boon, 'Education for Life or for Work?' (1987) 137 *New Law J.* 835, at 836.

to propose both sides of what have, hitherto, been seen as irreconcilable arguments. Thus, for example, in 1874, in his rectorial address to St Andrews, T.H. Huxley stated that faculties such as theology and law were '[t]echnical schools, intended to equip men who received general culture with the special knowledge which is needed for the proper performance of [their duties].'[16] His words were a response to John Stuart Mill's earlier rectorial address, delivered in 1867, in which Mill had stated that the university was not 'a place of professional education . . . [its] object is not to make skilful lawyers . . . but capable and educated human beings.'[17] Huxley would be delighted to find Dearing espousing, in recommendation 18, the notion that all programmes in higher education should 'help students to become familiar with work, and help them reflect on such experience'.[18] In turn, Mill would no doubt support at least one of the four purposes that Dearing sees for higher education 'to play a major role in shaping a democratic, civilised and inclusive society'.[19]

Dearing does not give liberal educational values the unequivocal support that is found in ACLEC. Nevertheless, it does allow room for such education. Given the positions taken in both these reports and given the stance taken by academics working in university law schools, this essay will therefore explore the changing nature of the law school in the context of its adherence to notions of liberal education. It is not clear that either ACLEC or academics in law schools wholly understand the implications of espousing law as a liberal education. This essay is premised upon the idea that '[t]he problem [for liberal education] is to produce specialists who are in touch with a humane centre, and to produce a centre for them to be in touch with . . .'.[20] A liberal education is thus seen as involving both a highly detailed technical education in an individual discipline and an attempt to facilitate students' appreciating the all-imbuing nature of, and involving themselves in assessing, questions of value and worth.[21]

THE LAW SCHOOL AND THE SOUL

Goodrich has explored the dispiriting effects of a traditional, doctrinal legal education:

16 T.H. Huxley, 'Universities: Actual and Ideal' in T.H. Huxley, *Collected Essays: Volume III* (1905) 215.

17 J.S. Mill, 'Inaugural address to the University of St Andrews' in *Collected Work of John Stuart Mill: Volume XXI*, ed. J.M. Robson (1984) 218.

18 Dearing, op. cit., n. 12, para. 9.32.

19 id., para. 5.11.

20 F.R. Leavis, *Education and the University* (1948) 28. Leavis's view was narrowly nationalistic. For 'centre' it would be better to substitute 'centres'.

21 See, further, A. Bradney, 'Liberalising Legal Education' in *The Law School: Global Issues, Local Questions*, ed. F. Cownie (forthcoming).

Law school stole my hopes of change and robbed me of any surviving sense of the relevance of my inner world, of poetry, desire or dream, to the life of the institution . . .[22]

Turow has written to similar effect about the immediate impact of studying law. Talking about a short holiday he took six weeks after starting as a student at Harvard Law School he wrote:

> I realized for the first time how great the pressure was which I'd been under. I was a different person here, the man I'd been six weeks ago. I was not trying to keep my language precise, or analyzing every spoken proposition to find its converse. I could look at mountains as well as words and books. I could live with nothing but the dull grey buzz of tranquillity passing through my head.
> 'I've stolen away from the brain thieves', I told Annette.[23]

Whatever its value in training the mind or in building a suitable intellectual base for the practitioner, there can be little doubt that the essential aridity of doctrinal study has a disabling effect on most of those who are subject to it.

DOCTRINAL ARGUMENT AND DOCTRINAL CONCEPTS

The disabling effect of doctrinal study arises because of two different, though related, matters.

First, in most instances, and for most people, doctrinal study teaches the student to particularize and narrow argument. It teaches close reasoning and the utmost attention to textual content. In themselves these things are important intellectual skills. But at the same time doctrinal study also forbids the making of the connections with the wider questions which lie at the root of human inquiry. Reasoning in doctrinal study must be about a particular range of questions. The question which cannot legitimately be answered by reference to a statute or a judgement lies outside the doctrinal gaze. Doctrinal study explicitly identifies questions outside the doctrinal range as being something not relevant for the doctrinal student. It implicitly devalues such questions and treats them as not being worthy of consideration within the precise, objective word of the law school. Moreover, the person skilled in doctrinal techniques is, by virtue of this skill, no better equipped to attend to non-doctrinal questions. But the student begins life as Aristotle's human being, driven and defined essentially by curiosity, by a desire to understand the world. This curiosity, involving as it does curiosity about questions of value and issues of assessment, cannot be assuaged by use of the seeming logic of doctrinal analysis. Kahn-Fruend argued that students 'must not be allowed to go around it [doctrinal argument] by escaping into talk about

22 P. Goodrich, 'Of Blackstone's Tower: Metephors of Distance and Histories of the English Law School' in Birks, op. cit., n. 1, p. 59.

23 S. Turow, *One L* (1977) 106.

politics . . .'.[24] But human beings are, precisely, in Aristotle's terminology political animals and cannot give up their constant process of political inquiry.[25] Doctrinal study thus builds a dissonance between the psyche of the student and his or her academic persona. To become a law student the student must ignore who he or she is.

The nature of doctrinal study and the effect that it has on students is highlighted by comparing it with something else in the academy that seems very similar, the techniques of close reading used in the study of literature by F.R. Leavis. Here again, as in the doctrinal method, in Leavis's close reading, there is the demand that the student pay close attention to the text and the dismissal of the idea that anything outside the text can be germane to what goes on in the analysis:

> It should, by continual insistence and varied exercise in analysis, be enforced that literature is made of words, and that everything worth saying in criticism of verse and prose can be related to judgements concerning particular arrangements of words on the page.[26]
> Literary history, as a matter of 'facts about' and accepted critical (or quasi-critical) description and commentary, is a worthless acquisition; worthless for the student who cannot as a critic – that is as an intelligent and discerning reader – make a personal approach to the essential data of the literary historian, the works of literature (an approach is personal or it is nothing . . .[27]

However, what Leavis seeks from this close reading is very different from that which is sought by the doctrinal lawyer:

> The essential discipline of an English School is the literary-critical . . . It trains, in a way no other discipline can, intelligence and sensibility together, cultivating a sensitiveness and precision of response and a delicate integrity of intelligence – intelligence that integrates as well as analyses and must have pertinacity and staying power as well as delicacy.[28]

Doctrinal study, in Leavis's terminology, trains intelligence. Leavis, pursuing a liberal education through the vehicle of literary studies, seeks more, addressing, through the development of sensibility, the questions of value that doctrinal study leaves out.[29]

24 O. Kahn-Freund, 'Reflections on Legal Education' (1966) 29 *Modern Law Rev.* 121, at 129.
25 Kahn-Freund believed that both doctrinal and non-doctrinal learning were possible together though he did concede that in the doctrinal method there was 'the danger that the discussion gets stuck in the perhaps intellectually very fascinating game of legal argument . . .' (Kahn-Freund, id.).
26 Leavis, op. cit., n. 20, p. 120.
27 id., p. 68.
28 id., p. 34.
29 Leavis has, of course, been widely criticized for the cultural and gender assumptions that lie behind his selection of material to be studied. (See, for example, M. King, *The New English Literatures* (1980) at 216–17.) Whatever the accuracy of these criticisms, they are criticisms of the application of the method rather than the method itself.

If Leavis's technique of close reading can allow students to address a wider range of questions than doctrinal study does this might suggest that doctrinal study can be adapted or improved so as to permit a wider engagement by the student. However, doctrinal study is personally disabling for students not just because of its argumentative technique.

Doctrinal study involves understanding, assimilating, and accepting given concepts which are particular to the discipline of law. The student must learn, for example, that the 'aggregate of a man's proprietary rights constitutes his *estate*, his *assets*, or his *property*' and that '[i]t makes no difference . . . whether a right is *jus in rem* or *jus in personam.* Rights of either sort are proprietary . . .'.[30] Such concepts are ways of seeing the world. They are concepts which are not only different to but also alien from concepts in other academic disciplines.[31] Moreover, they are ways of seeing which are at odds with what law students have previously experienced and continue to experience outside their studies. They are complicated, precise, abstruse and are learnt only at the expense of great personal effort. And their apparent solidity, objectivity, and neutrality cuts up the world in such a fashion as to forbid their use in any other kind of argument. Whereas in other disciplines within the social sciences and humanities concepts travel from one academic site to another, legal concepts remain isolated and isolating.

The alienating effect of doctrinal concepts has previously been noted in the context of women students, those from socially disadvantaged backgrounds, and those who hold radical political views.[32] It has, however, a resonance that is far wider than this. Doctrinal concepts, like the techniques of doctrinal argument, by their form, forbid all serious political, ethical or personal thought not just some kinds of such thought. Every student, no matter what their background and no matter what their political or other beliefs, is equally disadvantaged by 'the intellectual strait-jacket that is the traditional legal method'.[33]

The above is not to argue that doctrinal concepts do not have a political content nor is it to deny that that content can, at least in the past, frequently seem to have been slanted in a particular direction. Thus, for example, McAuslan may well have been right in arguing that:

30 *Jurisprudence by Sir John Salmond*, ed. G. Willliams (10th ed., 1947) at 256 and 257.

31 So much so that when other disciplines engage with law they must develop their own concepts to analyse law rather than rely on the concepts already developed in law. See, for example, E. Durkheim *The Division of Labour in Society* (1933) 68.

32 M. Le Brun and R. Johnstone, *The Quiet Revolution: Improving Student Learning in Law* (1994) 65. On the effect on women students, see 'Define and Empower: Women Students Consider Feminist Learning' (1990) I *Law and Critique* 47 at pp. 54–55. For a survey of CLS and feminist literature on this general point, see W. Conklin, 'The Invisible Author of Legal Authority' (1996) VII *Law and Critique* 173 at pp. 173–6.

33 R. Collier, 'Masculinism, Law and Law Teaching' (1991) 19 *International J. of the Sociology of Law* 427, at 429.

> the courts' general approach to judicial review in these matters [of health care and housing] – that it can all be reduced to a matter of individual rights versus the bureaucracy is very much in line with the ideology of the present [Conservative] government . . .[34]

Doctrinal concepts may well be inherently individualistic. They may well be patriachical. But to deplore their individualism or patriachy is to miss the point. It is not only those students who oppose or who are disadvantaged by individualism or patriarchy who are disempowered by the concepts. Doctrinal concepts not only do not teach us to oppose the philosophies they echo; they do not allow us to understand or defend the philosophies either. Because of this, doctrinal concepts are not simply a political difficulty; more importantly, they are also an educational problem. They reinforce certain attitudes and beliefs but they act as advertising slogans, not forms of reflection. If any thinking is to be done about their individualist or patriarchal nature, students must break through and break away from the doctrinal concepts they have been at such pains to learn. Thus the concepts are themselves a barrier to any student's education.

WIDER LEARNING

In their book on the manner in which students learn law, Le Brun and Johnstone argue that learning is not about the transfer of information from teacher to student but about students learning to construct knowledge in the context of a particular culture.[35] Learning is not simply learning facts; it is learning things in a particular context and learning to apply them in a way legitimated as correct by that social context. '[T]o learn law, law students must engage in activities and enter the community of practitioners and the culture of law.'[36] Le Brun and Johnstone go on to assert that this does not necessarily involve students 'buying into' all the cultural norms of that community.[37] However, many writers have argued that in the traditional process of legal education there is a strong pressure on students to not only assimilate but also accept the values of the community that they are studying. As Goodrich has put it, 'an institutionally managed trauma gives birth to a conforming or believing soul'.[38]

Engagement with socio-legal studies will assist a student in deciding whether or not to accept the cultural values of the legal community. Variety makes resistance more possible. This happens in three ways. First, whilst doctrinal study forbids many types of question, socio-legal studies embraces them. The range of questions that the socio-legal community asks about law

34 P. McAuslan, 'Administrative Law, Collective Consumption and Judicial Policy' (1983) 46 *Modern Law Rev*. 1, at 8.
35 Le Brun and Johnstone, op. cit, n. 32, pp. 71–5.
36 id., p. 74.
37 id., p. 75.
38 Goodrich, op. cit., n. 22.

is, precisely, the range of questions asked about anything within the academy. Some of the disciplines the student will study will directly and explicitly analyse values as one of the schedule of questions that constitutes the community. Others will raise matters relevant to law as a tangential part of the enquiry. Secondly, if Le Brun and Johnstone's analysis of the nature of learning is correct, in engaging in other disciplines the student will have to enter into each of the communities that constitutes the discipline. The hold that the legal community has on them is thus dissipated and other models of other communities with other values are put before the student. Finally, by engaging in other disciplines, students are freed to follow their own lines of enquiry. They are not constrained by the limits of an individual discipline. Rather, they can mix different disciplines in the way they choose. This promotes a form of student learning which is increasingly independent of course tutors and which can in principle continue beyond the life of the course.

THE LAW SCHOOL AND THE UNIVERSITY

Samuelson's comment on the relationship between American universities and their law schools, 'the same zip code often used to be about all the law school and the university had in common', is equally applicable to the British situation.[39] Historically, the law school has contributed little to the main body of the university except to provide large numbers of highly qualified students taught very cheaply. In particular there has been little curricular contact or cross-over between the law school and other departments. This academic isolation has not been not accidental. Rather, it is the logical and necessary outcome of the doctrinal method and the doctrinal concepts described above. The law school could not engage in the academic projects of other departments and disciplines because it lacked the necessary conceptual apparatus so to do. Other students could not engage in law because that which they had learned outside law was of no assistance in the study of law and their studies elsewhere was thought to leave them with insufficient time to study law adequately.

Superficial examination of British law schools' activities would seem to belie any charge of academic isolation. Harris and Jones' recent survey of law schools in England, Wales and Northern Ireland showed that, of the sixty-six law schools responding, only twelve did not have some kind of joint or mixed degree programme.[40] Moreover, there has been a 'considerable

39 P. Samuelson, 'The Convergence of the Law School and the University' (1975) 44 *The Am. Scholar* 256, at 258.

40 P. Harris and M. Jones 'A Survey of Law Schools in the United Kingdom, 1996' (1997) 31 *The Law Teacher* 38, at 46.

increase' in both the number of mixed and joint degree courses.[41] Equally, other disciplines are sometimes incorporated into the standard LLB programme and law courses are taught by members of the law school in other single honours programmes within the university.[42] A 1994 survey of the work of legal academics found that 78 per cent of all teachers taught non-law degree students.[43] However, despite this apparent width and depth of involvement, examination of the details and experience of such contact in fact confirms the charge of academic isolation.

Leighton, Mortimer, and Whatley found that 92 per cent of all legal academics they surveyed preferred to teach either law undergraduates or law postgraduates to any other form of student.[44] Teaching law outside the law school is often characterized as 'teaching law to non-lawyers'.[45] The teaching and the students are thus characterized as being both secondary and inferior to that teaching and those students that are found within the law school. Participation in courses is usually limited to teaching. Bastin's early small-scale study of law teaching in business studies degrees found that where the law teaching was done by staff from a law department they did not participate in the administration of the business studies degree even when they were given the opportunity to do so.[46] It is thus not surprising to find that those teaching law outside the law school 'are often isolated from colleagues who teach the core subjects relevant to the degree'.[47]

The reasons for the isolation identified above are easy to identify. As Cartan and Vilkinas note in their article on law teaching in MBA courses:

> [t]he traditional (and still more common) approach to legal education . . . emphasises legal rules and includes a plethora of cases'.[48]

Such teaching, which follows on the pattern of traditional doctrinal study, puts a premium on repetition and in its law school context requires the student

41 J. Wilson , 'A third survey of university legal education' (1993) 13 *Legal Studies* 143, at 152.

42 Thus, for example, Harris and Jones reported that 59.2 per cent of all particpating institutions offered foriegn language tuition as part of their standard LLB programme. (Harris and Jones, op. cit., n. 40, at p. 54).

43 P. Leighton, T. Mortimer, and N. Whatley, *Law Teachers: Lawyers or Academics?* (1995) 34. This would include teaching both non-law degree students and sub-degree students.

44 id., p 35.

45 L. Skwarok, 'Business Law for Non-Lawyers: Setting the Stage for Teaching, Learning and Assessment at Hong Kong Polytechnic University' (1995) 29 *The Law Teacher* 189, at 189.

46 N. Bastin, 'Law, Law Staff and CNAA Business Studies Degree Courses' (1985) 19 *The Law Teacher* 12, at 13.

47 A. Ridley, 'Legal Skills for Non-Law Students: Added Value or Irrelevant Diversion?' (1994) 28 *The Law Teacher* 281, at 282.

48 G. Cartan and T. Vilkinas, 'Legal Literacy for Managers: The Role of the Educator' (1990) 24 *The Law Teacher* 246, at 248.

to immerse themselves in law. Outside the law school, the student finds that law is only a small part of his or her course. They have little opportunity to engage in the repetition and no possibility of giving themselves wholly over to the study of law. The result is that study can become reduced to the rote learning of legal 'facts' where there is '[n]o real understanding of legal concepts [and] . . . no subtlety in the analysis of law . . .'.[49]

Teaching law as part of a joint or mixed degree is not the same as teaching law as one or two units within another programme. However, there is much in the normal pattern of teaching on joint or mixed degrees that replicates the experience above. Lecturers from the different disciplines that constitute the joint or mixed degree will rarely meet. There is usually little attempt to integrate the individual parts of the degree. The students learn something of law and something of another discipline. If there are any specific connections between the two, the student is left to find them.[50] If the degree is to be accredited by the Law Society and Bar Council for professional purposes then, under existing arrangements, the course must contain the seven foundation subjects. If the degree is to allow students an opportunity to study discipline other than law then it will frequently contain no more law than those seven subjects. The degree may then be criticized from within the law school on the ground that consideration of the law is carried on only at a superficial level.[51] Once again, these failings in contact between the law school and the rest of the university and the criticism of the content of mixed degrees stem from the same background of a theory of doctrinal study and the nature of doctrinal concepts. The degree, albeit that it is mixed or joint, is seen as being there to teach students some law. Law is perceived as a discrete, doctrinal subject. Contact with other departments who will be teaching the same student history or politics or whatever is thus otiose. The only question is whether or not the student can be taught enough law within the constraints of the joint or mixed syllabus.

New developments in teaching law to non-law students demonstrate some of the possibilities for new contacts between law schools and other departments if law is treated as a parasitic discipline. Ridley notes that, in the context of teaching law to accountancy students, studying law in its 'broader social and political context', rather than from a doctrinal perspective, resulted in a 6 per cent rise in those students who 'definitely' saw law as being relevant to their studies.[52] Similarly Cartan and Vilkinas have observed a change in the style of teaching law to managers. The new approach to teaching:

49 Ridley, op. cit., n. 47, at p. 284.

50 This, of course, is not always the case. For example, the BA Economics and Law degree at Leicester has a special course in each year given over to the consideration of the relationship between economics and law.

51 P. Birks, 'Short Cuts' in *Pressing Problems in the Law*, ed. P. Birks (1994) 10–24.

52 Ridley, op. cit., n. 47, p. 283.

views law as a living entity which has a future as well as a present and recognises law as an evolving process with important elements of history, sociology, politics and economics.[53]

The evidence presented by changes such as the above is limited but suggestive. Once law is presented in terms that students outside the law school can recognize its relevance to their studies becomes obvious. This is not surprising. If we believe that:

> empirically, law is a component part of the wider social and political structure, is inextricably related to it in an infinite variety of ways, and can therefore only be properly understood if studied in that context[54]

then the reverse proposition also logically follows. If law is a component part of the wider social and political structure, those who study that structure elsewhere in the university must, if they are to properly understand what they study, see the place that law has in the object of their study. Law, far from being an abstruse, technical discipline marginal to the university, is intricately involved in all that study in the university which involves either humanity, society or the state. This is not to say that law is, or should be, of dominant concern elsewhere. Nevertheless, it is part of the picture and, if it is painted using techniques and methods drawn from outside the law school, its place can become clear to non-law students.

ACLEC's support for the law degree as a form of liberal education underscores the need for the law school to use socio-legal material in teaching its students, Similarly, some of the conclusions of the Dearing report emphasize the need for the law school to use socio-legal techniques and thus involve itself in the curriculum of courses outside the law school. Dearing repeats the Robbins call for a wider range of degree programmes and states that:

> while many students will continue to welcome the opportunity to pursue a relatively narrow field of knowledge in great depth, there will be many others for whom this will neither be attractive, nor useful in career terms, nor suitable. In a world which changes rapidly, the nation will need people with broad perspectives.[55]

Law teaching using socio-legal material is ideally placed to play a part in such broader degree programmes.

CONCLUSION

The abandonment of the doctrinal project is seen to greatest effect in the research work of the law school. It continues to pervade much teaching and

53 Cartan and Vilkinas, op. cit., n. 48, p. 248.

54 P. Harris, 'Curriculum Development in Legal Studies' (1986) 20 *The Law Teacher* 110, at 112.

55 Dearing, op. cit., n. 12, para 9.3.

doubtless will do so for some years. As it gradually looses its grip on the law school so the law school will be able to take its proper place in the academy. The university, whatever else it is, is a conversation: a place for different people, and different discourses, to meet and, by their exchange, grow richer.[56] 'The carnival of understanding and judgement is open to all.'[57] Doctrinal study has held both students and the law school back from that conversation. Law as a parasitic discipline offers a much brighter future.

56 This is so, whether the exchange is characterized in enlightenment or in postmodern terms.
57 G. Steiner, *Errata: An Examined Life* (1997) 20.

JOURNAL OF LAW AND SOCIETY
VOLUME 25, NUMBER 1, MARCH 1998
ISSN: 0263-323X, pp. 85-101

New Wine in Old Bottles or New Wine in New Bottles?

PATRICIA LEIGHTON*

This chapter traces the origins of what became the new university law schools, paying particular attention to the creation, culture, and contribution of the United Kingdom polytechnics. It argues that the 'equal but different' philosophy of the polytechnics has special application to law teaching. In particular, it demonstrates that legal education outside the traditional universities has a commitment to vocationalism, innovation in teaching and learning, and to widening access to both legal education and the legal profession. Drawing on research findings, the chapter explores the nature and the professional norms of law teachers in new universities, as contrasted with their counterparts in the traditional sector.

INTRODUCTION

This essay explores the nature and contribution of the so-called new universities to legal education in the United Kingdom. It sets legal education in these institutions into the context of United Kingdom higher education generally, especially that of the contribution of their predecessors – the polytechnics.

Polytechnics and other higher education institutions have come under much recent scrutiny and yet analysis of law schools and legal education in them has had barely a mention. Indeed, in the increasing number of publications devoted to the history and celebration of individual new universities with large law schools, the lack of analysis of them is intriguing.[1] The neglect is also especially noticeable in policy documents and government publications on higher education generally. Similarly, in William Twinings excellent

* *School of Law, Elizabeth Gaskell Campus, Hathersage Road, Manchester Metropolitan University, Manchester M13 0JA, England*

1 For example, R. Pope and K. Phillips, *A History of the University of Central Lancashire since 1828* (1995); *Many Arts; Many Skills: A History of Manchester Metropolitan University* (1994); D. Daiches, *The Idea for New University: An Experiment in Sussex* (1964); T. Burgess, M. Locke, J. Pratt, and N. Richards, *Degrees East: The Making of the University of East London (1892–1992)* (1995).

analysis, *Blackstone's Tower*,[2] the hypothetical law school of the University of Rutland is clearly an 'old' law school, though the book does sometimes reflect more widely issues particular to new universities.

The reasons for this neglect in education literature are likely to be complex and merit exploration. However, this is outside the main focus of this essay. Its focus will be primarily an analysis of the evolution of new university law schools, with particular attention to curriculum and pedagogic matters, along with discussion of law teachers there and some thoughts on likely future developments. A number of important research projects which have tracked law schools and their work will be drawn on.[3] There is much data on student numbers, courses, resources, and some data on teaching methods, materials, and on the law teachers themselves.[4]

In questioning the particular contribution of the new universities, it is inevitable that issues of comparability with the old universities emerge. All too familiar 'league tables' relating to teaching quality and research have pushed this issue to the forefront. League tables and the like are generally presented on an institutional basis – but individual law schools may create a different picture. Nonetheless, it is impossible to dis-aggregate these issues of quality, comparability, and 'pulling power' from an analysis of law schools generally, and new university law schools in particular. It is also impossible to disregard the tensions that sometimes exist in the relationship between old and new universities. In legal education, the tensions manifested themselves in the necessary formation of the Association of Law Teachers (ALT) in 1965, a development which coincided with expansion of law degrees outside the old university sector. The ALT was formed in response to the refusal of membership by the Society of Public Teachers of Law (SPTL) for all those who did not teach on law degrees in old universities.

Much has now changed. The ALT and SPTL today have a cordial relationship. It would be wrong, however, not to see the formation of the

2 W. Twining, *Blackstone's Tower: The English Law School* (1994).

3 For example, see J. Wilson, 'Survey of Education in the United Kingdom' (1966) 9 *J. of the Society of Public Teachers of Law* 5; J. Wilson and S. Marsh, 'A Second Survey of Legal Education in the United Kingdom (1975) 12 *J. of the Society of Public Teachers of Law* 241 (with two supplements in 1978 and 1981); J. Wilson, 'A Third Survey' (1993) *Legal Studies* 143; P. Harris and S. Bellerby *A Survey of Law Teaching* (1993). For an official survey, see Her Majesty's Inspectorate (HMI) *A Survey of Undergraduate Legal Education 1987–1990* (1991).

4 Examples include R. Lee, 'A Survey of Law School Admissions' (1984) 18 *Law Teacher* 165; J. Craven-Griffith, 'Predicting Success: A Research Studies based on Law Degree Courses at Trent Polytechnic' (1987) 21 *Law Teacher* 156; K. Sear, 'The Correlation Between A-Level Grades and Degree Results in England and Wales' (1983) 12 *Higher Education* 609; D. Tribe and A. Tribe, 'Assessing Law Students (1986) 20 *Law Teacher* 160; F. Youngman, 'Report on Student Assessment of Staff' (1990) 4 *Higher Education Development Unit Bulletin* 7; P. Thomas, 'The Poverty of Law Students (1993) 27 *Law Teacher* 152; P. Leighton, T. Mortimer, and N. Whatley, *Today's Law Teachers: Lawyers or Academics?* (1995).

ALT as pivotal to an analysis of the particular contribution of new universities to legal education. This will be considered more fully later. It would be wrong also to deny the controversy, passion, and debate which has characterized the period during which old and new university law schools have co-existed. The binary divide has been a powerful factor in legal education in the United Kingdom. It has also been complicated by the key (some would say overbearing) role of the legal profession in influencing the content and delivery of the law degree curriculum and professional legal education. Of course, the relationship between the legal profession and legal education is an international concern. It is also one which is subject to considerable debate and changes across Europe and elsewhere. The new universities in the United Kingdom have, it will be argued, particular experiences to contribute to these debates and policy development. Before turning to this it is necessary to pose some basic questions.

NEW UNIVERSITIES: WHAT ARE THEY AND WHERE HAVE THEY COME FROM?

At one level these questions are easy to answer. The new universities are the product of the 1992 Further and Higher Education Act for England and Wales, which had equivalent legislation in Scotland and Northern Ireland. Thirty long-established English polytechnics and one Welsh polytechnic were converted into universities, followed by four more recent polytechnics – Bournemouth, Humberside, Anglia, and Thames Valley. Two other institutions, Luton and Derby were created universities in the following year. The total new university sector of England and Wales therefore comprises thirty-six institutions. There are four new universities in Scotland – Robert Gordon, Abertay, Napier, and Glasgow Caledonian. Ulster is the new university in Northern Ireland.

If the legislation which created the new universities was simple and direct their origins are far more complex and diverse. John Pratt's recent book traces the creation of polytechnics and clearly shows that the driving force for designation as a polytechnic was a recognition that there was a need for a type of institution which offered a new and distinctive experience for students.[5]

Most new universities have constituent elements, such as colleges of education and commerce and so forth, which go back into the nineteenth century. Indeed, these origins are in contrast to some of the United Kingdom's newer 'old' universities, such as Lancaster, Sussex, and Warwick which were built in the 1960s as new creations on green-field sites, generally in rural areas. Such universities, with a few notable exceptions such as York, now have law schools which have distinctive approached to studying law. Law teaching,

5 J. Pratt, *The Polytechnic Experiment 1965–1992* (1997).

in effect, developed from a blank sheet of paper in these universities, though clearly courses were developed by those familiar with the debates and issues of the time.

By contrast, law teaching in many of the polytechnics has had a long history, though not typically at undergraduate level. The first wave of polytechnics, established 1969 and 1970 had strong reputations for technology and art and design. Hatfield, Sunderland, Portsmouth, Kingston, and Lanchester (Coventry) typify this. However, the first wave of polytechnics also included a number of institutions with established reputations for teaching commercial subjects, such as law. These included Manchester, Leeds, Bristol, and Newcastle. The second wave of polytechnics from 1970 to 1971, included Liverpool, City, and Birmingham which had similarly absorbed colleges of commerce or the like.

The history of two polytechnics – Manchester and Preston – demonstrate the diverse and interesting origins of polytechnics. Although many new universities have recently published their histories, it is important to note again the very limited attention paid in virtually all to the development of law teaching and law schools. Interestingly, this is in stark contrast to the accounts of old universities where law often figures prominently.

The origins of the law school at Manchester Polytechnic (now Manchester Metropolitan University) can be gleaned not so much from its official history but from the handwritten minutes of the Law Department, starting from when it was part of Manchester College of Commerce.[6] These minutes, from 1963, reveal details of courses and course development, staff and, most interestingly, track the implications of the establishment of Council for National Academic Awards (CNAA) and then the move from law being taught in a college of commerce to a polytechnic in January 1970.

In the early 1960s the Law Department was running the London (External) LLB, the Law Society Finals part I and part II, and a range of other courses for managing clerks (legal executives), magistrates clerks, and short courses on specific legal topics. There were around twelve full-time staff members by the mid 1960s. A considerable amount of teaching on other programmes, for example, for accountancy and business studies went on and there is strong evidence of external links, for example, with Manchester Law Society and the Magistrates Association. The minutes are also an invaluable source of information about the application to obtain validation and then implement the BA Law (CNAA) in 1967.

A recent history of the University of Central Lancashire reveals some contrasts with Manchester.[7] The constituent elements of what became Lancashire Polytechnic in 1973 were similarly diverse, though Harris College, Preston offering a wide range of technical and commercial subjects dominated. In the 1890s a Mr Ernest Firth taught law at Harris College, possibly for

6 Pope and Phillips, op. cit. (1995), n. 1.
7 id. (1995).

articled clerks, but the numbers attracted were so low that the venture had to be abandoned. Law teaching was only established as a discrete undergraduate subject in the early 1970s in the pre-polytechnic era.

Outside the traditional universities law teaching was patchy. Many colleges relied on law teachers for professional courses; some taught the London External LLB and a few taught Law Society Finals. Law teaching in the 1960s was essentially an urban activity; law departments or discrete groupings of staff were rare – possibly only around eight law departments or so in the various institutions. It is important to note that law teaching, especially for the London External LLB, was provided by several private colleges and by correspondence courses at that time.[8]

THE NEW POLYTECHNICS: WHAT WERE THEY THERE TO DO?

To many people's surprise, in 1966 a plan for polytechnics was published by the then Department of Education and Science (DES), followed by the parliamentary statement by the Secretary of State in 1967 providing detail on implementation.[9] That this was a radical and innovative development cannot be denied. These new institutions were to be typified by their 'comprehensive range and character of work, especially to non-degree students and part-time courses'. Further, they were to have, 'closer and more direct links with industry, business and the professions.[10] In 1972 the White Paper, *Education: a framework for expansion*,[11] published immediately after most of the new polytechnics had been established, looked to the polytechnics to make the major contribution to the planned expansion of student places.

Possibly the most significant development had preceded polytechnic foundation. That was the setting up of the Council for National Academic Awards (CNAA) in 1964. The ability of colleges and then polytechnics to develop and award their own degrees released energy and innovation. This release was especially evident in law teaching institutions which had taught the London LLB and replaced it with deliberately different offerings. Whatever the virtues of the London LLB, and there were and remain many, most law teachers welcomed the opportunity of the CNAA degree. Pratt considers that law degrees exemplified the polytechnic revolution. He reports that, of the new CNAA law degrees, three were in business law (as opposed to straight law), one was a sandwich course, and others quickly developed in, say, law with public administration. Such developments were entirely

8 A number of colleges such as Woolsey Hall, Holborn Law Tutors, and several institutions which came and went prepared hundreds of students, especially from overseas.

9 Department of Education and Science (DES), *A Plan for Polytechnics and Other Colleges* (1966; Cmnd. 3006); DES Memorandum 8/67, *Polytechnics: A Parliamentary Statement* (1967).

10 id. (1966), p. 17.

11 DES, *Education: A Framework for Expansion* (1972; Cmnd. 5174).

consistent with the original objectives of polytechnics and in contrast to most old university law schools. They were practical and usually vocationally orientated. The first CNAA degree (at Manchester), though retaining some of the approach and content of the London LLB, introduced a contextual element – political institutions – in the first year. Other courses offered economics, languages, and business subjects.

Before going on to consider the contribution of the polytechnics/new universities to legal education more generally, it is vital to identify the nature of the institutions themselves and the people who taught or otherwise worked there. The polytechnics, though considered a part of the higher education structure, administratively remained firmly in the further education sector until the 1990s. They were funded and governed by local authorities. The literature abounds with examples of tensions between a polytechnic and its local authority. Some authorities were supportive and appreciated the fact that polytechnics were different from the usual further education college or school. But matters often came to a head over resources. Subjects which expanded greatly in polytechnics, such as law, were often victims of this uneasy relationship. In addition, the fact that staff were employees of the local authority, with all that that entailed, vividly re-enforced the binary divide with the universities. This is such a critical issue that it will be explored more fully below.

Local authority control also implied local or regional planning of course development. This, too, led to tension, this time between local authorities who each wanted 'their' polytechnic to develop the high profile and profitable courses. The process did not involve the universities so it was possible to have duplication of provision in relatively small geographical areas.

Overall, the 1970s and 1980s saw the polytechnics expanding. Law teaching developed dramatically in the period. It is vital, when reviewing this period, to observe also the major expansion of non-degree legal education, especially for the legal profession and the contribution of law teachers to other professional programmes. Indeed, in some cases, the contribution of law teachers to professional programmes such as engineering and property management was so great that law teachers became, in effect, law schools within another school/department.

This rapid expansion made huge demands for teachers of all sorts. What type of people were attracted to the polytechnics? Did they work differently and have different aspirations to their equivalents in the universities? An important study, undertaken in 1972–73 found, contrary to popular views today, that staff were well qualified (albeit with a slightly lower level of staff with first-class honours) and tended to hold more professional and teaching qualifications than their university counterparts.[12] They were strongly committed to innovation in courses and their delivery. Indeed, both students and staff were reported to be generally satisfied with the early polytechnic experience. Significantly, there was little evidence that staff wanted their

12 J. Whitburn, M. Melling, and C. Cox, *People in Polytechnics* (1976) ch. 3.

institutions to become universities.[13] However, the researchers record that many staff felt uncertain about the way they thought their sector should and would develop in the future.[14]

The overall picture of the polytechnics during the period of expansion and development is of enthusiasm and commitment 'on the ground' but of tensions and paradoxes at a higher level.[15] These factors have been extremely influential on the way law teaching evolved outside the universities. It is somewhat ironical that the polytechnic 'experiment' which was suddenly ended as a consequence of the Education Reform Act, 1988 was so admired and replicated outside the United Kingdom. Polytechnics continue to have highly regarded equivalents in Germany, the Netherlands, and several central European states, though they do not always have a discrete law degree programme.

A final broad issue to consider before turning to law courses, teaching, and so forth in polytechnics and new universities concerns the relationship between teachers in polytechnics and those in the universities. The rise of the CNAA, opening up the possibility of law degree teaching outside the old universities, raised expectations on the part of those planning or teaching such degrees. In early July 1965 leading law teachers from (then) further education sector met at Huntercombe Lodge, Slough, to discuss the future of law teaching.[16] It is important to note that this course was solely concerned with pedagogic issues. At its final session, the Association of Law Teachers was set up. It planned an inaugural conference in London in April 1966. After much debate it was agreed that membership should be predicated solely on the interest and enthusiasm for law teaching, regardless of teaching institution. It is interesting that at the inaugural and exciting meeting of the ALT in London the speakers and delegates were drawn from all sectors of legal education. Speakers included Professor John Wood (Sheffield), Professor Cyril Grunfeld (LSE), William Frank and Clive Schmitthoff from what became, respectively, Lanchester Polytechnic and City Polytechnic. Members of the judiciary joined the event which was attended by over eighty delegates. Interestingly, several members of HMI and various examination bodies were regular conference attenders in the early years of the ALT, further evidence of the strong links between education administration and law teachers.

At its inaugural meeting the ALT not only re-enforced its commitment to educational issues but also to the principle that membership was open to all. Today, membership is drawn mainly from the United Kingdom but it has a growing international representation. Law teachers in schools, adult

13 id., p. 177.

14 id., p. 39.

15 Whitburn, Melling, and Cox reported 'many courses were strikingly innovative' and polytechnics were making 'a distinctive contribution to meeting the 1966 objectives' (id., p. 175).

16 For an excellent account of the ALT see S. Marsh, *A History of the Association of Law Teachers* (1990).

education, and training organizations figure prominently. However, the driving force has been its committee, whose membership has been dominated by the new universities.[17]

The early years of the ALT coincided with the period of growth and innovation in the polytechnics. The various conferences and workshops, along with articles in the association's *Bulletin* and journal, *The Law Teacher*, reflected this activity. Articles in the *Law Teacher* covered the curriculum and pedagogic debates of the time. Typical were articles on the role of non-law subjects and the movements to clinical, critical, and other 'schools' of legal education.

By the early 1980s the pages of the *Law Teach*er reveal increased evidence of empirical research in legal education such as into admission policies and practices,[18] student assessment,[19] the careers of law graduates[20] as well as the major surveys of legal education in both further and higher education.[21] Overall, the pages of the *Law Teacher* are an invaluable source of data about the major debates and the evolving ideas and methods of teaching. A particular feature has been the willingness of authors to share the details of their teaching materials and techniques with readers. Typical here have been pieces on case-study approaches,[22] skills exercises,[23] and techniques and materials to introduce students to the study of law. Their authors have come from all sectors of law teaching and from outside the United Kingdom, but it has been the emphasis on legal education topics that has distinguished the ALT's journal from all others in the United Kingdom.

17 id. All but two of the Chairs of the ALT 1965–1990 were from polytechnics or their forerunners. One other was from Kings College, London and one from a further education college.

18 For example, V. Bermingham, C. Hall, and J. Webb, *Access to and Participation in Undergraduate Legal Education* (1996); R. Stone, 'Prediction, Prize or Profile: Three Models of Admissions Policy' 1988 22 *Law Teacher* 28; N. Duncan and N. Kibble, 'Excellence and Diversity: Admissions Policies in Law Schools (1986) 20 *Law Teacher* 36; M. Tzannes, 'Strategies in the 21st Century: Issues and Options for Admissions Policy Makers' (1995) 29 *Law Teacher* 43.

19 See P. Hassett, 'The Role of Assessment in the Continuing Professional Development of Lawyers in England and Wales' (1992) 26 *Law Teacher* 130. Tribe and Tribe, op. cit., n. 4; P. Harris and D. Tribe, 'The Impact of Semesterisation and Modularisation on the Assessment of Students' (1995) 29 *Law Teacher* 38.

20 For example, B. Read, 'Exit from Law Schools: Possibilities and Actualities' (1984) 18 *Law Teacher* 175.

21 P. Harris and M. Jones, 'A Survey of Law Schools in the United Kingdom, 1996' (1997) 31 *Law Teacher* 38.

22 P. Bergman, A. Sherr, and R. Burridge, 'Games Law Teachers Play' (1986) 20 *Law Teacher* 21.

23 For example, L. Squire and J. Chapman, 'Teaching Communication Skills on the Law Degree' in *The Silver Jubilee Collection for the Law Teacher,* ed. J. Macfarlane and J. Chapman (1990) 94; R. Grimes, J. Klaff, and C. Smith, 'Legal Skills and Clinical Legal Education – A Survey of Undergraduate Law School Practice' (1996) 30 *Law Teacher* 1.

Until recently there has been little research to facilitate both identification of trends and comparisons between old and new institutions. The 1996 *Survey of Law Schools in the United Kingdom* by Phil Harris and Martin Jones for the first time covers all types of higher education law school.[24]

The data reveal some differences. In comparison with old universities, new ones are far more likely to offer law degrees on a part-time basis, by distance learning, and to offer a degree which combines law with other disciplines. New university law courses are also more likely to be delivered on a modularized and/or semesterized basis. This last development has occurred as a consequence of university policy development, rather than as an initiative of law schools. Indeed, law schools have often fiercely resented and resisted modularization and semesterization.

Postgraduate academic work, especially taught programmes, is dominated by the old universities, though new ones are moving rapidly (only four new university law schools do not offer postgraduate provision).

There are some differences in the way in which students are admitted to law degrees. Although 'A'-level points and/or grades dominate there is a stronger tendency for new university law schools to accept non-'A'-level qualifications and to have access course arrangements, typically with a local further education college. Most old universities require a higher 'A'-level points score than do new ones, though the 'boundary' is becoming blurred as between some old and some new universities.

The major contribution of the new universities in terms of course provision is clearly in the vocational area. Bearing in mind the origins of many of the polytechnics this is not surprising. Today, the three major courses are the Common Professional Examination/Postgraduate Diploma in Law (CPE/PGDL), the Legal Practice Course (LPC) and the Bar Vocational Course (BVC). Although the last has only been taught outside the Inns of Court School of Law since 1997, the non-practising Bar Finals Course (now discontinued) was taught for many years by several new universities.

The LPC evolved from the Law Society Finals in 1993 and emphasizes legal skills and legal professional issues. New universities dominate provision in the public sector (twelve out of seventeen providers) and they are the only ones to offer it on a part-time and distance learning basis. With one exception, the Bar Finals Course is taught in new universities, aside from private providers. Provision of the CPE/PGDL is again largely confined to the new universities. It should also be remembered that although the picture is complex, professional development courses, such as the mandatory Professional Skills Course (PSC) for the Law Society and the New Practitioner Programme

24 Harris and Jones, op. cit., n. 21.

(NPP) for the Bar Council are typically offered by new universities, often in partnership with local professional bodies.

The major contribution of new universities to vocational legal education has great significance for staffing, resources, learning methods, and research. Law schools which have staff involved in this work inevitably have a different culture from those that do not or have it as a marginal activity. It is highly relevant that postgraduate students on vocational programmes pay high fees (almost at MBA level) and have comparable expectations and demands. All of these courses are (and always have been) strongly externally regulated and have made considerable (some say, relentless) demands on both staff and students. Learning processes, assessment, and learning materials are also heavily prescribed. Providers of vocational programmes must necessarily establish effective relationships with legal professional bodies but also, increasingly, with other vocational course providers. This degree of control over courses and their delivery is in marked contrast to the diversity and relative autonomy and diversity of old universities regarding their academic programmes.

To sum up on course provision and delivery: it can be argued that the emphasis on vocational and skills based programmes, often available on part-time and other flexible bases, has been the particular contribution of the new university sector. This provision has derived from a relatively long tradition in colleges of commerce and the like. This emphasis has clear implications for styles of teaching, the type of publications generated by staff, and many other aspect of professional life.

The case for a distinctive contribution by new universities to law teaching cannot be made so easily by research findings. There is, though, some recent evidence that law teachers in new universities are far more likely to be professionally qualified as teachers than their old university counterparts.[25] They are similarly more likely to participate in staff development with an educational (as opposed to law) focus. They are also far more likely to use education technology (such as overhead projectors, cameras, and videos) and computers. Because of the emphasis on skills-based education, techniques such as role-play, simulation, and group work of various sorts have been long developed in the sector. This is not to say that institutions outside the new universities have not developed these features; it is simply that so many new university law schools have.

Until relatively recently, a criticism of some law schools was their failure to share this good practice which has evolved on vocational programmes with colleagues on academic programmes. This might well be changing, in part because of the growing emphasis on skills on degrees. If so, a critical mass of innovation in these law schools offering both academic and vocational programmes will have evolved.

25 Leighton et al., op. cit., n. 4.

WHAT OF THE LAW TEACHERS AND THEIR WORK?

Much of the energy and direction of those early law schools in the polytechnics and colleges came from some particular individuals. Is there a definable new university man or woman? The names Marsh, Seabrooke, Tillotson, Tribe, P.A. Jones, Bailey, Collins, and so forth may not be as well known as Treitel, Twining, Sherr or others but it is arguable that their contribution has been no less to legal education. The former group were the pioneers of polytechnic/new university law schools or have great significance in terms of developing and analysing innovative learning methods and student assessment.

An understanding of the 'people' issues of law teaching in new universities is vital. This is not least because the new university sector is relatively stable. Staff movement between the two university sectors is still rare. To some extent the different nature of course provision in new universities, especially the LPC, has required recruitment of staff with different skills and qualities than those in the old universities. But this cannot be the whole story.

That there is clear evidence of the divide cannot be denied. The research report of 1995, *Today's Law Teachers: Lawyers or Academics?* provides data on a range of issues. Some were relatively straightforward. There was a markedly stronger likelihood of teachers in old universities having research degrees, but having less experience of non-academic work. They also were more likely to be academic authors, to subscribe to journals, and to define themselves as active researchers. Law teachers in new universities were more likely to be qualified teachers, to teach more hours per week, and place a higher priority on staff development and research on professional legal education matters.

The survey which generated the 1995 research report was much concerned to identify the attitudes of law teachers towards their work, both in terms of what their priorities were and what were their aspirations for the future. Old university law school respondents were more enthusiastic than their new university colleagues about being a part of an academic community, about research opportunities, and the maintenance or improvement in library/learning resources. However, the contrasts were observable in other ways. If the question is posed as to what was important to new university law teachers, it was improved staff development, especially for further qualifications, to improve teaching and learning resources, and better administrative and other support. New university law teachers also attached a higher priority to providing advice to students, in particular, for careers. They also wanted fewer class contact hours (and more pay). This finding was not surprising in the light of the Harris and Jones report which shows the disparity between new and old universities in class contact hours.[26]

The picture clearly emerged of law teachers in new universities having

26 Harris and Jones, op. cit., n. 21.

different working conditions (usually worse), priorities, and aspirations. The relatively poorer performance of most new university law schools in the 1992 and 1996 research assessment exercise (RAE) compounded the situation. Indeed, in virtually every league table generated, for example, by the *Times*, old universities will be higher up.[27] It has to be said, however, that league tables and even official quality assurance agencies are primarily concerned with publicly funded courses and exclude analysis of law school performance on vocational courses. Here, the Law Society, the Bar Council, and the CPE Board undertake the assessment but the results tend not to achieve the same level of popular awareness.

Many will argue that the whole process of law school assessment is flawed and biased towards the old universities. (Critics point to the low level of representation on assessment panel of people from new universities.) Ask the training partner of a medium or large firm of solicitors which is the 'best' law school and answers would be far more diverse than the much quoted league tables suggest!

There may well be unfairness in the system in terms of resources, teaching demands and quality assessment. It is especially stark in relation to value added, in that formal assessments make no allowance for the achievement of many 'new' law schools in taking mature, disadvantaged or non-traditional law students and turning them into creditable graduates. Many new universities, such as South Bank, Westminster, and Central England, typically in urban areas and ones with high representation of ethnic minorities, have an honourable record in this area and although the policy is seen as valuable, the reality is that in league-table terms it can operate to their disadvantage. Equal opportunities sit well in mission statements but can have obvious downsides!

NEW LAW SCHOOLS OR MIMICS OF OLD ONES?

Less research, longer teaching hours, an emphasis on legal skills rather than scholarship, and often inadequate learning and working environments can lead some to see new university law schools as inevitably second-rate. However, whilst it cannot be denied that the emphasis on and output of works of scholarship in general is lower in new universities, on the other hand, the contribution to professional legal education, teaching and learning skills, and in providing a wider access to legal education is higher. Thus, new university law schools are not second-rate but, rather, are different.

The search for the factors which have led to a different culture in new

27 See J. O'Leary (ed.), *The Times Good University Guide* (1997). This ranks all universities according to specified criteria. Of the ninety-six institutions, the 'highest' ranked old polytechnic/new university is Ulster at no. 53. No new university is ranked higher than an old one.

university law schools must start with their origins. These have been sketched in earlier, but need now to be expanded. Most new universities are derived from several further education colleges, which may or may not have had law courses. However, most importantly, the law teachers' terms and conditions of employment, including their management framework was drawn from local government. This means that law teachers were part of huge bureaucracies which, typically, included administrators, manual workers, social workers, schoolteachers, housing managers, and a wide range of professional and craft groups. Terms of work were arrived at following collective bargaining with some powerful unions. Law teachers tended to join and be represented by what became the National Association of Teachers in Further and Higher Education (NATFHE). This has been a radical union with its roots firmly in further education colleges. Its policies and practices have long been in marked contrast to the Association of University Teachers (AUT) which covers 'old' universities. In both cases, union density in the respective workforces has been very high.

Law teachers in new universities have therefore been part of a complex and often fraught structure of management and resourcing, with industrial relations being especially tense. Over the years, law teachers in new universities have often felt and expressed frustration with the situation and, for example, in 1971 some joined a rival Association of Polytechnic Teachers (APT). Given the different bargaining and employment structures as between new and old universities, it is not surprising that the movement of individuals has been limited and that different cultures emerged.[28]

It is worth exploring specifics such as grading structures. Grading and pay in old universities is based on a longer scale. Junior lecturers have been relatively poorly paid, but can move along a long incremental scale. At the other end, readers and professors can achieve relatively high salaries. The salary structures in new universities have more individual grades but, whereas in the 1960s and 1970s movement between grades was by promotion, this has tended to be replaced by seniority overcoming the grade 'bars' in recent years. At a senior level, salaries are generally lower than in old universities.

Most importantly, the head of a law school in a new university was traditionally designated as a permanent post with specific terms and conditions. Typically, in old universities, deans have been selected from professors on a rotational basis. Essentially, therefore, those aspiring to leadership in a new university school have joined a well defined management structure. Appointments to headship in new university terms has meant self-identification as an administrator or manager. One suspects that in the old universities such choices are not so stark. However, the idea of the law school as a business and the entrepreneurial imperative has probably been most keenly felt in the new universities.

28 See R. Cuthbert, *Looking into Higher Education* (1996).

There are, therefore, a number of powerful reasons why the culture of the new university is distinctive from that of the old, and why movement of teaching staff between 'new' and 'old' has been so limited. Indeed, the distinctive culture of new and old universities as a whole has made a series of proposed mergers between new and old universities difficult to achieve.

WHAT HAS BEEN THE DISTINCTIVE CONTRIBUTION OF NEW UNIVERSITY LAW SCHOOLS? A SUMMARY

Some matters are relatively straightforward. First, new universities have, broadly, spearheaded legal professional courses and skills development. They have not had a monopoly (some old universities, along with the private providers, especially the College of Law, have made a major contribution) but have been extremely important. A relatively rarely discussed matter, but one of rapidly growing importance, is that of continuing professional development (CPD) for lawyers and other professional groups. This is often undertaken in conjunction with local law societies and circuits. New university law schools have been prominent. Second, they have provided many opportunities for the non-standard applicant to law courses. Third, they have given priority to effective teaching and learning strategies. Fourth, they are the major providers of degree programmes on a part-time basis. Indeed, in the United Kingdom, only four old universities offer a part-time law degree. But most importantly, they have provided legal education at a far higher staff-student ratio (SSR) than their old university equivalents. This last point has made new universities attractive to government in economic terms. Indeed, the proposals of the Dearing report[29] for an emphasis on part-time and shorter full-time programmes continues the tradition that government has mainly looked to the new university sector for the major expansion in student numbers.

The success of new universities, including their law schools, in providing education for high numbers has, on the one hand, brought pressure to develop innovative learning methods (for example, using information technology effectively) but, on the other, made it difficult for new university law schools to compete in the traditional areas of scholarship. At the same time the pressures of old universities to research and publish is less evident in new universities (though growing in many).

Some new university law schools have responded to the vocational versus the 'academic' challenges by setting up separate units within schools or establishing graduate schools. It is clear that the outcomes of the 1992 and 1996 RAEs has caused considerable heart-searching in new university law

29 The National Committee of Inquiry into Higher Education, *Higher Education in the Learning Society* (1997) (the Dearing report).

schools as to what to do about research in the future. A particular problem has been the emphasis to date on scholarship, refereed journals, and monographs, with the relatively low accord to empirical work, practitioner materials, and probably even research into legal education itself. A particular problem for universities, especially new university law school management, has been the implications of the analysis by McNay of the 1992 RAE.[30] This shows, broadly, that the teaching function has separated from the research function in many university schools. The former has tended to have less status.

Compared to the position of law schools outside the United Kingdom which provide postgraduate professional legal education and emphasize effective teaching and learning strategies, the status of university law schools in the United Kingdom, especially in the new university sector, appears relatively low. So, we have a complex conundrum. New university law schools have, predominantly, provided more diverse and professional legal education; they have done so economically, often with innovation. However, despite the need for professional legal skills, the key formal indicators of legal education continue to reward law schools which emphasize scholarship and intellectual debate.

THE FUTURE?

All law schools are currently facing massive challenges and changes, some arising from the funding and structure of higher education itself but many from developments in the legal profession and legal education. Few commentators expect a massive cash injection into higher education. Indeed, the likelihood is of law as a subject remaining as one of the 'cheapest' subjects and the cost burden moving yet further from the State to the student. Student demands will increase. In this climate, the new universities with their high SSRs, and generally lower-quality working environments will face particular problems.

It is possible that despite the best endeavours of the Advisory Committee on Legal Education and Conduct (ACLEC), the legal profession will continue to bring pressure for law degrees to comply with their demands in order to achieve qualifying law degree status.[31] Similarly, the profession will continue to closely supervise the vocational programmes – the LPC and BVC.

Arthurs has commented recently:

30 I. McNay, *The Impact of the RAE,* 1992 (1996).

31 ACLEC, *The Lord Chancellor's Advisory Committee on Legal Education and Conduct' First Report* (1996). For a summary, see P. Leighton, 'Government and Education News' (1996) 20 *Law Teacher* 201 and for a commentary, see H. Arthurs, 'Half a League Onward' (1997) 31 *Law Teacher* 1.

> The . . . academy and the profession exist for different reasons, have different values, do different work, even operate on different understandings of what is meant by 'law'. They are in certain respects each other's inevitable adversary.[32]

However, in this situation those new universities with long experience of delivering professional courses are well used to this type of regulation and live easily with it. They will continue to work closely with the legal profession both locally and nationally.

We know that there has been much recent change and speculation about the future of professional courses in the United Kingdom. Recession in the early 1990s, unfortunately coinciding with the introduction of the LPC, has led to a severe decline in the number of training contracts available to intending solicitors. Recent statistics from the Bar Council and the College of Advocates reveal a similar trend in opportunities for potential barristers/advocates. Students, unsurprisingly, are selecting vocational courses which appear to offer the best career opportunities. Often this means courses in institutions with a large legal 'hinterland'. It is possible, therefore that there will be a move to urban university law schools. Interestingly, this move will tend to be towards those new university law schools which provided the old vocational courses (Law Society Finals (LSF) and so forth) such as Trent, West of England, University of Northumbria, and so on.

In this likely structural change, the role of the private providers of vocational legal education must be considered. The College of Law provides by far the highest number of LPC places and the Inns of Court School of Law the highest number of BVC places. Indeed, both institutions have plans to move into 'academic' courses. Competition between public and private providers will continue and even intensify, especially if the number of applicants, say, for the LPC, declines further.

If there are to be binary divides (whether formal or not) will old university law schools always be in the premier league? We do not know, but the next few years will be interesting to watch.

New university law schools will need to respond effectively, possibly by developing radical learning strategies which provide students with a broad range of learning opportunities, such as postgraduate study. More importantly, they will need to prepare students on vocational courses for the professional and business world of the next millennium. Much has been written about the future direction of professional legal practice. Much, though, fails to appreciate not only the gobalization of various professional market places but also likely competition from non-law professionals who have the skills and experience to compete with traditional lawyers. Somehow, law schools will have to prepare students for a world increasingly dependent on information technology, for new types of business opportunities and threats.

To say that this will give law schools a lot to do is a grotesque under-

32 id., p. 8.

statement. However, many new university law schools are within faculties or other groupings which teach those skills and knowledge lawyers will need. Strategies will need to develop or be expanded to draw on them. At the same time, these will be a continuing demand for the 'High Street' practitioner, able to deal with consumer, property, family, employment, and other non-corporate, more personal problems. The danger here will be of preparing students to practice in a relatively cosy and stable world but where the reality is also of change and increasing competition from non-law professionals.

The pressure on law schools offering vocational programmes from the profession is often to do 'more' law, to cover a wider range of legal knowledge which can only be at the expense of non-law material and even skills. One has to question the wisdom of this. There will be lots of discussions and debates to be had and choices to be made. New university law schools will have to work hard to ensure their graduates are truly well prepared for professional life. They will need to work closely with the legal profession but also other professionals both within the United Kingdom and abroad. These thoughts apply especially to schools which provide courses for the Bar/Advocates and, most importantly, for CPD.

What of new university law schools who provide few or no vocational courses? One option, which is declining, is to provide legal vocational courses. Unless current market trends reverse there is likely to be continuing over-provision of student places. Such law schools will instead probably continue to provide degree courses using diverse and innovative delivery methods. Specialist law degrees might become more popular as might more mixed degrees. One senses that the energy and creativity which characterized the early years of the CNAA will need to be recaptured.

There are several issues which will affect new university law schools of all types. They will only thrive with an adequate investment in staff and staffing. The combination of low pay with job insecurity clearly detracts from building up a highly qualified and motivated cadre. If the situation does not change and there is a continuing increase in students numbers, higher SSRs, and a growing emphasis on evening and week-end teaching with longer teaching terms, problems will be compounded.

Finally there is the spectre of universities being categorized as research or teaching universities. Most have assumed that new universities will populate overwhelmingly the second group. Some even fear that several new universities will slip back into the further education sector or become the equivalent of many United States liberal arts universities or colleges. Whether this happens will depend on United Kingdom government policy and the ability of institutions to respond to new challenges.

JOURNAL OF LAW AND SOCIETY
VOLUME 25, NUMBER 1, MARCH 1998
ISSN: 0263–323X, pp. 102–15

Women Legal Academics – A New Research Agenda?

FIONA COWNIE*

Women academics have been the subject of suprisingly little academic research; this is particularly true of women legal academics. This article argues that it is important that research into women legal academics is carried out, not just to gain empirical evidence about the working lives of these women, but because in exploring these members of the 'academic tribe' of lawyers, important insights may be gained into the university as an institution, the development of law as a discipline, and the nature of law itself.

INTRODUCTION

It is a truth almost universally acknowledged that there is very little research which examines the position of British women academics.[1] The Hansard Society Commission on Women at the Top, commenting in 1990 on the disturbingly low number of female academics who gain promotion, noted that:

> [t]here is little empirical evidence available about the processes which bar women's progress at Oxford and Cambridge, or at any other university: academics have only just begun to research themselves.[2]

These sentiments are echoed by, for example, Sandra Acker, in several of the studies which constitute part of her major contribution to the field and, more recently, by Ann Brooks, in her detailed study, *Academic Women*.[3]

* *Faculty of Law, University of Leicester, University Road, Leicester LE1 7RH, England*

1 There is not a lot of research into women academics per se, but a more extensive literature does exist in the United States of America, Canada, and Australia, some of which is referred to later in this article.

2 Hansard Society, *The Report of the Hansard Society Commission on Women at the Top* (1990) 67.

3 See, for example, S. Acker, 'Contradictions in Terms; Women Academics in British Universities' in *Feminism and Social Justice in Education*, eds. M. Arnot and K. Weiler (1993) 146 and S. Acker, *Gendered Education* (1994); A. Brooks, *Academic Women* (1997).

If there is a noticeable dearth of research about academic women in general, the same is even more true if the focus is on female legal academics. Margaret Thornton's study of women in the legal profession, *Dissonance and Distrust,* is a noticeable exception; her book contains a chapter on women legal academics. However, forming only one chapter out of eight, the discussion is necessarily brief.[4]

It is in this context that this article seeks to address the current lack of knowledge and attempts to set out a possible new research agenda as we approach the next millennium.

RESEARCHING WOMEN LEGAL ACADEMICS – WHY BOTHER?

One reaction to the absence of research on women legal academics might be that this is unsurprising, because such research is of little interest or value. There are a number of reasons why this view is mistaken. Most fundamentally, there is the Aristotelian view that the search for knowledge is part of being human, that, as Houseman wrote, ironically in somewhat sexist terms:

> curiosity, the desire to know things as they are, is a craving no less native to the being of man, no less universal through mankind, than the craving for food and drink.[5]

However, there are many other reasons for pursuing research in this area. Information about legal academics (women as well as men) is important in terms of the development of the university as an institution; as Bourdieu has shown in his analysis of the academic world, the academy is not just a site of intellectual debate and critical dialogue, but is a sphere of power. The ways in which academic careers are made, defended, and destroyed have implications for the development of higher education as a whole:

> the partial and partisan views of the agents engaged in the game, and the individual or collective struggles through which they aim to impose these views, are part of the objective truth of this game, playing an active part in sustaining or transforming it.[6]

In the same way, the behaviour, attitudes, and values of legal academics have implications for the future development of the discipline of law. Members of the academic tribe which inhabits the territory of law will have a profound effect on the research which is carried out and valued, the subjects which are taught, the people who are influential in this sphere; to

4 M. Thornton, *Dissonance and Distrust: Women in the Legal Profession* (1996).

5 A.E. Houseman, *Selected Prose* (1961) 16. Houseman's 'Introductory Lecture', from which this quotation is taken, is an extended meditation on the nature of the search for knowledge.

6 P. Bourdieu, *Homo Academicus* (1988) xiv.

acknowledge this is to indicate the importance of studying what Martin Trow has called the 'private life' of higher education.[7]

It goes without saying that these arguments do not merely justify research into legal academics; they apply to knowledge about all academics; so what is especially interesting or valuable about researching legal academics? If we take seriously the work of Bourdieu and Becher, it soon becomes apparent that research into the members of one particular academic tribe can provide fascinating insights into the relationship between people and ideas. What Becher tries to do in *Academic Tribes and Territories* is to explore the ways in which disciplinary practices, the ways in which particular groups of academics organize their professional lives, are intimately related to the intellectual tasks on which they are engaged.[8] In a study like Becher's, however, the treatment of any particular discipline is necessarily somewhat broad-brush, since the whole point of his work is to make comparisons across a range of fields. There is much work to be done in exploring individual disciplines and sub-disciplines, and we have already seen the potential value of this approach in William Twining's Hamlyn Lectures.[9] *Blackstone's Tower*, with its visit to the department of law in the fictional University of Rutland, points up the potential insights which could be gained from really detailed, qualitative research into real law schools. How many of us recognize the description of Rutland's law faculty, founded in 1934 to provide part-time instruction for local articled clerks, progressing to teaching the external London LLB and finally, in 1950, to offering its own LLB? More importantly, if we carried out such an enquiry into real law schools, what could we find out about the development of the discipline of law, who influenced it and why, and what could those discoveries tell us about where the discipline might go in the future?

All of these arguments could lead to the conclusion that it is important to know more about all legal academics, and not just women. This is undoubtedly true; we know virtually nothing about the everyday experience of male legal academics. In focusing on women my suggestion is merely that we should start with the most under-researched part of the legal academy, where ignorance is greatest. In making this suggestion, however, I want to acknowledge the post-structuralist concern that researching anything in relation to the category 'woman' is problematic. Once it is recognized that women, like men, are possessors of multiple subjectivities based on race, class, age, sexual orientation, religion, and so on, it follows that there are limits to the conclusions which can be drawn for all women, or, in this context, for all women legal academics. In recent years, there has been considerable debate among feminist writers as to how differences between

7 M. Trow, 'The Public and Private Lives of Higher Education' (1976) 104 *Daedelus* 113.

8 T. Becher, *Academic Tribes and Territories* (1989).

9 W.L. Twining, *Blackstone's Tower: The English Law School* (1994).

women can be accorded their rightful place without destroying the integrity of the concept of 'woman'.[10] In the context of research into women academics Ann Brooks has attempted to address such concerns by her use of the concept of 'discourse' within a feminist post-structural analysis to facilitate '. . . an understanding of the different responses of academic women to the discourses of power in the academy in both challenging, resisting and in some cases, accepting the sexism of the academy'.[11]

A fundamental aspect of the research agenda for investigating women legal academics is the construction of a theoretical framework which will allow the voices of individuals to be heard, and provide insights into the future of the discipline and the potential contribution of women legal academics to the development of the academy as a whole. It is also possible that in addressing this very specific research agenda, scholars will necessarily find themselves involved in discovering more about all legal academics, not for the purpose of making invidious comparisons between women and men, an approach which has been largely discredited in the relevant literature, but in order to allow us to gain an accurate, rich picture of the cultural context in which women legal academics live their lives.[12]

BASIC INFORMATION – GATHERING QUANTITATIVE DATA

A common theme among commentators when writing about women academics is that they, of all women, should in theory have the best possible chance of succeeding in their career to the same extent as male academics. 'If there is anywhere that women professionals should be successful, it is the universities. We think of teaching as a woman's forte and universities as meritocratic institutions.'[13] However, there is plenty of evidence that the position of women in academia is far from equal to that of men, and that the higher one goes up the academic ladder, the fewer women one will encounter.[14]

An obvious place to begin any exploration of women legal academics is

10 See, for example, M. Arnot, 'Introduction' in *Feminism and Social Justice in Education*, eds. M. Arnot and K. Weiler (1993) 2; J. Butler, *Gender Trouble: Feminism and the Subversion of Identity* (1990); M. Halberg, 'Feminist Epistemology : An Impossible Project' extracted in S. Hall, D. Held, and D. McGrew, *Modernity and Its Futures* (1992).

11 Brooks, op. cit., n. 3, p. 5.

12 Thus, for example, see Thornton's comment that '. . . the experiences of women in the legal profession are far more than the mirror images of the experiences of men of law . . .' (Thornton, op. cit., n. 4, p. 5) and Acker's observation of '. . . the practice of making invidious comparisons between advantaged and disadvantaged groups so that the superiority of the advantaged group's characteristics is never questioned.' (Acker, op. cit., n. 3, p. 131).

13 Acker, op. cit., n. 3. There are similar comments in Hansard Society, op. cit., n. 2, p. 64 and in Brookes, op. cit., n. 3, p. 1.

14 See statistics in Higher Education Statistics Agency (HESA), *Resources of Higher Education Institutions 1994/95*, June 1996, and comments in Hansard Society, op. cit., n. 2.

to gather some basic quantitative data. Overall, it is easy to find out, for instance, that in 1994/95, of all full-time academic staff, women made up 7 per cent of professors, 15 per cent of senior lecturers, 30 per cent of lecturers, and 32 per cent of other grades.[15] One can also find, without much effort, that between 1983/4 and 1993/4 the proportion of women within all full-time academic staff in 'old' universities increased from 15 per cent to 23 per cent.[16]

However, gathering similar data on women legal academics is not so straightforward. Those same published sources do not appear to regard law as an important category of information. It is the task of the Higher Education Statistics Agency (HESA) to collect data about all aspects of institutions of higher education, including staff.[17] In its annual statistical publication, we find that although data on staff includes information about gender, it is generally collected globally, so that it is impossible to identify information specifically attributable to women legal academics. Even in the table which purports to show full-time academic staff by departmental group, grade, and gender, we find that the departmental groups chosen do not include law.[18]

If we look at studies of legal academics, we find a similar picture. There have been a number of surveys of law schools which have gathered data about law-school staff. These include the three 'Wilson' surveys, published in 1966, 1975, and 1993 which were extremely valuable in making available information about law schools which informed debates in legal education over a number of years, but they do not include information related to the gender of staff.[19] More recently, the detailed survey carried out by Harris and Jones, published in 1996, while containing information about different grades of law school staff and their teaching hours, does not relate this to gender.[20] There is a small amount of information in the survey of law teachers by Leighton and others but gender is not a major concern of this study.[21]

Clearly one aspect of a new research agenda in this area would be to gather quantitative data specifically relating to women legal academics. There are many aspects of the working lives of women legal academics which

15 HESA, id., table 13.

16 Universities Statistical Record, *University Statistics 1993–94 Vol. 3 Finance* (1995).

17 Before 1994 that task was carried out for old universities by the Universities Statistical Record and for new universities by the Department for Education.

18 HESA, op. cit., n. 14, table 13.

19 See J. Wilson, 'A Survey of Legal Education in the United Kingdom' (1966) 9 *J. of the Society of Public Teachers of Law* 1; J. Wilson and S. Marsh, 'A Second Survey of Legal Education in the United Kingdom' (1975) 18 *J. of the Society of Public Teachers of Law* 239; J. Wilson, 'A Third Survey of Legal Education in the United Kingdom'(1993) 13 *Legal Studies* 143.

20 P. Harris and M. Jones, 'A Survey of Law Schools in the United Kingdom, 1996' (1997) 31 The Law Teacher 38.

21 P. Leighton, T. Mortimer, and N. Whatley, *Law Teachers: Lawyers or Academics?* (1995) 11.

it might be interesting to explore: quite apart from basic questions about numbers of women at different academic and research grades, there are questions to be asked about the other ways in which women are represented on law-school staff – as clerical staff, cleaners, law librarians. As far as academic staff are concerned, questions might focus on research interests, publication patterns, membership of research networks; similarly on teaching interests and responsibility for course design, lectures and tutorials, as well as welfare and pastoral responsibilities. Administrative responsibilities, their nature and their status within the hierarchy might also prove a fruitful area of exploration. Quantitative data alone is insufficient to allow analysis of the culture of law schools, or the working lives of female legal academics in the way which has been suggested above, but it could provide a wealth of information which could serve to indicate the direction in which qualitative enquiries might be directed.

WOMEN LEGAL ACADEMICS AND THE ACADEMY

I argued above that one of the benefits of studying women legal academics is that it might tell us more about the nature of the university itself. Bourdieu's analysis of the social backgrounds and professional activities of his fellow academics, his examination not only of the quantity of publishing they engaged in, but also where they published, their institutional connections, media appearances, political involvements, and so on, enabled him to analyse the forms of capital and power, the lines of conflict, and the patterns of change which characterize contemporary French higher education.[22] In the same way, a new research agenda of the kind I am proposing might use an examination of women legal academics to explore issues relating to the notion of 'cultural capital'.[23]

It has been noted by many commentators that higher education in Britain has been subject to a great deal of change in the late 1980s and 1990s, largely as a result of government policies directed at introducing concepts such as the 'free market' and 'efficiency' to the sector.[24] There have been repeated attempts to impose 'managerialism' and bureaucratic control on universities. Martin Trow has noted that the advocates of such approaches:

> argue that higher education must be reshaped and re-formed by the introduction of management systems which then become a continuing force ensuring the steady improvement in the provision of higher education.[25]

22 Bourdieu, op. cit., n. 6.

23 P. Bourdieu, *'Les trois etats du capital culturel'* (1979) 30 *Actes de la Recherche en Sciences Sociales* 3–6.

24 For example, see, generally, *Working in Higher Education*, ed. R. Cuthbert (1996).

25 M. Trow, 'Managerialism and the Academic Profession : The Case of England' (1994) 7(2) *Higher Education Policy* 11, at 11.

What could work on women legal academics tell us about the effects of such policies? Margaret Thornton has argued that the congruence between bureaucratic power and masculinity is central to organizational structuring, making this interface a site of particular interest for those exploring the relationship between the academy as an institution and the women legal academics within it.[26] Thornton goes on to argue that there has been significant resistance to women carrying out authoritative functions within the academy and that the acceptance of women into the academy is possible only if they slot themselves into one of the limited positions available which reify the sexual regime. 'Such positions are characterised by conventional notions of the feminine, in that they emphasise appearance, sexuality, deference, docility, diligence, care and self-sacrifice.'[27] Thornton's interviews with women legal academics provide evidence for her analysis of the power structure in the Australian context; much could be learnt about the power structures of British legal academia by carrying out similar work in that context.

In considering the effects of institutional bureaucratization, it would be particularly interesting to discover more about the role of women legal academics may (or may not) play in resisting the bureaucratic process. In his recent analysis of the Dearing report, Martin Trow takes issue with the report for its authoritarian assumption that 'management' within the university sector can unproblematically impose its will on individual academics. Dearing's recommendation eight reads as follows :

> We recommend that, with immediate effect, all institutions of higher education give high priority to developing and implanting learning and teaching strategies which focus on the promotion of students' learning.[28]

Trow comments:

> I like particularly the intensifier 'with immediate effect': the phrase suggests how strong is the committee's illusion that universities are organised like firms, bureaucratically, with clear lines of authority that can ensure that instructions down the line will be obeyed 'with immediate effect'.

The truth of the matter is quite to the contrary. As Trow goes on to argue:

> Such generalised assertions about what must or should happen . . . do not reflect the actual processes by which decisions are made about teaching and learning in universities, or the very considerable authority over teaching that still inheres in the teaching staff itself . . . The bureaucratic assumptions of the report are reflected in its absence of concern about how that willing assent can be evoked; implicit in much of what is recommended is the assumption that if only the senior administrative staff can be persuaded about a course of action, then it can find the means to introduce and implement new policies.[29]

26 Thornton, op. cit., n. 4, p. 108.

27 id., p. 112.

28 National Committee of Inquiry into Higher Education, *Higher Education in the Learning Society* (1997) (the Dearing report) para. 8:10.

29 M. Trow, 'More Trouble Than it's Worth' *Times Higher Education Supplement*, 24 October 1997, 26.

What Trow is focusing on is his underlying belief that academic life cannot be controlled by a central agency, and that to assume that it can shows a complete lack of understanding of the nature of academic life.

> Academic life is continually bursting out of any pre-defined boundaries, and never more than just now. That is just what makes centralised efforts to manage and control intellectual life hopeless.[30]

I have argued elsewhere that it is possible for academics to find methods of resistance to what Foucault would call a 'disciplinary culture'.[31] The interesting question for the new research agenda currently under discussion is whether one of those sites of resistance might be found among women legal academics.

WOMEN LEGAL ACADEMICS AND THE DISCIPLINE OF LAW

Studying women legal academics may contribute not only to our knowledge of the university as an institution, but also to our knowledge of the discipline of law. Given the almost total lack of knowledge about the female members of the academic tribe which inhabits the territory of law, we have much to learn. Becher argues that, 'the ways in which particular groups of academics organise their professional lives are intimately related to the academic tasks on which they are engaged.'[32] His exploration of the social aspects of knowledge communities also leads him to look at the way in which such communities influence the epistemological properties of knowledge forms and vice versa. It is this interplay which suggests that research into women legal academics may have important things to say about the discipline of law itself.

Becher's work is especially valuable to lawyers, because it is one of the few examples of an examination of academic disciplines which encompasses law within its survey. He investigated twelve different disciplines, including academic law, looking at the relevant research literature and also conducting 221 semi-structured in-depth interviews across the twelve disciplines.

However, from the point of view of the research agenda which I am addressing, it is interesting to note that when discussing academic careers, Becher's methodology does not allow him to examine possible gender differences. He notes, nevertheless, that in terms of women's career patterns, the literature suggests that there are different patterns as between different fields. This phenomenon is well documented in the literature, and is reflected, for example, in Margherita Rendel's historical overview of the position of women academics. Margherita Rendel found that in the first half of this century women academics were not only a small minority of all academics,

30 id.

31 A. Bradney and F. Cownie, 'Working on the Chain Gang?' (1996) II(2) *Contemporary Issues in Law* 15.

32 Becher, op. cit., n. 8, p. 1.

but they tended to be concentrated in a small number of disciplines, law not featuring among them.[33] By the time she came to examine the position in the 1970s, she found that the number of both female and male academics employed full-time in universities had increased, but that there was increasing vertical and horizontal segregation; that is to say, increasing differences as between the sexes in the grades and subjects in which growth had occurred.[34] Becher has to rely on his reading of the literature in order to make comments about the careers of women academics. His discussion of this topic is entitled 'Addendum : A Note on Gender', which might say something about the importance he attached to this issue. However, in his appendix on methodology he writes that while there were no particularly revealing discontinuities in perception or response across respondents of different ages, experience or from different institutions, when it came to the question of academic careers he had insufficient material to draw any meaningful distinction between men and women. If he were to start again, he writes, he would want to build in some more systematic allowance for gender differences.[35] There is certainly room here for further work.

But it is not just in terms of examining the career patterns of academics that work on women may be valuable in enlightening us about the culture of a discipline. In relating gender solely to career patterns, Becher is missing the point. Work on women as members of a particular academic tribe may also have important things to tell us about other aspects of disciplinary culture. How do women fit into the competitive aspects of their discipline, for instance? Becher notes that this may be manifested, in the words of a biologist, by 'an emphasis on publication, aggressiveness at meetings and a high degree of single-mindedness.'[36] It may also result in secrecy, arising out of fears that someone else may exploit one's ideas more effectively, or in the production of hasty, careless work in order to generate frequent and rapid publications. The question for the new research agenda under discussion here is how, if at all, does the presence of women academics in law schools affect the competitive practices of legal academia? Do women legal academics behave differently, in terms of competition, secrecy, publication patterns or any other aspects of the disciplinary culture? And if they do, what does this mean for the disciplinary culture as a whole?

The potential for exploration of the culture of legal academia, informed by a gender perspective, can be appreciated if we examine in more detail some aspects of William Twining's *Blackstone's Tower*. The appendix to the book is entitled 'English Law Teachers as Academics : A Preliminary Analysis'. In it Twining raises the question, '[a]re there any salient characteristics that

33 M. Rendel, 'How Many Women Academics?' in *Schooling for Women's Work*, ed. R. Deems (1980).

34 M. Rendel, 'Women Academics in the Seventies' in *Is Higher Education Fair to Women?*, eds. S. Acker and D. Warren Piper (1984) 164.

35 Becher, op. cit., n. 8, p. 174.

36 id., p. 91.

differentiate English law teachers from the academic profession as a whole?'[37] He suggests that there is anecdotal evidence at least that some law teachers sense an underlying hostility from fellow academics and administrators, especially in the context of university politics. He notes that in Becher's work, perceptions of academic lawyers were generally unattractive:

> The predominant notion of academic lawyers is that they are not really academic – one critical respondent described them as 'arcane, distant and alien : an appendage to the university world'. Their personal qualities are dubious: they are variously represented as vociferous, untrustworthy, immoral, narrow, arrogant and conservative, though kinder eyes see them as impressive and intelligent. Their scholarly activities are thought to be unexciting and uncreative, comprising a series of intellectual puzzles scattered among 'large areas of description'.[38]

Twining argues that the picture of legal scholarship presented here is largely out of date, but more importantly, that on the basis of currently available information, it may be the case that academic lawyers are not very different from other types of academics. Twining had access to data on academic lawyers extrapolated from Halsey's 1989 survey, which he is then able to compare with the data on all academics. His interpretation of these data leads him to conclude that in almost all key respects the profile of academic lawyers very closely resembles the profile of the academic profession as a whole, especially colleagues in the Humanities and Social Sciences.[39]

However, Twining is clear that there is a need for further research into the academic legal profession, pointing out that Becher and Halsey are almost unique in providing a basis for comparing academic lawyers with colleagues in other disciplines, their samples are small and relate to different times (1980 and 1989) in a rapidly-changing context. Further work which included a gender perspective would arguably be even more informative. Twining speculates that work on sub-disciplines might prove very fruitful in making discoveries about the culture of academic law. Even on a superficial consideration of the issues, one could speculate that women legal academics may encounter different experiences according to their specialism, and that their contribution to the development of different sub-disciplines may vary considerably, with significant consequences for the discipline as a whole.

CHALLENGING MASCULINITY IN THE LAW SCHOOL

The relationship between women legal academics and the discipline of which they are part arguably has particular resonances in terms of gender. Law, it is often argued, is a particularly masculine domain. Richard Collier has drawn attention to the importance of 'rendering visible . . . the masculism

37 Twining, op. cit., n. 9, p. 201.
38 Becher, op. cit., n. 8, p. 30.
39 Twining, op. cit., n. 9, p. 202.

of the institutions of legal education', pointing out that the masculinity of law, in terms of the power of both law and men, has been a central concern of feminist legal theorists such as Smart, Mackinnon, and Stang-Dahl for some time.[40] He draws on Smart's work to draw attention to the mutual resonances, or overlaps, in the constitution of law and of masculinities; one of the most obvious of these is the idea that both of these are constructed as rational and that this correlation is based upon naturalistic, essentialist presuppositions.[41] Collier goes on to argue that:

> a further connection between masculinism and law lies in the fact that the power of each can be seen to relate to their ability to exclude that which would challenge their hegemonic power, their univocality and claims to authority. There is, it would seem, a convergence between the construction of both masculinity and law in that both are enmeshed within notions of hierarchy, authority, rationality and abstraction, and involve a distancing of the personal, the emotional and the sexual in the constitution of a univocal authoritative voice.[42]

For women legal academics, the fact that they work within a discipline in which such intimate connections can be made between that discipline and masculinity is something which should be a central concern of any research agenda in this field. As Collier notes:

> The politics of masculinity involves recognising that historically specific institutional practices – for example how we behave as legal academics, how we interact with colleagues and students, how the 'working' lives relate to the 'home' lives – each contribute to, draw upon and transform a gender order in which at present hegemonic masculinity constitutes the dominant ideology.[43]

It is a realization of the close relationship between the legal profession (including the academic branch of the profession) and masculinity which also lies behind Margaret Thornton's analysis of women in in the legal profession, when she asks, '[c]an women in law transcend the oppressive misogynism with which the legal culture . . . is saturated?'[44] In her examination of the legal academy, she argues that the increasing bureaucratization of universities favours the promotion of masculinist values and that women find it very difficult to be accepted as authoritative knowers within the academy, in a context in which, '[t]he fiction that neutrality is the distinguishing characteristic of benchmark men is the underlying presumption of the masculinised norm'.[45] While docile women, who conform to the prevailing norms of masculinity may be accommodated, feminist scholars, who challenge maculinist knowledge and modes of behaviour, feel

40 R. Collier, 'Masculinism, Law and Law Teaching' (1991) 19 *International J. of the Sociology of Law* 427, at 428 and 429.
41 See, generally, C. Smart, *Feminism and the Power of Law* (1989).
42 Collier, op. cit., n. 40, p. 321.
43 id., p. 433.
44 Thornton, op. cit., n. 4, p. 2.
45 id., p. 6.

unwelcome.[46] It is important that any new research agenda pays attention to these issues, asking, for instance, how women legal academics perceive their position as academics working with a subject which many have analysed as pervasively masculine, and how their position is undermined or strengthened by the structures of the institutions within which they work.

Experience from Canada points up the importance of addressing such issues. *Breaking Anonymity : The Chilly Climate for Women Faculty*, published in 1995, is a book composed of articles which describe and analyse the 'chilly climate' experienced by a number of women academics in universities across Canada. It includes analysis of reactions when women document the climate they work in and try to bring it out into the open for discussion.[47] For those interested in the idea of challenging masculinity within the law school, the most interesting chapter is that written by Sheila McIntyre about her experiences in the law school at Queen's University in Ontario.[48]

In 1985, Sheila McIntyre was hired on a two-year non-renewable contract to teach law at Queen's University. A year later, she wrote a memo, detailing and analysing incidents of sexism and anti-feminism which she had experienced and observed during her first year of teaching. She distributed the memo to the student representatives who sat on the law school's Faculty Board, and to all her colleagues. Copies of the memo circulated widely at Queen's and ultimately it became a national news story. Her autobiographical account paints a particularly vivid picture of a range of exclusionary and devaluing practices, some intentionally so, some not; she also describes the effects which occur when such practices converge on one individual.

One of the incidents which Sheila McIntyre chronicles is sufficient to illustrate the point which is being made; the importance of a research agenda which explores the need to challenge sexism/anti-feminism within law schools. McIntyre describes how, in her torts class, several male students agreed 'to take a run at Sheila'. They were angered by her use of gender-neutral vocabulary, and construed her linguistic usage to be 'shoving her politics down students' throats'. In addition, they objected to the fact that she had used two gender-loaded hypotheticals during the first six weeks of classes to explore the question of intentional torts. They were also angered by her use of a case on battery called *Fillipovich*.[49] *Fillipovich* stands for the proposition that so long as civilization exists, men will resolve disputes with their fists, that the injuries suffered from punches are *de minimis* and would cause '. . . amused discussion in a pub but no litigation'. Sheila McIntyre asked students to consider whether the ratio applied to 'men' or 'people',

46 id., ch. 4.

47 The Chilly Collective (eds.), *Breaking Anonymity: the Chilly Climate for Women Faculty* (1995).

48 S. McIntyre, 'Gender Bias Within the Law School; "The Memo" and Its Impact', id., ch. 7.

49 *Fillipovich* v. *Nahachewsky* (1969) 3 D.L.R. (3d) 544 (Sask. Q.B.).

and whether the trial outcome would have been any different if any of the parties had been women. In class, about six men were deliberately disruptive, uncooperative, interruptive, and angry. They endorsed the propositions in *Fillipovich* and belligerently tried to prevent students who disagreed with their position from speaking, by a combination of insult, interruption, hostile gestures, and increasingly voluble but untenable argument. When Sheila McIntyre tried to legitimate the contribution of other students, the 'troublemakers' were equally abusive to her.

There was never another incident of this type in the torts class, and during the rest of the course other gender-loaded cases were studied without disruption. However, the incident became legendary, and was used for the remainder of the academic year by some students to fuel opposition to the hiring of more women faculty.[50] They cited McIntyre's torts class to illustrate their claim that current hiring policies were undermining academic excellence in the law school.

Sheila McIntyre also chronicles an aggressive verbal attack from a male colleague. It was an isolated incident, but she reports that in general she did not experience overwhelming support from her colleagues (the vast majority of whom were male) and that she felt her views were not generally respected either. Reflecting on the impact of 'The Memo', she notes that at Queen's and several other academic institutions anti-sexism initiatives have sprung up, and the consciousness of individuals across faculties has shifted. Women are breaking their silence, forging new alliances and using a range of strategies to translate activism into permanent gains towards achieving substantive equality. However, as McIntyre is quick to point out, all this progress has its costs, in terms of the courage needed by individuals who speak out, and in confronting the inevitable backlash.

The importance of challenging masculinity within the law school, and of making this a specific focus of a new research agenda, is summed up by Sheila McIntyre when she writes:

> Women's equality cannot be secured if women continue to embody and personify all that male culture has projected on and into 'woman'. Nor can women be role-models to anyone when we operate with self-contempt, self-effacement or self-deceit . . . When we settle for scraps, why should the women who look to us as precedents imagine themselves qualified for more? Relative to most women watching us with hope and envy, we are privileged. We already have academic/professional training, hierarchical platforms from which to speak, (qualified) social status. If we sell our integrity in any form – our dignity, our right to freedom from physical, intellectual or emotional violation; our principles; our womanhood – in the search for external (male) acceptance or reward, at best we secure empty, fraudulent stature at all women's expense. Institutional acceptance on such terms ought to be unthinkable.[51]

50 Sheila McIntyre reports that at the time there were twenty-six permanent and six non-permanent men compared with three permanent and three non-permanent women on the staff of the law school at Queen's.

51 MacIntyre, op. cit., n. 48, pp. 220–1.

The work of McIntyre and Thornton, extremely valuable though it is in raising a number of important issues relating to women in the legal academy, nevertheless has its limitations. The experience of Canadian or Australian legal academics, working in very different political and economic situations, is very interesting, and offers insights which may be valuable in other contexts. However, it does not necessarily reflect the experience of similar legal academics working in Britain; a new research agenda, while drawing on such work as a source of issues to explore, should address the British experience, not in any parochial sense, but because, as has been argued above, the experience of academics working in a specific context, whether local or national, is very particular, and it is important that research in future should take as much account as possible of such variations in experience.

CONCLUSION

Researching women legal academics has enormous potential, not just for exanding our sum of knowledge as such, but for allowing us to learn more about the discipline of law and its place and influence in the academy as a whole. A research agenda such as that outlined here has the potential to contribute much to the challenging of masculinity not only within the law school but within the university as an institution, by exposing areas where oppression is greatest, as well as those where resistance is already well established.

In examining what Malinowski called 'the imponderabilia of everyday life', research into women legal academics could allow professional lives to speak out, and set within a firm theoretical perspective, make a contribution to the sociology of knowledge which should not be underestimated.[52]

52 A. Kuper, *Anthropologists and Anthropology: The British School 1922–72* (1973) 27.

JOURNAL OF LAW AND SOCIETY
VOLUME 25, NUMBER 1, MARCH 1998
ISSN: 0263–323X, pp. 116–33

Gazing into the Future through a VDU: Communications, Information Technology, and Law Teaching

PETER ALLDRIDGE* AND ANN MUMFORD*

The article deals with the interaction of computers, information technology, and legal education. It considers the technical achievements of communications and information technology (C&IT) in the practice and teaching of law, then the jurisprudential paradigms which underlie these issues. To the extent to which law is conceived as a form of information, existing assumptions about the theory, practice, and teaching of law are challenged. Where, on the other hand, law is regarded as a collection of rules, reversal to formalism, driven by C&IT, is identified as a concern for socio-legal scholars. Other concerns addressed by this article include the exclusive economics of the C&IT revolution, the power dynamics of technophobia, and the interaction of computers and gender. The article concludes with suggestions for alternative visons of the future of C&IT and legal education.

INTRODUCTION

Compared to the many other changes he would have spotted,[1] a nineteenth-century legal academic deposited in a law school in the last quarter of the twentieth would have found the working methods of his successors in the 1970s and even the 1980s surprisingly familiar. He would, however, require significant explanation of the changes effected over the last ten years. In contrast, while the theoretical terminology considered by some of his latter-day colleagues might be difficult for him to understand, the questions addressed by the most technologically advanced of his colleagues would provide him little trouble. To date, the advent of the Communications and Information Technology (C&IT) revolution has significantly changed the mechanisms by which academics communicate with each other and with students, the way in which they handle materials, and the experience

* *Cardiff Law School, University of Wales, Cardiff, PO Box 427, Museum Avenue, Cardiff CF1 1XD, Wales*

1 'Have pale blue trousers replaced gowns?'

of students. It has not yet, however, significantly changed the nature of the law school enterprise. It must be acknowledged that computers have failed to deliver the kinds of changes to the law curriculum which were predicted by their most enthusiastic advocates. The virtual law school is some way from being developed.

Our general thesis is that the most significant changes in law teaching over the next ten years will not arise in consequence of the advent (and subsequent assimilation or demise) of, for example, critical legal studies or autopoeitic theory, but from the changes which technology has brought, and that socio-legal studies has not engaged sufficiently with those developments, especially information technology and (though we shall not deal with this) in biotechnology. The changes effected by computers are not trivial, and they are not merely technical. They are substantial and demand our consideration. Developments in technology have made available many techniques (word processing/document assembly, electronic mail, legal databases, whether CD or Internet access, Internet more broadly, teaching programmes) which radically alter the ways in which people try to learn about law. On some accounts, C&IT will transform the very nature of narrative, of criticism, and of text-based education in general.[2] At the very least it presents alternative versions of the future between which choices must be made.

The article will examine the contribution which C&IT has made to law schools thus far, and the sorts of things to which it is, and to which it is not, suited. It will consider the conflicting jurisprudential paradigms which govern C&IT and the problems with the way in which it has been received in law schools in the United Kingdom. At various points in the analysis, legal education in the United States of America will provide a contrast. This is because the C&IT revolution in general is United States-led, because of the significant United States literature on C&IT in law teaching and because of the shared experience in developing software for teaching law.

THE TECHNICAL ACHIEVEMENTS OF COMMUNICATIONS AND INFORMATION TECHNOLOGY IN LAW

The 'killer ap'[3] in law teaching has yet to be found. None the less, many indisputable gains have been made. The following is a non-exhaustive list.

2 G. Landow, *Hypertext: The Convergence of Contemporary Critical Theory and Technology* (1992) quoted in J. Pickering, 'IT and Legal Education' (1996) 2 *J. of Information, Law and Technology* (Work in Progress section).

3 The application of C&IT which revolutionizes the way in which the profession works by compelling – usually by economic force – its adoption, as the spreadsheet did for accounting.

1. *Datasets*

Electronic datasets grant a legal scholar mediated or unmediated access to vast amounts of information. The task of 'looking something up' can be performed on an electronic as on a printed text, frequently with greater speed. This changes the nature of legal scholarship because electronic datasets enable searches of unprecedented amplitude. Datasets are now a standard tool for legal research.[4] Law Reports are available not only on-line but also on CD-ROM.[5] The decisions of the House of Lords are available on the Parliament Web Site the same day as they are delivered.[6] All new statutes are available free from the HMSO web page.[7] Major practitioner works are now available on CD-ROM with hyperlinks and search facilities of increasing value. Different United Kingdom law schools have opted for different on-line and CD packages but the differences between packages is relatively insignificant and dates very quickly. The significant difference is between using and not using one.

Electronic versions of standard texts, casebooks, and major practitioner works are now available on CD-ROM with hyperlinks. The value of these resources to (American) law students was investigated by the Chicago-Kent Law School, which sponsored research into the use of electronic casebooks.[8] The experimental programme involved equipping one hundred students with electronic 'casebooks', and, more crucially, fostering '. . . an environment and school culture that affirmed the use of computers as essential professional tools'.[9] The provision of electronic casebooks was, in many ways, a sophisticated take on the practice of providing lecture notes at the beginning of a term. Advantages for participating students included the ability to open the outline for the entire course, and to type notes into spaces provided for that purpose.[10] Lecturers were consequently free to depart from whatever set text they had felt obliged to follow, and then to experiment with material presented, in safe knowledge of the fact that the 'basics' of the law were within student's possession.

Although the project was a qualified success, its results support the observation that the availability of such research tools is, in some areas, a

4 See W.G. Harrington, 'A Brief History of Computer-Assisted Legal Research' (1985) 77 *Law Librarian's J.* 543 for an interesting discussion of the introduction of computers into the range of standard legal research tools.

5 Electronic Law Reports Context Ltd.

6 At http://www.parliament.the-stationery-office.co.uk/pa/ld/ldjudinf.htm

7 At http://www.hmso.gov.uk/acts.htm

8 P.W. Martin, 'What Do Law Students with Laptops and Electronic Casebooks Do? – The Chicago-Kent Computer Section' (1995-96) May 1996 (Internet version 15 October 1996) http://www.law.cornell.edu/papers/index.html.

9 id.

10 id.

clear advantage.[11] For example, by the 1980s, checking whether a particular section of a given statute was in force, which is an intellectually trivial task, had become a serious bugbear, because it was very time-consuming to search through the statutory instruments which brought them into force. There is now enough confidence in the authority of LEXIS and Lawtel that this problem, at least, has dissipated.

This does not mean that those resources are beyond criticism. Questions of editorial selection are clearly important. The unresolved issue with any data resource is how much the user needs to know about before one can search properly. If electronic research is the norm, the skills of electronic research are critical to legal education. The student must have a conceptual structure within which to search, and must be trained in searching techniques. Adequate training must instil skills which are capable of being easily upgraded as the software and datasets are enhanced. An ideal search will produce from the database all, and only, the relevant documents.

2. *Electronic mail*

The growth in popularity of electronic mail, or e-mail, amongst students presents a paradigm of student-initiated learning. After word processing, the first unequivocal success of the C&IT revolution in law schools was the use of electronic mail. Indeed, e-mail has radically altered the nature of the academic community.

There are few operations which are performed by e-mail which could not be performed otherwise but its efficiency permits an exceptional range of operations to be performed. And soon automation becomes innovation. In law teaching, particularly, written communication of many types with, and between, students becomes possible. Electronic mail also has been used in various imaginative ways in teaching. Any activities which require the dissemination of documents or discussion amongst groups can deploy e-mail. Asynchronous discussions can take place during the course of any designated time period. For example, the Chicago-Kent experiment noted that, whereas students who received paper handouts in class were unlikely to type notes about those handouts into their laptops, these same students (and even students who had neither laptops in class, nor access to electronic

11 'In response to the question "Did the use of so many laptops in the classroom have an effect on class discussion or class atmosphere?" 39 said "no" and 25 "yes". While the faculty do not see negative effects on engagement, a fair number of the "yes" group are persuaded that the computers reduce the quality of reflection and discussion, that "people get engrossed in trying to type everything the professor says rather than participating in class". However, "None of those who had this novel teaching experience would shy away from another like it, indeed some would volunteer. None thought the computers had a measurable negative impact on the kind of teaching they try to do".' See http://www.law.cornell.edu/papers/kentrptf.htm

casebooks) were, as a majority, more likely to request that future handouts be distributed via e-mail.[12]

3. *Teaching and learning software – the IOLIS disk*

From 1995 onwards, the IOLIS disk, published by the Law Courseware Consortium, has been in use in universities, and in other further education establishments. It is used in the University of London External LLB, and apparently is to be used in the Open University law courses.[13] The subjects covered thus far are: introduction to law, contracts, criminal law, torts, property law, public law, and European law. The objective is to provide coverage, at least, of the 'core' curriculum. This, and other, computer-assisted learning (CAL) programmes for law require the student to answer questions or to perform other exercises.

4. *Distance learning*

One communications value of e-mail and the Web is that, so long as most communication is conducted in electronic form, it does not matter where in the world the students are. An obvious advantage of distance learning is that it extends to people who simply would not be able to attend an institution of full-time higher education. The pedagogic model of C&IT provision in legal education may be particularly appropriate for part-time and distance-learning students. This observation, however, implies a further dichotomy. If the methods used in distance learning are really as effective as those used in more traditional teaching and learning, then there is no reason for them to be the sole preserve of distance learning. If they are not as good, then that is a matter of concern.

A more positive view would be to accentuate the advantages of the distance. Many jobs are performed now by telecommuters, and the employer chooses to employ people in that capacity because it is cheaper and/or more effective.[14] It is worthy of note that these sorts of jobs are often preferred by women, many of whom claim to have benefited immensely from the liberations from venue confinement that telecommuting allows.[15] Distance learning presents other questions, however, and ultimately the question

12 Martin, id.

13 The list of subscribers is at http://www.law.warwick.ac.uk/html/subscribers.html.

14 See, among others, 'Pacific Bell offers tips to begin telecommuting; Telecommute America week is Oct. 23-27' *Business Wire*, 13 October 1995; B. Husted, 'Is telecommuting the answer? Web sites address the question' *San Diego Union-Tribune*, 19 November 1996, 13; and 'Telecommuting' *Los Angeles Times*, 16 July 1989, part 2, p. 11. See, also, A. Rajan, 'Flexibility the key for a new breed of worker' *Evening Standard*, 4 August 1997, 36, and C. Pepinster 'Big title, big pay, no desk' *Independent*, 23 March 1997, 20.

15 See, among others, L.A. Fox, 'Flexible Homes Wave Of The Future: Survey' *Toronto Sun*, 12 March 1997, 62, and J. Mcclellan 'Cyberspace: Doodles From Deskland' *Observer*, 24 December 1995, 43.

whether distance learning can ever emerge from the shadow of face-to-face teaching and learning will depend upon the extent to which interpersonal interactions are replaceable. This is a matter to which we shall return.

THE JURISPRUDENTIAL PARADIGMS: LAW AS RULES VERSUS LAW AS INFORMATION

In a study carried out across disciplines for the Dearing committee, it was found that where C&IT had successfully been applied to assist teaching and learning, there was a predominance of subjects where:

(a) routine or mechanical skills play an important part;
(b) the knowledge component can be precisely specified; and
(c) there is a well-defined professional base.[16]

On the other hand, it was found that C&IT has not been successful where the subjects are:

(a) creative or performing arts; or
(b) subjects where the skills/knowledge less easily defined or specified.

In order to determine whether law is a subject in which C&IT can play a larger role or not, it is necessary to decide into which category law falls. The idea of law as being part of the first group is well established. That is the traditional doctrinal 'black-letter' approach in which the student is required to identify and apply rules to facts. Law as a more discursive discipline encouraging divergent thinking has, still, a tenuous foothold. Having spent years at the margins, only to be brought forward (oddly enough, by research assessment exercises in the United Kingdom), socio-legal studies and other perspectives which do not satisfy the Exeter criteria for ease of importation of C&IT may once again be forced to the wall by a reversion to formalism driven by C&IT.

1. *Law as rules*

One of the troubling aspects of the advance of C&IT in the legal sphere is a jurisprudential paradigm which seems frequently to travel unchallenged. The advent of the technology combines the most innovative techniques with the most reactionary jurisprudence. Susskind's acclaimed, and in many ways excellent, *The Future of Law* is informed by cutting-edge work in managerial theory, studies of the role of C&IT in organizations and specific developments in C&IT applications, but also by legal theory which, to a legal theorist, would have looked seriously out of date in the late 1970s.[17] In a bibliography,

16 Consortium of Telematics for Education Information, University of Exeter et al., *Information Technology Assisted Teaching and Learning in Higher Education*, HEFCE Research Series, July 1997 (hereinafter 'Exeter') 12.

17 R. Susskind, *The Future of Law* (1996) 293.

Susskind records the seven books on the nature of law by which he was most influenced[18] as:

Author	Dates	Work	Date of Publication
Bentham	1748-1832	*Of Laws in General*	(Written c.1810) 1945 or 1971
Ehrlich	1862-1922	*Fundamental Principles of the Sociology of Law*	1913 (German); 1936 (trans.)
Kelsen	1881-1973	*General Theory of Law and State*	1922 (German); 1946 (trans.)
Frank	1889-1957	*Courts on Trial*	1949
Hart	1907-1992	*The Concept of Law*	1961 (2nd ed. 1992)
Harris	1943-	*Law and Legal Science*	1979
Dworkin	1931-	*Law's Empire*	1986

If an author were to produce a book on law and *x*, (where *x* is history, geography, economics, literature, politics, sociology, popular culture), have the presumption to entitle it *The Future of Law*, but in it to acknowledge that the most important theoretical influences upon them, concerning law, were these seven books, the reviewers would have a field day. What, they might ask, about Foucault, Habermas, Teubner, MacKinnon, Derrida, Coase, Unger or Posner? It might be said that *because* a scholar is dealing with computers they have, by that very fact, unquestionable credentials. Susskind's list represents the dominant jurisprudence of many people in computers and law. It is a paradigm with serious limitations. The problem is that this list is not just out of fashion. It also tends towards a highly formalistic positivism. In many ways the distinctive book on Susskind's list is Harris's, which is one of the few serious attempts since his death to revive Kelsen's jurisprudence.[19] Kelsen's essential tenets include the view that rules are directed at officials not citizens (legal rules are all, in their essence of the form 'if *p* then an official ought to *q*') and that the principle of imputation (the relation between the triggering facts and the obligation upon the official) operates to produce the legal 'ought'.[20]

Why is this view of law one which sits well with the movement for computers and law? Conceiving law as rules of the form *if p then q* is something which is enormously constraining. Even those interested in teaching or writing doctrinal law might well be more interested in

18 And see, for their influence, R. Susskind, *Expert Systems in Law* (1986) part III.

19 Also R. Tur and W. Twining, *Essays on Kelsen* (1986).

20 Thus, for example, the law of murder would be expressed in Kelsen's terms, 'If a person has been shown to have [followed by a full definition of murder] then the judge *ought* to sentence him/her to life imprisonment.'

questioning whether *q* is invariably an appropriate sequitur to *p*, or whether a particular set of circumstances should actually be classified as *p*, than with the mechanics of rule application. But the advantage in computers and law is that as soon as the 'legal' operation is characterized as an *if p then q* operation, then it becomes easy to perform it with a computer. At least in computing, *if p then q* can be an enormously complicated operation. In the sphere of law even relatively complicated statutes (those which expressed algorithmically would have a good many junctions) the application (failing logical inconsistency) of clear rules to clear facts is a relatively mundane, mechanistic operation.[21] If you are going to use computers in legal contexts, the pressure which computers generate is towards a rule-bound framework, because it is what they do best. There does seem to be a link, if not a logical one then a practical one, between technological innovation and jurisprudential reaction. It is no coincidence, for example, that the IOLIS disk has yet to engage with sociology of law or socio-legal studies. Marginal attempts on it at 'Law in Context' have fallen pretty flat. It would not be impossible to produce such materials. Good interactive materials have been produced in qualitative social sciences. It is just less easy.

2. *Law as information*

Susskind is not himself committed to such an highly positivist formalism. There is an alternative vision of law evident in his book and elsewhere in the C&IT literature – of 'law as information'. The essence of this position is there is nothing particularly to distinguish law from other form of information and that 'Lawyers do not know so much more law than other people, but they know better where to find it'.[22] The richer paradigm of law to which information technology gives rise is law as information, and the study of law is the study of techniques of information delivery and manipulation. This view threatens to blow the gaff on a well-kept secret, which is that, in terms of the intellectual operations which are demanded of its students, law is not a particularly difficult academic subject. It breaks down the 'priesthood' view of lawyering (the idea that there is some special thing that lawyers know, or know how to do, which escapes the common

21 This was seen in the Latent Damage System developed in the late 1980s. Susskind, op. cit, n. 17, p. 199. The kinds of aspirations for such systems expressed in the late 1980s – as to which, see E.L. Rissland, 'Artificial Intelligence and Law: Stepping Stones to a Model of Legal Reasoning' (1990) 99 *Yale Law J.* 1957, at 1957 – have largely been disappointed.

22 This remark has been attributed to King George II. See F. Hicks, 'The Teaching of Legal Bibliography' (1918) 11 *Law Library J.* 1, 2, cited by L.A. Silecchia, 'Designing and Teaching Advanced Legal Research and Writing Courses' (1995) 33 *Duquesne Law Rev.* 203, at 203. See, also, T.A. Woxland, 'Why Can't Johnny Research? or It All Started with Christopher Columbus Langdell', 81 *Law Library J.* 451, at 451 (1989) ('Legal research is not an unimportant skill. It is not something one can get along without: no attorney can go through life only arguing the equities; sooner or later he or she has to find the law.')

run of humanity). Legal texts, as non-linear texts, and the uses to which they are put matches what C&IT can do. For instance, the dense cross referencing in some legal texts matches the web-like structure of hypertexts. Here, what C&IT can do to a text corresponds quite well with what the users of that text wish to do. Legal techniques will become techniques of using information delivery systems. The distinction between lawyers and others becomes blurred, and scope arises for the introduction of a range of paralegal occupations and of hybrid skills.

3. *The value of the 'human touch'?*

Community is important in universities, but the C&IT revolution has altered radically the nature of the communities to which members of universities belong, and raised serious questions about the potentially dehumanizing effect of the introduction of computers into the workplace. The question is whether personal contact is a vital component of a university education either as learning or as socialization, and if these things are important, to what extent they can be emulated by electronic communication? In what way does it matter whether students having similar experiences do so in the same place and at the same time?

C&IT has redefined teaching and learning interaction. As Kramarae has written, United States law teachers, due to the traditional importance placed on argumentative exchange as a learning tool, strictly construed valuable teacher/student interaction as that which occurred within the walls of the classroom.[23] The same may be said of legal education in the United Kingdom, with the caveat of intimacy. The tutorial is traditionally viewed as a far more familiar environment than the United States law-school lecture. As a result of C&IT, however, 'interaction in classes today is often explicitly more dispersed, with much of the interaction taking place asynchronously among students and teachers in many locations'.[24]

So far as concerns teaching and learning, notwithstanding its general commitment to C&IT, there is a slightly misty-eyed reference in the Dearing report of the value of personal contact:

> . . . personal contact between teacher and student, and between student and student, gives a vitality, originality and excitement that cannot be provided by machine-based learning, however excellent.[25]

What is naïve about Dearing's observation is the assumption that these three 'human' qualities, whilst admittedly desirable, are in any way possible in the current production-line approach to legal education in the United

23 C. Kramarae, 'Technology Policy, Gender, and Cyberspace' (1997) 4 *Duke J. of Gender Law and Policy* 149, at 151.

24 id., at fn. 10.

25 National Committee of Inquiry Into Higher Education, *Higher Education in the Learning Society* (1997) (the Dearing report) para 8.21.

Kingdom. '[V]itality, originality, and excitement' are obstructed by a system which demands that the majority of law teachers engage in mind-numbing repetition of tutorials. Computers do not tire. They are capable of taking a student through the same ten questions, ten times each if necessary. Law teachers are capable of more than this, of course, but the present system does not allow them enough time with their noses raised from the grindstone to inject the specifically human qualities which Dearing mentions. In terms of the measurable educational outcomes, what we need is research on the relative effects upon the vast preponderance of students of, on the one hand an hour interacting with an IOLIS module or similar program, and, on the other, an hour of what sometimes seems little short of sullen indifference with a tutorial of ten to twelve covering material which the tutor has already dealt with many times. If indeed it is the case that interpersonal interaction scores more highly, then the case is made out. What is surprising is that Dearing was prepared to take this as an article of faith rather than of evidence.

The second, stronger, reservation about C&IT in law schools centres on the function of community in education, and the value of students communing, perhaps in a library, as opposed to shutting themselves away, with their law school networked computers, at home. One response is that e-mail could discharge the socialization function. The Mead report notes:

> It may well be that faculty and students will replace the socialization process that has traditionally taken place in the hallways and student centers of the law school with a new kind of socialization that occurs through computer mediated communication or that physical presence at the law school actually increases because of computer mediated communication. Perhaps students will continue to come to an aesthetically pleasing and functional law building [sic]. Perhaps they will come because they are so competitive as a group that they could not function believing that they were 'missing out' by not being physically present at the law school. Experience suggests, however, that this is probably not the case. In any event, the answer is certainly unclear at this time. It remains a significant concern that the law school community will have to address and resolve.[26]

The Mead report focused on the extent to which C&IT has decentralized access to, and consequently altered our 'current conceptions of legal education'.[27] The report considered the function of community in education, and the value of students communing in a library, as opposed to shutting themselves away, with their law school networked computers, at home.[28] Thomas Bruce of the Legal Information Institute argued that an increase in 'free beer' was hardly going to be necessary to foster student community, as e-mail would appear to be enhancing the amount and quality of student interactions.[29]

26 *Interim Report of the University of Dayton School of Law Mead Data Central Joint Committee to Study Computer Technology in Legal Education* (http://www.law.cornell.edu/mdc udsl/toc.html) (hereafter Mead), citing letter from Thomas R. Bruce, Research Associate and Director of Educational Technologies, Cornell Law School, to the Mead/Dayton Joint Committee (May 12 1993)

27 id., s. 2f.

28 id.

29 Bruce letter, id.

In an article which displays a great deal of resistance to C&IT, Thomas has described e-mail as '. . . the new high-tech water cooler, where people exchange important messages or sometimes gossip in an all-day conversation.'[30] Thomas's primary objection to e-mail is that it is not 'real'. Real, in the human, interactive sense of what Thomas has dubbed 'The Question', that is, 'Did you get my e-mail?'. 'The Question', on his account, is actually the expression by the speaker of:

> . . . a subconscious desire to form the bond which e-mail, however convenient, cannot provide – a sign of implicit dissatisfaction with the transmission medium itself, and an attempt to form the human connection essential to communication.[31]

There is no denying that oral queries regarding e-mail receipt are annoying. Thomas's submission that these queries indicate 'implicit dissatisfaction with the transmission medium itself', however, lacks plausibility. A better interpretation is that 'did you get my e-mail?' translates, quite consciously, as 'why haven't you done what I've asked yet?' – hence, the irritation which it engenders. Thomas's larger concerns, however, focusing on the extent to which e-mail hinders 'real' human interaction, merit serious consideration. His primary thesis is that, in a profession such as law, where clients, in particular, often bemoan the extent to which its practice is an intensely alienating experience, the introduction of a further dehumanizing factor is to be discouraged.[32]

The C&IT revolution need not be construed as a threat to traditional concepts of community; rather, it may more productively be accepted as a challenge to produce different notions of community. In a business setting, the asynchronous interpersonal transaction is firmly established without computers: the overwhelming proportion of telephone transactions have only one participant. Of course, e-mail and the Internet have altered the communities to which academics belong. It is far more productive to try to profit from the abolition of distance and the availability of a wider community at differing times than to complain about the personal contact which is lost.

THE ECONOMICS OF THE COMMUNICATIONS AND INFORMATION TECHNOLOGY REVOLUTION

The economics of the introduction of C&IT into law schools have now become relatively clear. In the introductory phase, it was imagined by some

30 R.H. Thomas, '"Hey, Did You Get My E-Mail?" Reflections of a Retro-Grouch in the Computer Age of Legal Education' (1994) *J. of Legal Education* 233, at 240.

31 id., at p. 242.

32 'In the rush to accept technology, we must not lose sight of the dehumanizing effects of the computer and e-mail communication. Being a lawyer, thinking like a lawyer, is an intensely human enterprise' (id. at p. 245). Rather endearingly, Thomas adds, 'Kingsfield notwithstanding, sometimes mushy thinking is just what the client may need.'

that there would be easy short-term gains in efficiency with little outlay, and that it would pay for itself, in the way that it has (for example) in the banking or travel businesses (where essentially very simple operations are performed with huge databases in such a way as to make greatly more efficient the conduct of the operations). It rapidly became clear that this was a hopelessly optimistic and unrealistic view to take in the context of law teaching and learning, even where (as was generally the case) no proper quantification was made of the commitment of time of enthusiasts (which was, for the opening period of the C&IT revolution, the major driving force). In universities, the changes which were able to be made – where made at all – were only in administration. To keep hardware provision in C&IT up to a minimum standard is going to cost a great deal. The major factor preventing development for the foreseeable future will be funding.

Although there are some jobs which can be done viably for smaller numbers,[33] anything which requires substantial software authoring to be performed cannot efficiently be achieved within one institution. It is the nature of the C&IT revolution that ease of communication means that the product perceived as best drives out competitors with great speed. The only way, in the foreseeable future, in which the production of teaching materials in interactive, electronic format can be supported in the United Kingdom is by collaboration between institutions. Writing software is a more labour-intensive process than writing linear texts, because it involves writing texts, creating links, writing responses to alternative student responses, and checking that all the relations work. Writing linear texts is, of course, in itself an operation which is done only for a larger audience than one law school.

The cost of C&IT is considered more of a barrier in the United Kingdom than in the United States of America for two primary reasons. First, more universities have invested funds towards the advancement of C&IT in the United States than in the United Kingdom. Secondly, the expectation of debt as a consequence of higher education in the United States of America is far more common, than in the United Kingdom. But even (better funded) United States law schools have not been able to go it alone. No single law school has so many students that it can support the writing of software just for its own students. In the United States, co-ordination and standardization has been achieved by the CALI consortium working at Chicago-Kent University, using the Warwick IOLIS authorware.[34]

At any given moment, there is an argument specific to C&IT which militates towards delay in the commitment of resources in individual schools. This is that C&IT is getting cheaper. The decline in hardware prices per unit of performance is well known. As to software, the fact that the techniques

33 For example, the examination of appropriate courses, as to which see P. Alldridge, 'Multiple Choice Examining in Law' (1997) 31 *Law Teacher* 167.

34 http://www.cali.org/

of C&IT have been getting rapidly easier has the effect that skills which even two years ago were necessary and sought-after are now redundant, and so the time spent in their acquisition can be viewed as having been wasted. For example, the relatively complex task which web-authoring was has now become the production of a more sophisticated than usual word-processed document. In consequence, just as the economics of law schools make it difficult to commit to buying hardware, so there is both an institutional and a personal unwillingness to commit to the investment of time required in learning software skills.

There are many difficulties in arriving at accurate costings of the respective cost and benefits of introducing C&IT in universities. These difficulties led to research on cost *perception*, which was described in the Exeter study to 'be characterised as a monotonically non-decreasing function of perceived distance of observer from point of ITATL delivery'.[35] People who use the computers and do not pay directly for them think that they cost less than the people who do not use them. This difference in perception may be a function of the degree to which the people in senior managerial positions have been ignorant of anything which is achieved by computing.

The obvious issues which are created by the economics of C&IT are those of centralization and uniformity. The introduction of CAL is a threat to the academic freedom of the individual teacher to teach a course in the way in which they judge best, and to the autonomy of an institution which attempts to create a discrete intellectual identity. A CAL program seems to raise greater anxiety about academic freedom than a textbook, because it is easier (and, as it happens, less work) to be selective within a textbook than from a teaching module, because there is usually a range of textbooks from which to choose, and because it always possible to choose not to have a textbook in any given course. An institution attempting to carve out a discernible identity must either adopt commonly used CAL (reducing the potential for distinctiveness) or eschew it, losing whatever efficiency savings can be generated.

The Higher Education Funding Councils created the Computers in Teaching Initiative (CTI) Centres with briefs to develop teaching materials in their respective domains. The CTI Law Centre is located at Warwick.[36] The most recent step towards centralization is the establishment of the National Centre for Legal Education (NCLE), also at Warwick. The object of the centre is that it will provide a repository for teaching materials, hypertext links, and so on which could not economically be maintained in individual institutions.[37] It is impossible to say, at the moment, how it is likely to develop.

Even among the community of computers and law, centralized production

35 Exeter, op. cit., n. 16, at p. 23.

36 http://www.law.warwick.ac.uk/html/ltc.html

37 The aims are set out at http://www.law.warwick.ac.uk/ncle/html/aims.html

of teaching software has occasionally met with resistance. Although the modules on the IOLOS disk vary in quality, quality has not been one of the primary obstacles to their introduction into the 'core' courses to which the IOLIS disks aspire.[38] Rather, the concerns would appear to centre upon control. If the only teaching software in a particular subject is that which is produced by the Warwick consortium (notwithstanding that their authors come from disparate institutions), then that will give the people responsible significant influence over the curriculum in all law schools. The choice – which may be uncomfortable – will be between using CAL to discharge teaching obligations more effectively and efficiently or to commit greater resources to teaching the courses for which CAL is not used, perhaps at the expense of research output. In the light of the range of pressures being exerted upon university departments, this is not an easy choice.

COMPUTERS AND GENDER

Kramarae has stressed that perspectives of women are not included in the growing discussion in United States law journals to questions concerning computers and the curriculum.[39] She wrote '[w]e need to pay attention to women's lack of equal access to money, economic independence, and computers.'[40] She argues that not only are poorer children largely disadvantaged by school systems responding to the C&IT 'revolution', but the C&IT training of girls is frequently ignored in favour of boys.[41] This is perhaps due to the fact that C&IT fits many traditional assumptions squarely: for example, computers are machines, and are hence the province of (whether concerning school-age children, or law teachers) boys or men; or, that computers involve logic and maths – fields in which, according to gender-based prejudices, men, and not women, are supposed to excel.

This latter stereotype has particular resonance for law teachers. The age group which for the most part manages legal education in the United Kingdom today recalls when the most notable function of computers was to assist with spreadsheets. The next notable evolution of computers for this age group was the advent of word processors, and it is this development which hits at one of the most stubborn gender paradoxes plaguing the evolution of IT. If computers are viewed simply as very powerful typewriters, it is unsurprising that both women and men in legal education should react so strongly against them. For male legal academics, the tradition is that the law teacher constructs the materials, and the secretary types them up. For women legal academics, this is the same tradition, although it is accompanied

38 P. Moodie, 'Law Courseware and Iolis: Assessing the Present and Constructing the Future' (1997) 1 *J. of Information, Law and Technology.*

39 Kramarae, op. cit., n. 23.

40 id., at p. 150.

41 id., at p. 151.

by often widely defined concepts of 'admin' with which, more often than not, women law teachers are burdened. It is unsurprising that a women law teacher who has managed to achieve liberation from typewriter-related duties should be loath to re-engage with a 'super typewriter' voluntarily. All of these factors have contributed to an environment in which both male and women law teachers may boast about a lack of competence in C&IT, for so to so brag is to indicate empowerment.

Yet if women law teachers reject C&IT, the implications both for them and their students are dire. Law teachers who reject C&IT for themselves nonetheless can appreciate that it is valuable for students to acquire IT-related skills. Law teachers should be concerned with exactly what is being acquired without their input. Kramarae has indicated, for example, that many aspects of cyberspace are less than gender tolerant.[42] What is not supportable is for law teachers to appreciate the value of IT-related education for students, and then to refuse to engage with it.

DEALING WITH TECHNOPHOBES

What may be identified as the great, and largely unspoken, fear underpinning the C&IT debate is summarized in the Mead report's observation that 'advancing technology may quite literally change the face of the law school faculty'.[43] At any gathering of people involved in law and C&IT the (usually negative, or resistant) responses of colleagues are a constant theme, and the difference in this respect between the United Kingdom and other jurisdictions notable. The complaints are unified, and focus on the extent to which the efforts of 'pro-IT' colleagues to improve the efficiency of how they do what they do are hindered by their 'IT-resistant' colleagues. Martin hints at reason behind this in the relations between academic staff and other members of law schools.

> [E]ffective use of digital technology in the educational and research activities of a law school will necessitate far more collaborative working relationships among faculty members and these and other professionals. Given the status/power structure of our schools and the model of every professor a star on his/her own stage, this shift will be difficult if not impossible for many schools to pull off. But finding the right way to integrate these new professionals into the institution in the same way that librarians were brought into the profession during the first half of this century is critical.[44]

Another reason lies in the differences between high- and low-status academic staff. At the latest from the 1970s, it became a badge of status to be able to command sufficient secretarial facilities not to be obliged to type, and to have access from colleagues mediated by women.

42 id., at pp. 151-6.

43 Mead, op. cit., n. 26, s. 3B.

44 id., s. 3bf, citing letter from Peter W. Martin, Jane M.G. Foster Professor of Law, Cornell Law School, to the Joint Committee (20 April 1993).

The issue of the extent to which C&IT skills should be required of law faculty is controversial. Traditionally, what is desired in a legal academic is that they research well, and that they teach well. In the twenty-first century, it is unlikely that either of these will be achievable without the assistance of IT.

DEARING

In the summer of 1997 the Dearing inquiry reported. Notwithstanding that the report was infused with an economist's scepticism as to the relative costs and benefits which are involved, the Dearing report was unequivocal in its explicit commitment to C&IT. Its educational philosophy accords most clearly with that of one of its members.[45]

> As will be clear from other chapters in this report, we believe that the innovative exploitation of Communications and Information Technology (C&IT) holds out much promise for improving the quality, flexibility and effectiveness of higher education. The potential benefits will extend to, and affect the practice of, learning and teaching and research. C&IT is also, we argue, needed to support high quality, efficient management in higher education institutions. There is scope to reduce costs in the future and the potential is great, but implementation requires investment in terms of time, thought and resources in the short term.[46]

Dearing recommends the foundation of an Institute for Learning and Teaching in Higher Education which is to be responsible for setting standards for teachers in higher education.[47] Competence in C&IT will be among the required skills for newcomers to the profession. A number of specific issues arise from the report. They will be considered in turn.

1. *Student purchase of equipment*

Importantly, on the issue of cost, the Dearing report acknowledges that:

> [w]e are also aware that students will need access to high quality networked desktop computers that permit the use of the latest multi-media teaching materials and other applications. . . . We expect that students will soon need their own portable computers as a means of access to information/networks.[48]

The question which must be considered is whether students should ever be asked by their institutions to purchase the own computers. Students have always been expected to buy books, so there is no categorical prohibition about imposing expenditure upon them. There are United States law schools which require students to buy a computer of a given specification. Obviously,

45 D. Laurillard, *Rethinking University Teaching: a framework for the effective use of educational technology* (1993).

46 Dearing, op. cit., n. 25, para. 13.1.

47 id., rec. 14.

48 id., para. 68.

from the point of view of the institution, it would represent a great saving to shift the major part of the hardware burden onto the student body. If there is to develop a practice of making this requirement of students, institutions cannot change the policy too soon, because any expenditure on provision of hardware for students before the policy is introduced will turn out to have been wasted.

2. *University management*

Dearing sees effective management (in terms of a clear information strategy and the provision of training and support) as providing the essential link between, on the one hand, the communication infrastructure (network, support staff, hardware) and the context (electronic information, learning materials, management systems software, and teaching and research databases) for the deployment of C&IT.[49] Likewise the Mead report concludes that:

> [l]eadership will require a tremendous commitment of time and resources by law schools and their faculties, a commitment that many commentators fear will not occur. Those doubters may not have adequately accounted for the increasingly intense competition for students which may develop during the remainder of this decade and which we believe will powerfully motivate law schools to embrace technology.[50]

Dearing requires that all higher education institutions in the United Kingdom should have in place overarching communications and information strategies by 1999-2000, that higher education institutions should develop managers who combine a deep understanding of C&IT with senior management experience, and that funding bodies should encourage institutional management to review their C&IT strategy, and its implementation, as a matter of urgency and importance.[51] University management has not, in general, been among the earliest in large organizations to adapt to C&IT. The recognition that things have advanced as far as they will on the basis of individual efforts, and that managerial impetus is now required, is a welcome one.

3. *Skills and graduates*

For many years, the guiding model of a university education was as training in being an academic. This has been taken over by the skills model. The consequences may well be that the nature of the law school enterprise will change. Fewer law graduates now practice of law than in previous years. The model of a university education as training to be an academic – always a curious one – is clearly insupportable. Serious attention is being given to

49 id., para 13.1.
50 Mead, op. cit., n. 26, s. 8A, conclusion.
51 Dearing, op. cit., n. 25, rec. 41; rec. 42; para 13.13.

the sorts of transferable skills which all graduates need. Skills in C&IT should be high on any list. In the context of C&IT, the Dearing focus on 'learning throughout life' could not be more relevant.[52]

CONCLUSION – ALTERNATIVE VISIONS OF THE FUTURE

Increasingly, students have been arriving at institutions of higher learning with increased C&IT skills. The period during which institutions of Higher Education have had to supply training in a trivium of word processing, electronic mail, and net-surfing will shortly be gone – indeed, '[t]he successor to print literacy will be the set of skills needed to locate and usefully organise information for ourselves and others in cyberspace'.[53] The question will then be how the C&IT skills which incoming students have can be deployed in law. This will depend upon how courses are to be designed for them.

In a time of shrinking provision, C&IT may be a way to preserve quality of teaching and learning. It may also, however, be regarded as a threat to the way in which teaching and learning was previously conducted. Consequently predictions as to the value of C&IT in law schools in the twenty-first century fall broadly into two camps. The optimists assert that C&IT will produce better educational outcomes, a richer working life for academics freed from the drudgery of repetitive tutorials and better able to concentrate on research and teaching at a higher level. The pessimists regard the advent of C&IT as the ultimate victory of Kubrick's Hal, as a mechanism for replacing academic staff by machines, leaving only a few jobs for academics as the writers of CAL software.[54] What is certain is that the drawbacks of what we have, in terms of the capabilities of C&IT, are only temporary. New advantages, and new problems, are likely, and in a more immediate context than law teachers will be able to control.

52 id., introduction, para. 2.

53 Pickering, op. cit., n. 2, quoting J. Lemke, 'Education, Cyberspace and Change' (1993) 1(1) *Arachnet Electronic J. on Virtual Culture*.

54 *2001: A Space Odyssey* (1968).

JOURNAL OF LAW AND SOCIETY
VOLUME 25, NUMBER 1, MARCH 1998
ISSN: 0263–323X, pp. 134–50

Ethics for Lawyers or Ethics for Citizens? New Directions for Legal Education

JULIAN WEBB*

The Lord Chancellor's Advisory Committee on Legal Education and Conduct (ACLEC) has called for the reconstruction of the ethical foundations of legal education. However, it has not justified its premise that teaching legal values at the initial stage will enhance professional legal ethics. It is argued that the present system of education, given its technocratic, individualistic, and authoritarian tendencies, cannot meet ACLEC's challenge. A more ethical legal education can be envisaged within a neo-Aristotelian framework. This perspective emphasizes the reflexivity between micro and macro ethics, and utilizes the active and participatory learning approaches which should enable students to engage in meaningful moral discourse and problem solving.

As Zygmunt Bauman has so powerfully argued, we are entering a world of modernity without illusions in which we are assailed by *fin de millennium* doubts and fears of moral decline.[1] Ethics has once more come to the fore in debates about the protection of the environment; the future of our communities, the education of our children, and standards in public and professional life.

The recent calls for a renewal of legal ethics are symptomatic of these events, and particularly of 'the backlash against professional society'.[2] The attack by academics, by clients, consumer groups, and by state authorities antagonistic to the monopoly power of professions, has resulted in the initiation of a substantial renegotiation of the relationship between profession, state, and civil society.[3] In such an age of doubt and deregulation

* *Faculty of Law, University of the West of England, Coldharbour Lane, Bristol BS16 1QY, England*

1 Z. Bauman, *Postmodern Ethics* (1993).
2 H. Perkin, *The Rise of Professional Society* (1989) ch. 10.
3 For example, I. Illich, *Disabling Professions* (1977); P. Wilding, *Professional Power and Social Welfare* (1982). See the Green Paper, *The Work and Organisation of the Legal Profession*, (1989; Cm. 570) paras. 1.1-1.2, and P.A. Thomas, 'Thatcher's Will' in *Tomorrow's Lawyers*, ed. P.A. Thomas (1992); A.A. Paterson, 'Professionalism and the Legal Services Market' (1996) 3 *International J. of the Legal Profession* 137, notably at 145-8; J. Levin, 'An Ethical Profession?', Inaugural Lecture, University of Wales, Swansea, October 1994.

there is therefore a certain inevitability in the growing calls for legal education to develop a more distinctively moral voice.[4]

In England and Wales emphasis on the ethical dimension has emerged only relatively recently. The creation, in 1991, of the Lord Chancellor's Advisory Committee on Legal Education and Conduct (ACLEC) has been an important catalyst. Though its role is primarily advisory, it is the first single body to take significant responsibility for much of the education, training, *and* regulation of the English legal profession. It is therefore ACLEC's proposals for legal ethics that I will take as a starting point for this analysis.

ETHICS AND ACLEC

ACLEC's vision has been spelt out in its two reports on legal education and training.[5] Taken together these represent a significant attempt to reconstruct legal education and training in England and Wales into a system that is both more progressive, more coherent, more flexible and accessible than that which operates today.

The crux of ACLEC's position on ethics is the belief that:

> no amount of external regulation of professional practice will serve as an adequate substitute for the personal and professional values and standards that lawyers should internalise from the earliest stages of their education and training.[6]

As a consequence, ACLEC calls for a greater emphasis throughout legal education not just on the standards and codes of professional conduct, but on developing commitment to fundamental legal values of 'justice, fairness and high ethical standards'.[7] Potentially, this would seem to signal a number of emphases, particularly at the undergraduate or 'initial' stage of English and Welsh legal education.

First, it indicates some acceptance of a broad definition of legal ethics which is capable of incorporating both a macro and micro perspective.[8] At

4 For evidence that this is an international phenomenon, see D. Pearce, *Australian Law Schools: A Discipline Assessment for the Commonwealth Tertiary Education Commission* (1987); B. Cotter, *Professional Responsibility Instruction in Canada* (1992); American Bar Association (MacCrate report), *Legal Education and Professional Development – An Educational Continuum* (1992).

5 ACLEC, *First Report on Legal Education and Training* (1996) and *Continuing Professional Development for Solicitors and Barristers: A Second Report on Legal Education and Training* (1997).

6 id. (1996), para. 1.19.

7 id., para. 2.4; in addition, ACLEC calls for compulsory continuing education in professional ethics for the first three years of practice – (1997) para. 2.33.

8 D.R.F. O'Dair, 'Ethics by the Pervasive Method – the Case of Contract' (1997) 17 *Legal Studies* 305.

the macro level, I suggest, we are concerned with the 'system ethics': an ethics that functions at the institutional interface of law and society and explains the values underpinning legal processes and structures. It therefore incorporates but goes beyond the institutional dimension of professional ethics to the ideals that, in ACLEC's approach, seem to correspond to Fuller's 'inner morality of law' – the principles of justice and due process implicit in the concept of law itself.[9] By contrast a micro legal ethics focuses more conventionally on professional legal ethics in terms of the roles and responsibilities of individual lawyers.

Secondly, it endorses *in part* the liberal ideal of university education. By this I mean the view that the initial stage is first and foremost about intellectual, as opposed to strictly vocational, development; what the Arthurs report calls 'the cultivated ability to stand at a distance from conventional wisdom'.[10] For ACLEC, the 'humane' study of law implies an emphasis on 'contextual' approaches to law and a commitment to the direct teaching of legal values as part of the processes of developing intellectual integrity and the skills of problem solving.[11]

Thirdly, however, ACLEC's first report also suggests a rejection of the *classical* liberal approach which treats professional training and formation as only an indirect and, perhaps, unintended outcome of the educational process. ACLEC, like the American MacCrate report, stresses the need to treat legal education as a continuum rather than a set of more or less discrete stages. This in particular begs the question, what is the scope and purpose of ethics teaching at the initial stage? Is the ethical dimension of the law degree to be viewed primarily as enabling legal professional formation, or does it have a wider function? In essence are we teaching ethics for lawyers or, in more conventional liberal fashion, ethics for citizens? To some degree, these are manifestly not the same thing, but the differences are not necessarily easy to define. That I have a detailed understanding of the rules regulating conflicts of interest in non-contentious business may make me a better conveyancer; whether it makes me a 'better person' is far more doubtful. Equally, can we say that a wider appreciation of ethics might make me both a better citizen and a better lawyer (if that is what I choose to be)? ACLEC does not provide an answer. In this paper, however, I will show how ethics might be positioned in the curriculum in a way that acknowledges and exploits creatively the possible tensions between ethics for lawyers and ethics for citizens.

9 L.L. Fuller *The Morality of Law* (1969).

10 Consultative Group on Research and Education in Law, *Law and Learning: Report to the Social Sciences and Humanities Research Council of Canada* (1983) at 49.

11 At least, this is how I interpret the overall intent of ACLEC's first report (op. cit. (1996), n. 5), see paras. 1.15, 1.19, 2.2, 2.4 and 2.16 for support.

THE NATURE OF THE ETHICAL CHALLENGE

The underlying problem is that 'Law' as a discipline has built up a relatively substantial and formally coherent internal epistemology, in which, beyond the realms of normative jurisprudence, ethical knowledge has played little part.[12] As Toddington argues, almost at best, there is a strong tendency within the legal academy to 'sprinkle moral and political comment over the top of ["legal" facts] like so much icing sugar'.[13] In this context, I see five key challenges to the development of an 'ethical curriculum'.

1. *Challenge 1: law as rules*

Enough has already been said over the years about the limitations of doctrinalism, so I will pass over this terrain as quickly as I decently can.

Basic black-letter scholarship is clearly not without some value. It serves to transfer a degree of substantive knowledge and technique, it should also enhance the translation of law-as-rules into law-as-system. But this is still rather like suggesting a degree in 'tennis studies' should constitute three years of close, systematized analysis of the rules of the Lawn Tennis Association and its institutions. It neither fully equips one to play nor to locate the rules and institutions meaningfully in the social world. This formalistic approach has two further consequences.

First, it encourages a pedagogy in which students are merely 'theoretical spectators'; the teaching is often didactic and the ideas 'challenging' in only the most abstract, intellectual sense of that term.[14] We seldom stop to address how students are to find meaning in that knowledge, make it their own, and use it transformatively for their purposes, not ours.

Secondly, emphasis on the rules generates 'legalism', an ethical attitude which encourages individuals to treat moral conduct as rule-following and to use rules manipulatively through forms of creative compliance.[15] I suggest one of the aims for undergraduate legal education should be to place this kind of unthinking legalism constantly under the spotlight. This has been one of the self-appointed tasks of the Critical Legal Studies movement,

12 The jurisprudence presented by English universities before the mid-1950s offered little serious challenge to this perspective, because it too was of a particularly narrow and formalistic kind, see Raymond Asquith's comment: '[it is] the most irritating quasi-science that ever was begotten by bad philosophers upon an intractable material.'- letter to H.T. Baker, 17 November 1901 in *Raymond Asquith: Life and Letters*, ed. J. Jolliffe (1980) at 85. For a recent, more balanced, analysis, see W. Twining, 'General and Particular Jurisprudence -Three Chapters in a Story' in *Positivism Today*, ed. S. Guest (1996) at 130.

13 S. Toddington, 'The Emperor's New Skills: The Academy, The Profession and the Idea of Legal Education' in *What Are Law Schools For?*, ed. P. Birks (1996) 69, at 74.

14 J. Dewey, 'Experience and Thinking' in *The Philosophy of John Dewey*, ed. J. McDermott (1973) at 496.

15 J. Shklar, *Legalism* (1964); compare also Luban's analysis of 'rule/application theory' in D. Luban, 'Epistemology and Moral Education' (1983) 33 *J. of Legal Education* 636, at 638.

though in so doing it has often failed to move beyond the deconstructive turn. By contrast, as Jack Balkin persuasively argues, for reconstruction to take place there must be a dialectic between social science, philosophy, and legal doctrine in which values can be acknowledged as moments within that dialectic, and understood as immanent within a culture and within the life experiences of individuals.[16]

2. *Challenge 2: skills*

The shift towards more skills-based legal education has enabled the law schools to make a critical contribution to thinking about the legal process. However, much of that potential has yet to be fulfilled. The more technocratic (often vocational, competency-based) skills training may enable students to 'do', but it does not necessarily encourage them to question the uses to which those skills are put.[17] This constitutes a major failure to acknowledge that thinking ethically about actions and their consequences is itself an essential part of skilled problem-solving. Conversely, undergraduate skills teaching has tended to focus chiefly on its contribution to student learning rather than its potential for transforming notions of legal practice. As Julie Macfarlane has recently argued, this is an abnegation of the academic responsibility to help shape, progressively, the legal profession of tomorrow.[18] No one is better placed than the academics to make the necessary early links between reflective learning and reflective practice.

3. *Challenge 3: roles and relationships*

The adoption of a rule-centred paradigm in legal education also sends out powerful signals about the nature and relative unimportance of individual roles and relationships in legal problem-solving. The criticisms are well known: the education process commonly replicates the competitiveness and individualism associated with the adversarial paradigm; classroom legal problems treat facts, and often preferred outcomes, as given and non-negotiable, in particular there will often be an artificial closure of the problem domain so that the 'non-legal' or 'human' considerations are excluded; 'clients' are two-dimensional and frequently made absurd in name and/or in behaviour; opponents are non-existent; third party or wider 'social' interests are likely to be ignored, unless they raise some particular technical issue. As a consequence students learn early on that the instinctive *moral* reaction of the first year student – '. . . but that's not right' is simply not

16 J. Balkin, 'Taking Ideology Seriously' (1987) 55 *University of Missouri Law Rev.* 392.

17 D. Barnhizer, 'Of Rat Time and Terminators' (1995) 45 *J. of Legal Education* 51. C. Maughan et al, 'Sharpening the Mind or Narrowing It? The Limitations of Outcome and Performance Measures in Legal Education' (1995) 29 *Law Teacher* 255, at 265-7.

18 J. Macfarlane, 'The Legal Skills Movement Ten Years On: Triumph or Compromise? (1997) 29 *J. of Law and Society* 440, at 443.

valued by the system.[19] They become detached from the wider non-technical issues and often increasingly passive or plain cynical in the face of attempts to get them to respond to a situation. This is a fundamental failure in any system that proclaims itself to be 'liberal' and humane. It disregards the extent to which:

> the human phenomena of importance to us are initially *relational* phenomena; thus we aren't seeking to explain what they really 'are' in themselves, but to grasp their 'point', how they work to relate us to each other and to our surroundings . . .[20]

The challenge is to encourage our students to appreciate the situatedness of their understanding, and the importance of locating decision-making in the fundamentally dialogical reality of human relations. This leads also into my next point, concerning the relationship between thought and action.

4. *Challenge 4: from seeing the right to doing right*

If an education is to be liberal, it needs to be liberating. It needs to create in us the ability and confidence to make judgement calls and to act upon them in the social world. In terms of ethics education, there is the need to balance a knowing of what is right and the capacity for motivating right conduct. In teaching legal ethics it is easy to get locked into either a defensive professional ethics that is philosophically banal, or a 'pure' philosophy that is remote from professional practice. The first, by engendering a crude appreciation of rules and sanctions, may ensure some degree of technical compliance, but little deeper appreciation of the issues and values involved, or of the extent to which ethical action is inevitably underdetermined by the rules.[21] The second may develop some deeper philosophical understanding, but not necessarily any clear connection to 'real world' issues. At the risk of an over-generalization, this distinction about sums up the present gap between the teaching of professional conduct at the vocational stage and much academic jurisprudence. Neither by itself seriously addresses the problem of moral agency, namely, what do I do when faced with a moral dilemma?

If we are to prepare our students for this task, we must appreciate that it begs an explicit educational focus on the skills involved in developing moral judgement competence. It is not enough to treat 'ethics' as a knowledge attribute (as we tend, narrowly, to understand that term).

19 See, for example, C. Stanley, 'Training for the Hierarchy? Reflections on the British Experience of Higher Education' (1988) 22 *Law Teacher* 78; K. Economides, 'Cynical Legal Studies' in *Educating for Justice: Social Values and Legal Education*, eds. J. Cooper and L. Trubek (1997); W.L. Felstiner, 'Professional Inattention: Origins and Consequences' in *The Human Face of Law: Essays in Honour of Donald Harris*, ed. K. Hawkins (1997).

20 J. Shotter, 'Dialogical Realities: The Ordinary, the Everyday, and Other Strange New Worlds' (1997) 27 *J. for Theory of Social Behaviour* 345, at 348.

21 J. McDowell, 'Virtue and Reason' (1979) 62 *The Monist* 331; compare O. O'Neill, *Towards Justice and Virtue: A Constructive Account of Practical Reasoning* (1996) at 77-89.

Following Rest and Narvaez, ethical decision-making can be said to depend on four elements: (i) a perceptive ability to recognize ethical problems and their consequences for ourselves and others, which requires both cognitive and affective[22] (especially empathic) capacities; (ii) a judgemental capacity to select and justify morally appropriate courses of action; (iii) the motivation to prioritize ethical concerns over other factors (for example, personal advantage or organizational constraint); and (iv) the character to 'see things through', that is, to convert ethical thought into ethical action. If ethics education is to have a chance of influencing real-world choices, it needs to address each of these elements.[23]

5. *Challenge 5: the problem of institutions*

In introducing this particular challenge I want to turn to what may seem a rather extreme example: Hannah Arendt's famous discussion of the 'banality of evil'.[24] Arendt reaches the conclusion that the extreme evils committed routinely by minor functionaries such as the Nazi Adolf Eichmann are not the result of great wickedness and hatred as such, but of a diffuse mixture of unconditional obedience, a lack of spontaneity, and pure thoughtlessness.[25]

The relevance of Eichmann for an everyday legal ethics lies in two things. First is the fact that moral wrongs may be perpetrated through normally acceptable motives – the desire to do one's job, to avoid criticism in one's role, to show loyalty to superiors – and, secondly, that moral judgement seems to fail us dramatically when we need it most.

Legal education and practice become problematic in this light because they contain within their structures a number of 'authoritarian' and other tendencies which potentially reduce our capacity for moral judgement. First there is the sense in which law begs an habitual deference to certain formally legitimate kinds of authority in a way that perhaps restricts our capacity to question its moral legitimacy.[26] Second, there is the extent, as I have said, to which it conventionally objectifies legal problems so as to exclude the emotive and interpersonal dimensions of decision-making from consideration.

22 This point is still insufficiently acknowledged by much 'conventional' psychological theory on moral development , but compare *Moral Development and the Social Environment*, ed. G. Lind et al. (1985) and, from a more purely philosophical perspective, A.J. Vetlesen, *Perception, Empathy and Judgement: An Inquiry into the Preconditions of Moral Performance* (1994).

23 J.R. Rest and D.F. Narvaez, *Moral Development in the Professions: Psychology and Applied Ethics* (1994) at 23-4.

24 See, particularly, H. Arendt, *The Origins of Totalitarianism* (1951) at 456-9.

25 Albeit operating within a social structure in which 'evil . . . [has] lost the quality by which most people recognise it' – H. Arendt, *Eichmann in Jerusalem* (1963) at 150.

26 Compare Wittgenstein's observation that obeying rules is not a matter of choice but an exercise in blind obedience: L. Wittgenstein, *Philosophical Investigations*, trans. G. Anscombe (1973) at 219.

Third, there is the feeling, at least in some quarters, that the process of legal education and training can actually be antithetical to the development of a creative or critical autonomy.[27] Lastly, there is its failure to encourage students to consider, either at the level of macro ethics or of moral agency, the cultural and institutional settings in which moral dilemmas arise, and to prepare them for dealing with those settings.[28] By no means all dilemmas are 'natural' in the sense of deriving 'from enduring features of human nature' and much ethical decision-making is to a large degree contingent on the institutional setting.[29] Organizations themselves are often insulated against acts of individual conscience, either by a bureaucratized 'floating responsibility', whereby ethical problems are disguised and dissipated by the division of labour, or by distorted notions of professional ethics which enforce collective loyalty and responsibility to the institution.[30] In these contexts amoralism all too easily dominates the normal modes of thinking and doing.

6. *Conclusion: re-negotiating 'liberal' legal education*

The ethical challenge I have presented is thus to transform a system of legal education that too often conceives of the law in technical-rational, individualistic terms, that underplays the ethical significance of legal institutions, that separates personal moral development from intellectual and professional formation.

If we are even to begin to prepare students for this challenge, we need to do more than just ensure that they have argued about law and morality in jurisprudence classes, and are familiar with the conduct rules and able to apply them. It demands that we seek to develop the morally engaged individual, prepared to question whether she has done enough under and, perhaps, beyond the law.[31] In so doing, I suggest it is likely to be extremely difficult, as a matter of educational practice, to separate the micro ethics from both macro ethics and from consideration of personal values and particularistic moral behaviour. This calls for some significant reshaping of the undergraduate curriculum.

27 Compare J.R. Elkins, '*Rites de Passage:* Law Students "Telling Their Lives"' (1985) 35 *J. of Legal Education* 27, at 43-4. Also, to quote one of my own student research subjects: 'you lose some of your personality doing a law degree . . . it disciplines you'. For a brief discussion of this project, see J. Webb, 'Where the Action Is: Developing Artistry in Legal Education' (1995) 2 *International J. of the Legal Profession* 187, at 188.

28 Part of the same research (so far unpublished) suggests students may be overly willing to adopt an accommodationist stance to institutional dilemmas.

29 B. Jennings, 'The Regulation of Virtue: Cross-Currents in Professional Ethics' (1991) 10 *J. of Business Ethics* 561, at 563.

30 Z. Bauman, *Alone Again: Ethics After Certainty* (1994) at 8-9.

31 Compare ACLEC, op. cit. (1996), n. 5, para. 1.21

Underlying the model I wish to present is a single key assumption: that the traditional separation of moral theory from moral practice is self-limiting. Every goal-directed human activity (what John Dewey calls 'acts of great content') has some moral theory behind it; while such theory may be thought of as an abstraction, divorced from 'practice', it may also be conceived of as a *practical* knowledge of the human self, which helps us to analyse the required conditions of right action.[32] To be morally engaged we need deeply to understand who we are and this in turn requires the opportunity to know, to do, and to reflect on what we do.[33]

Our new direction, then, might begin by defining the ethical objectives of legal education through an activist, (neo-)Aristotelian framework of 'virtues'.[34] While each of these objectives might in itself raise complex ethical issues, for the purposes of this discussion I intend to present them only briefly before exploring implications of the model for teaching and learning.

1. *To develop a sense of community*

An Aristotelian approach considers human beings to be inherently social, and treats moral character as a social construct. To this extent it starts by acknowledging that we are members of a community with some common *locus* and culture.[35] The idea of community emphasizes that our individual identities and mutual interests are situated or embedded within the institutions and social groups to which we belong.[36] Both the law school and (as Durkheim noted long ago) the professions clearly constitute moral communities and serve as guardians and transmitters of cultural capital and values; the implications of this – both positive and negative – warrant consideration in the curriculum. At the same time, we cannot forget, either individually or collectively, that we are simultaneously members of wider communities (defined by cultural ties, ethnicity, and so on), so that we need also to be sensitive to the priorities that might be assigned to our obligations to these different communities.

32 J. Dewey, *The Early Works: 1882-1898*, vol. 3, ed. J.A. Boydston (1972) at 94-9.

33 Similarly, D.A. Schon has made the point that sometimes experience provides the only form of meaningful learning, because what the teacher knows how to say, the students cannot *at that stage* understand: see 'Educating the Reflective Legal Practitioner' (1995) 2 *Clinical Law Rev.* 231 at 249.

34 Compare, also, Luban, op. cit., n. 15; G.J. Postema, 'Moral Responsibility in Professional Ethics' (1980) 55 *New York University Law Rev.* 63; R. Tur, 'Accountability and Lawyers' in *Ethics and the Professions*, ed. R.F. Chadwick (1995) 58, at 81-3.

35 This much can be accepted, I suggest, without also denying the heterogeneity of communities.

36 See, for example, M.J. Sandel, *Liberalism and the Limits of Justice* (1982).

2. *To consider the importance of role*

A central characteristic of the Aristotelian good life is that one fulfils one's function or role well. This acknowledges that to take an ethics wholly out of context is to rob it of meaning. Of course, there are problems with the idea of what it means to perform 'well'. Especially in the context of professional ethics, 'role morality' can become an argument for infringing the moral rights of others in ways that would otherwise (that is – but for the professional 'justification') be thought unacceptable. This in turn is sometimes used to suggest that professional ethics can be defined as somehow outside or exempt from the standards of 'ordinary' morality.[37] While this is a position I would personally wish to question, the debate should not create insurmountable problems for us as teachers. The nature of one's role, and the underlying ethical assumptions of role morality can simply be viewed as fertile ground for discussion. Having said that, an Aristotelian approach may be particularly useful in enabling us to juxtapose the notion of role with ideas of what I shall call 'integrity' and 'connection'.

3. *To enhance integrity*

The word 'integrity' conveys a number of meanings that are of value in describing an ethical sensibility. It is commonly used in the lawyering context to convey the personal traits of honesty and trustworthiness that are classically thought to be central to the role.[38] It also conveys, more generally, a commitment to fairness, and an idea of 'wholeness' that we have become perhaps less accustomed to apply to people than things.[39] Yet it is 'wholeness' that I think is critical, particularly as a counterbalance to the morally deadening consequences of too close an adhesion to a narrowly defined role morality. There is no virtue in blind adherence to a role or a rule. By 'wholeness' I am thus trying to convey a sense of being true to oneself, not as a metaphysical being, but as an embodied self in constant interaction with others.

4. *To value 'connection' and responsibility*

It may be argued that certain 'social virtues', commonly expressed in such terms as friendship, care, beneficence, sympathy, and solidarity, are an

37 Compare, for example, A. Gewirth, 'Professional Ethics: The Separatist Thesis' (1986) 96 *Ethics* 282; B. Williams, 'Professional Morality and Its Dispositions' in *The Good Lawyer*, ed. D. Luban (1983) at 259-69 and D. Luban, *Lawyers and Justice: An Ethical Study* (1989) chs. 6 and 7.

38 S. Steir, 'Legal Ethics: The Integrity Thesis' (1991) 52 *Ohio State Law J.* 551.

39 This might be interpreted to warrant a greater emphasis on substantive/distributive justice as opposed to the present primary focus of the curriculum on matters of formal/corrective justice.

ethical requirement of the good life, because the institutions and rights-talk of justice are not enough to protect from harm those to whom we are socially connected.[40] Acknowledging the place of the social virtues can help us explore the nature and limits of social and professional responsibility. Special relationships (like the lawyer-client relationship specifically, but also relationships such as employer-employee, or those who, in tort, are connected by a duty of care) give rise to special rights granted by legal institutions.[41] But these measures of connection may in many circumstances legitimize indifference to others: for example, the innocent third party who may suffer loss because of my, or my client's, actions. The social virtues generally demand a receptiveness and attentiveness to the needs of others,[42] they expect a commitment to maintaining social relationships, to social participation, and to what O'Neill calls 'acts of solidarity' in support of strangers.[43] Indeed, a social virtues perspective may thus go further and become a useful tool for analysing the limits of law itself, for example, by looking at the way concepts like 'citizenship' or 'discrimination' may be legally constructed to push 'outsiders' to the margins of or beyond the bounds of 'community'.

5. *To develop the capacity for judgement*

An Aristotelian ethics places at its heart the capacity for judgement or phronesis. Judgement in this sense is both a form of understanding and a practical skill.

Judgement as a form of understanding: the ability to make sound moral judgement depends on the acquisition of virtue, that is, the predisposition to behave according to standards that are intersubjectively recognized and accepted. Judgement is not predicated on a simple application of accepted rules and principles, however. Rather, it involves the exercise of 'perception' – the ability to discern acutely and respond, with discrimination, to the features of a given situation.[44] The idea of judgement thus brings together many of the themes we have already explored. It is a particularistic form of understanding, developed through experience, and grounded in our ability to deal not just rationally but relationally with others.[45] *Contra* Arendt,

40 See O'Neill, op. cit., n. 21, at 189-94 for a development of this argument.

41 Compare C. Fried 'The Lawyer as Friend: The Moral Foundations of the Lawyer-Client Relation' (1976) 85 *Yale Law J.* 1060.

42 See, especially, the work on an ethic of care which has developed out of C. Gilligan's *In A Different Voice* (1982); see, for example, V. Held (ed.), *Justice and Care: Essential Readings in Feminist Ethics* (1995); R. Jack and D.C. Jack, *Moral Vision and Professional Decisions: The Changing Values of Men and Women Lawyers* (1989).

43 O'Neill, op. cit., n. 21, at 197.

44 M.C. Nussbaum, *Love's Knowledge: Essays on Philosophy and Literature* (1990) at 37.

45 Aristotle, *Nichomachean Ethics*, trans. T. Irwin (1985), at 1142a25. This particularist interpretation has increasingly been emphasized in recent historicist (as in the work of Alasdair MacIntyre) and more radical, Wittgensteinian, readings of Aristotle – for example, McDowell, op. cit., n. 21. On experience, see 1143b6-10.

ethical failures may not just be 'thoughtless', but failures in the capacity to feel for or empathize with the other.[46] In this light, most deliberations about 'justice' or 'the merits' cannot be reduced to some mechanistic process of formal analysis that will guarantee a 'right' answer. Disputes about justice are inevitably judgement calls, drawing on a complex interplay of cognition and affect.

Judgement as a practical skill: by recognizing the centrality of judgement to ethics, we are acknowledging that ethics is ultimately about making real as opposed to abstract decisions. The exercise of *phronesis* is grounded in an activist epistemology. It assumes that we can know the right and be motivated to do right.[47] It also turns particularly on our capacity to respond to a new situation 'imaginatively', that is, in a way that recognizes the mutability and uncertainty of situated problem-solving.[48] In this way it corresponds closely to Donald Schon's concept of 'artistry', in which propositional knowledge is bounded by and utilized through our capacities to improvise solutions and reconstruct ('re-frame') problems through processes of reflection.[49]

The function of education in this model is thence to enhance the capacity for judgement by developing both an understanding of and motivation towards the good, and the capacity to translate that motivation into action. The question is, how?

FROM PRUDENCE TO PRAXIS

Despite the somewhat abstract and idealistic slant of the argument so far, I suggest that many of these ideals can be made concrete and introduced into the curriculum at the initial stage through a combination of techniques that are already in use within the legal academy. In stepping from theory to practice we need to consider both the 'knowledge' that is to be created and how the learning environment might operate to enhance ethical understanding.

1. *Knowledge*

If the ethical challenge is to be taken seriously, legal ethics cannot be treated as an optional extra, but that still begs the question of what ethics and where? There are signs that ACLEC's thinking prioritizes professional ethics, even at the initial stage.[50] It is important that we do not respond too

46 id., 1109a23; see also Vetlesen, op. cit., n. 26, at pp. 81-2, 99-107; M.C. Nussbaum, *The Fragility of Goodness* (1986) 361-2.

47 See Luban, op. cit., n. 15, at p. 647.

48 See Nussbaum, op. cit., n. 47, at pp. 71-2.

49 See D.A. Schon, *The Reflective Practitioner* (1983), and *Educating the Reflective Practitioner* (1987).

50 The ethical challenge is thus first and foremost presented by 'the complex ethical issues that lawyers . . . face in modern practice' – ACLEC, op. cit. (1996), n. 5, para. 1.19.

formalistically. It does not necessarily imply a narrow focus which treats professional legal ethics as just another substantive, black-letter, domain. As Richard O'Dair argues, professional ethics is not just about training in professional standards; because the development of legal institutions reflects, among other things, the ethics of the legal profession, knowledge of the micro ethics will enhance understanding of legal institutions.[51] However, I also suggest that there is a need to assimilate more of the 'system ethics', because the structure and institutions of the legal system are also an important influence on ethical conduct.[52] The essential point is that there is a reflexivity within the legal system which generates a symbiosis between the macro and micro ethical domains.

How should we build this understanding into our teaching? The American experience suggests that free-standing courses on professional ethics are (even where they adopt a more reflexive understanding) relatively ineffective at inculcating legal values and easily marginalized within the curriculum.[53] As Deborah Rhode suggests, the answer most likely lies in a pervasive approach which seeks to link issues of professional conduct, macro ethics, and personal values across the curriculum.[54] This model suggests a number of changes to the contents of conventional courses.

First, and this is hardly a radical suggestion, macro ethical contexts might be introduced into substantive modules, to address, for example, the assumptions of personal responsibility underlying an area of law, the ethical basis of compensation or other legal rights, or perhaps to focus on problems associated with the adversarial process, or the delivery of legal services.[55]

Secondly, and at the same time, some element of professional legal ethics can also be relatively easily assimilated into the substantive courses, often by way of discussion or role-play. Activities such as negotiating a contract, or pursuing settlement of a personal injury action, or plea-bargaining a crime can all generate learning at the levels of substantive law, professional ethics, and personal responsibility/social virtue.[56]

Thirdly, if this approach is not to be too particularistic or fragmented, there needs to be at least one 'foundation' course ('English Legal System' perhaps?) which is capable of setting out in general terms some major ethical assumptions underlying the due process model and the provision of legal

51 O'Dair, op. cit., n. 8, p. 310.

52 A. Ashworth, 'Ethics and Criminal Justice' in *Legal Ethics and Professional Responsibility*, ed. R. Cranston (1995) at 145.

53 D.J. Rhode, 'Ethics by the Pervasive Method' (1992) 42 *J. of Legal Education* 31; 'Into the Valley of Ethics: Professional Responsibility and Educational Reform (1995) 58 *Law and Contemporary Problems* 139.

54 id.

55 See, for example, A. Ashworth, *The Criminal Process: An Evaluative Study* (1994); P. Cane, *The Anatomy of Tort Law* (1997); R.E. Goodin, 'Theories of Compensation' (1989) 9 *Ox. J. of Legal Studies* 56, and, as a teaching model, O'Dair, op. cit., n. 8.

56 O'Dair, id., pp. 316-7.

services, and possibly also introducing the core principles of professional legal ethics.[57] This may help overcome problems which will inevitably arise in trying to co-ordinate a pervasive curriculum in a culture in which teachers are used to having considerably curricular autonomy. Fourthly, there may be a strong case, as I have argued elsewhere, for expanding the use of clinical teaching as a vehicle for ethics education in which students must confront and reflect on the pragmatics of legal practice.[58]

Lastly, I suggest that we need to reconsider the role of the 'legal humanities' – legal history, legal philosophy, and, in more (post)modern vein, perhaps law and literature also. In the hands of law teachers these have often been both subverted to and diminished by the Anglo-American positivist tradition, leading to marginalization in the average curriculum. Yet they ought to be central to the 'liberal' vision of humane professionalism, by virtue of their capacity to provide an understanding of legal culture and of the concepts and language of ethical criticism.

2. *Understanding and participation*

The development of understanding needs to be recognized as a more complex and relational process than the law curriculum has conventionally allowed. I suggest that an emphasis on judgement as the primary form of understanding privileges what one might call a constructionist epistemology.[59] This recognizes four things: (i) that understanding is distinct from bare knowledge acquisition – I can 'know' without understanding; (ii) that understanding is constructed out of shared social action and discourse – that is, theoretical knowledge ultimately becomes meaningful through use; (iii) that understanding is not purely a cognitive activity but draws heavily on affective ('feelings') and situational factors and (iv) that understanding is in turn creative – it may transform not just what we know but our ability to define a position for ourselves in the social world. In making ethical judgements we intelligently reinterpret our culture in the light of changing circumstances.[60]

Judgement is largely acquired through the transformation of theory by processes of what we now tend to think of as active and experiential learning. There are a number of such techniques which might prove useful.

57 Compare J. Webb, 'Inventing the Good: A Prospectus for Clinical Education and the Teaching of Legal Ethics in England and Wales' (1996) 30 *Law Teacher* 270, at 293.

58 id. Insofar as students may be encouraged in such contexts to reflect on the efficacy of codified ethics, this may have some 'transferability', given the recent growth of ethical regulation in professional and quasi-professional occupations generally.

59 See, for example, J. Shotter, *Cultural Politics of Everyday Life: Social Constructionism, Rhetoric and Knowing of the Third Kind* (1993); H. Haste, 'Communitarianism and the Social Construction of Morality' (1996) 25 *J. of Moral Education* 47.

60 See the discussion in S. Fesmire, 'The Social Basis of Character' in *Ethics in Practice: An Anthology*, ed. H. LaFollette (1997) 282, at 285; also J. McDowell, 'Are Moral Requirements Hypothetical Imperatives?' (1978) LII *Proceedings of the Aristotelian Society* 18, at 21.

First, conventional seminars can be used to enable group work involving 'Socratic' discussion of ethical issues. These can expose students to a plurality of views and lead them to a deeper, more hermeneutic, understanding of concepts and roles.[61]

Secondly, we could make more sustained use of 'non-legal' literature and narrative devices. Encouraging students to engage with the metaphors, parables and exemplars provided by varied forms of literature offers the 'imaginative provocation . . . [of] a poetic interpretation' that may particularly be exploited in, say, ethics classes or jurisprudence.[62] Social and professional identities may also be explored in a range of both clinical and non-clinical settings through legal ethnography and the personal narratives of lawyers, clients, and students.[63] Creative writing exercises and personal journals ('learning diaries') could be used in many contexts, not just as a vehicle to aid reflection, but to help expose the dialogical relation which underpins the intersubjective dimension of the ethics I have described.[64]

Thirdly, deep engagement with problems through role-taking must be seen as a central activity. Experience of moral decision-making plays an essential part in making moral development self-sustaining through exposure to moral-cognitive conflict.[65]

Lastly, at the same time, the tutor's role cannot be ignored. For moral development to take place students need to receive guided reflection as well as opportunities for taking responsibility.[66] This demands that, in key courses at least, tutors roles are perhaps closer to a mentoring rather than traditional teaching function. They may challenge students' understanding and interpretation of problems; they may help students re-frame and work creatively through problems, and concentrate on providing appropriate role-models, not just solutions.

61 Aristotle, *Politics* (1992), III, xi; see also M.C. Nussbaum, 'The Uses and Abuses of Philosophy in Legal Education' (1993) 45 *Stanford Law Rev.* 1627, at 1640.

62 R. Needham, *Exemplars* (1985) at 2; also Nussbaum's claim, op. cit., n. 44, at p. 27 that 'moral philosophy requires attentive and loving novel reading': compare I. Ward, 'From Literature to Ethics: The Strategies and Ambitions of Law and Literature' (1994) 14 *Ox. J. of Legal Studies* 389, at 398. See also, for example, Webb, op. cit., n. 57, and K. Green et al., 'The Indeterminate Province: Storytelling in Legal Theory and Legal Education' (1994) 28 *Law Teacher* 128.

63 See, for example, A. Boon, 'Skills in the Initial Stage of Legal Education: Theory and Practice for Transformation' in *Teaching Lawyers' Skills*, ed. J. Webb and C. Maughan (1996) at 114-24; P. Maharg, '(Re-)Telling Stories: Narrative Theory and the Practice of Client Counselling' (1996) 30 *Law Teacher* 295

64 Boon, id; Webb, op. cit., n. 27, at pp. 201 ff.

65 L. Kohlberg and A. Higgins, 'Continuities and Discontinuities in Childhood and Adult Development Revisited – Again' in *Essays in Moral Development, Vol. II: The Psychology of Moral Development*, ed. L. Kohlberg (1984); G. Lind, 'Educational Environments Which Promote Self-Sustaining Moral Development'; revised version of a paper to the meeting of Division E, American Educational Research Association, April 1996; available at http://www.uni-konstanz.de/ag-moral/.

66 Lind, id.

3. *Power*

We cannot leave the issue of what we teach without exploring the question of how we teach. The problem of teacher power weighs heavily over the law school.[67] Its symptoms may include an apparent unwillingness to negotiate large elements of the teaching and learning process; a lack of reflexivity about the curriculum and its delivery; disinterest in the students' subjective experiences of learning; a lack of transparency of the criteria governing, say, learning outcomes and assessment processes, as well as the small daily acts of intellectual and personal arrogance, of unthinking discrimination and discourtesy which can sometimes mark out the respective statuses of student and teacher.

It is not enough for law schools to proclaim that they teach ethics, they must also try to behave as ethical institutions. I suggest this requires a number of things. First it demands some shared commitment to teaching law in an 'ethical voice'. Without this ethics, and perhaps ethics teachers, will become marginalized in the curriculum.[68] Second, core values (such as 'integrity', 'independence' and 'respect') need to be reflected in institutional structures and practices; oppressive social practices will foster cynicism, conformity, and passivity.[69] Thirdly, participation in the learning process needs to be constructed to enable teachers and learners to proceed as 'moral friends'.[70] There need to be explicit and commonly understood goals and some shared vision of the human good arising out of intellectual and practical activities.

CONCLUSION

I am deeply conscious that a piece such as this must leave much unsaid and undone, not least because it is difficult to write meaningfully about teaching at a time when much of the debate about what we, in Britain, mean by legal ethics has still to take place. I am also conscious of the practical hurdles to developing such a curriculum. It undoubtedly begs questions of teacher competence, resource availability (particularly if a greater degree of small-group teaching is required), and curriculum co-ordination, though I also suspect the scale of such problems is easily overestimated.

Nevertheless, I hope I have been able to share some sense that legal education can be positioned to provide an ethical education for the citizens of the new millennium. This is not simply a matter of saying, in true

67 J. Macfarlane, 'Teacher Power in the Law School Classroom' (1996) 19 *Dalhousie Law J.* 71; Stanley, op. cit., n. 19.

68 Rhode, op. cit., n. 53.

69 Haste, op. cit., n. 59, at p. 53.

70 M.C. Nussbaum, 'Non-relative Virtues: An Aristotelian Approach' in *The Quality of Life*, ed. A.K. Sen and M.C. Nussbaum (1993) at 243.

Aristotelian fashion, that the virtuous lawyer is, by definition, a good citizen. It is, rather, an acknowledgement that the capacity for ethical thought and action is both a socially desirable attribute and a transferable skill. Moral judgement and the capacity for reflection underpin both social and professional decision-making; both are likely to be enhanced by a deeper philosophical and experiential understanding of the situated self.

At the same time, such a conception presents 'ethics for lawyers' with some radical challenges, and this is exactly how it should be. A much more informed debate needs to take place about the institutional values of the profession, the nature and role of codified professional ethics, the need for continuing professional education in ethics, and about the nature of the workplace and the kinds of training and mentoring necessary to sustain ethical development in practice. The professional project should ultimately be strengthened rather than undermined by a creative but critical dialectic between the academy and the profession. Whether we can genuinely create the space for just such a discourse is, perhaps, the first ethical challenge we must face.

JOURNAL OF LAW AND SOCIETY
VOLUME 25, NUMBER 1, MARCH 1998
ISSN: 0263–323X, pp.151–69

History is Past Politics: A Critique of the Legal Skills Movement in England and Wales

ANDREW BOON*

In the past thirty years legal practice changed so significantly that a fundamental response was demanded of legal education. Making legal skills a compulsory component in the vocational stage was an incomplete response. It addressed the technical competence of lawyers but left significant gaps in professional preparation in terms of content and methodology. By focusing on the educational and pedagogic implications of the skills curriculum the clinical movement contributed to these gaps. The Lord Chancellor's Advisory Committee on Legal Education and Conduct has facilitated the consideration of a curriculum organized around a more imaginative integration of legal skills in order to begin to tackle these failings and prepare lawyers for the new economic and social challenges facing them. Solutions, however, must permeate every stage of legal education, requiring unprecedented levels of co-operation and interaction between the profession and the academy.

INTRODUCTION

The past ten years has seen a rapid incorporation of 'legal skills' into the education and training of lawyers in common law jurisdictions, particularly in the vocational stage. The theme of this article is that the structure of training to become a lawyer, usually a law degree followed by a vocational course, a period of apprenticeship, and continuing professional development, is the result of historical accidents and jursidictional compromise between the profession and the academy which allows significant gaps in professional preparation. It is argued that, in order to achieve wider objectives, including developing the values of legal practice, there is a need for continuity and integration in legal education. This calls

* *School of Law, University of Westminster, 4 Red Lion Square, London WC1R 4SR, England*

I thank Robert Abbey and John Flood for their helpful comments and suggestions and Avis Whyte for research assistance.

for unprecedented co-operation between the profession and the academy. In order to pursue this proposition it is necessary to consider the historical, political and social pressures which have created, and which will continue to shape, legal education.

EDUCATION AND PROFESSIONALISM: VOCATIONAL LEGAL EDUCATION

Some so-called caring professions, those that see individual client needs as significant, prioritize 'scientific knowledge' ('knowing that') while others have focused on the interaction with the client ('knowing how').[1] In the last ten years both branches of the legal profession have adopted new courses built around skills. The significance of this step was emphasized by two facts. First, it was a brave attempt to reverse a conservative pedagogic tradition. Legal education had distinguished itself by absent or unclear educational aims, adherence to a 'banking concept' of education and, consequently, a heavy reliance on a pedagogy of instruction.[2] Second, the 'know-how' embraced by the vocational stage went far beyond that required to manage the interaction with the client. It also embraced activities, such as advocacy and negotiation, which concerned action on behalf of the client. This is not to suggest that such a heavy emphasis on legal skills is novel. Viewed historically, a strong practical and craft element in professional preparation was a key to the success of the profession. Since this success was originally founded on apprenticeship it is appropriate to begin this account at the end of legal education, the vocational stage, rather than the start, currently the undergraduate stage.

The problematic role of skills in professional preparation needs to be confronted in order to locate the history of skills and to explain continuing impediments to the development of legal education. The starting point is to recognize the importance of the functional and symbolic role that education played in the English legal profession's claim for respectability and status.[3] At the earliest opportunity both branches of the profession established apprenticeship as the main route into the profession. It is significant to the argument developed in this essay that articles of clerkship were a moral

1 R.A. Barnett et al., 'Models of Professional Preparation: Pharmacy, Nursing and Teacher Education' (1987) 12 *Studies in Higher Education* 51.

2 See, further, M.F. Fitzgerald, 'Stirring the Pot of Legal Education' (1993) 27 *Law Teacher* 4 and P. Freire, *Pedagogy of the Oppressed* (1972) 39.

3 See, further, M. Burrage, 'From a Gentleman's to a Public Profession: Status and Politics in the History of English Solicitors' (1996) 3 *International J. of the Legal Profession* 45; D. Sugarman, 'Bourgeois Collectivism, Professional Power and the Boundaries of the State: The Private and Public Life of the Law Society, 1825 to 1914' (1996) 3 *International J. of the Legal Profession* 81 and W. Prest, 'Lawyers in the Professions in Early Modern England' in *The Professions in Early Modern England*, ed. W. Prest (1987) ch. 3.

rather than a cognitive training.[4] The decline of professionalism in law was brought about by prospective entrants forsaking the five-year articled clerkship in favour of the law degree.[5] The personal relationships of solicitors had been the cement of the profession, and the means by which it continuously reproduced itself as a club of white, middle-class males.[6] More importantly, articles of clerkship guaranteed the commitment and values of entrants to the profession. They offered 'a period of hardship, drudgery and semi-servitude' which '. . . instilled respect for one's elders, for their experience, for their manners, conventions and ethics and for their sense of corporate honour' and offered 'cast-iron guarantees about the attitudes, demeanour and commitment of those who were to enter the profession.'[7] Wider access to educational opportunities, and a rapidly changing practice environment, precipitated a search for new means of ensuring professional inclusiveness and the reproduction of professional values.

Until 1962, and the creation of the College of Law, both branches of the profession regarded university-style lectures, at best, as supplementary to their own apprenticeships. The Law Society Finals Course (LSF), however, concentrated all the worst aspects of university education in one course. It was a six-month cramming course with the suspected aim of limiting entry to the solicitors' branch. The LSF was remodelled in 1980 and yet remained a 'bastion of old-style legal education'.[8] It is fairly clear that the pressure for these changes, and the advocacy of them, came from outside vocational legal education. The introduction of the Bar Vocational Course (BVC) in 1989 was significant because the curriculum was based around a core of 60 per cent skills. The Law Society followed suit in 1993 with the launching of the Legal Practice Course (LPC). This was a shift, essentially, from a pedagogy of instruction to one of performance. The solicitors' branch also took the opportunity to widen the number of providers of vocational training thus including many universities which had not previously provided the LSF. The Bar increased the number of providers in 1996 so that, currently, twelve new university and five old university law schools offer the LPC and six institutions or consortia, in addition to the Inns of Court School of Law, now offer the BVC.[9]

The Inns of Court School of Law established the BVC's revolutionary curriculum with some apprehension but little difficulty. The LPC had a more public and hostile reception. Divisions were apparent from the start, relating to the increased numbers of those delivering the course and the course

4 Burrage, id., p. 53.
5 id., p. 68.
6 id., p. 71.
7 id., p. 54.
8 A. Sherr, 'Professional Legal Training' (1992) 19 *J. of Law and Society* 163.
9 P. Harris and M. Jones, 'A Survey of Law Schools in the United Kingdom, 1996' (1997) 31 *Law Teacher* 38, at 71.

content, particularly in relation to skills. The eventual shape of the LPC owed much to the Law Society's permanent officers who had been dissatisfied with the initial proposals of the Law Society's Training Committee. These were said to have taken insufficient account of, among other things, 'the extent to which the final course is dominated by the requirements of the written examination at the expense of training in practical skills' and the fact that the Lord Chancellor's Green and White Papers opened the way for increased rights of audience and the development of opportunities for advocacy. Strong arguments were made against repeating the mistakes of the LSF with its reputation for over-teaching and the dominance of the examination. The touchstone of the new course, it was said, must be the 'competencies that are needed to be an effective member of the profession'. It was argued that the:

> relationship between skills and knowledge is central to the validity of the examination . . . [and] that the primary purpose of the vocational stage of training should not be to add to the body of factual knowledge but to develop the analytical skills and to add to them the practical skills that will be needed in practice.[10]

Proposals considered by the training committee of the Law Society in May 1990 identified two principal forces for change:

> . . . the continuing needs to improve the quality of entrants to the profession and to increase the system's ability to respond flexibly to changes in demand for solicitors' services.'[11]

The report recommended a substantial increase in the 10 per cent skills teaching provided on the LSF with the intention that this would be further increased as institutions 'develop their expertise in this field.'[12] The training committee was particularly aware of the need to assess because:

> . . . there cannot be a greater emphasis placed on the development of practical skills without a proper and workable means of assessing whether the teaching of those skills has been successful.[13]

In the event, and unlike the BVC which had opted for grades for skills work, with competence as the basic pass grade, the Law Society concluded that assessment should be on a pass/fail basis. It reasoned that, like most other skill assessments (for example, the driving test), grading was inappropriate.[14] At the same time, the Law Society also introduced measures

10 The nature of the proposals by the Law Society's Training Committee in their Review of Legal Education may have been influenced by the fact that the review took place at the time of a recruitment crisis (Law Society Training Committee, *The Recruitment Crisis: A Report by the Training Committee of the Law Society* (1988); J. Randall, *Review of Legal Education – An Alternative Approach* (1989) at 5).

11 Law Society Training Committee, *Training Tomorrow's Solicitors: Proposals for Changes to the Education and Training of Solicitors* (1990) para.1.2.

12 id., para, 5.10.

13 id., para. 1.3.

14 id., para. 7.2.21.

to monitor training contracts, which were to replace articles of clerkship. Firms would be authorized to take trainee solicitors only if they agreed to observe a code of conduct incorporating monitoring and appraisal of trainees. Trainees were also required to undertake the Professional Skills Course (PSC), comprising four weeks building on issues of 'professional conduct, ethics, interviewing skills and accounts rules'.[15] The rationale for the content of PSC was that trainees need not have more than a passing acquaintance with some topics before entering the office or that others could not be sensibly taught until they had an understanding of how legal offices operate.

The declining fortunes of the profession was the catalyst of the move to a vocational education built around skills. Until the 1970s the legal profession assumed that there was nothing to fear from the state. It acted as if there was a tacit agreement which secured its privileges in return for a commitment to act in the public interest. From the end of the decade, however, the notion that lawyers' perception of the public interest was at best misconceived, or at worst partial and self-interested, gained ground. Sociologists came to see professions as a means of concentrating and exercising power, and their ethical commitments as elements of an ideological weaponry which operated to justify privilege.[16] The benefits offered by professions to clients as consumers, and the wider society, were called into question.[17] The profession's record in relation to conveyancing and criminal legal aid were particularly important for they implied that lawyers systematically exploited two of its main constituencies; the middle classes on the one hand and the state on the other.[18]

The undermining of the profession's public image prepared the ground for the political onslaught on the profession's jurisdiction by the Thatcher governments of the 1980s.[19] In the environment of uncertainty created, competition and levels of competence were causes of deep concern.[20] Until that time professional knowledge had always been inextricably linked with professional power. Professions were seen to exercise market control through the construction of a 'professional commodity' spanning the technical and

15 Sherr, op. cit., n. 8, at p. 167.

16 R.M. Rich, 'Sociological Paradigms and the Sociology of Law: An Overview' in *The Sociology of Law: A Conflict Perspective* (1978) at 148-9 and 178; R.L. Abel, *The Legal Profession in England and Wales* (1988) 4; H. Jamois and B. Peloille, 'Changes in the French University-Hospital System' in *Professions and Professionalisation*, ed. J. A. Jackson (1970) 117; P. Bordieu and L. Wacquant, *An Invitation to Reflexive Sociology* (1992) 242.

17 See, generally, T.J. Johnson, *Professions and Power* (1972); E. Friedson, 'The Theory of Professions: State of the Art' in *The Sociology of the Professions*, eds. R. Dingwall and P. Lewis (1983, reprinted 1992); R.L. Abel, 'The Decline of Professionalism?' (1986) 49 *Modern Law Rev.* 1.

18 A.A. Paterson, 'Professionalism and the Legal Services Market' (1996) 3 *International J. of the Legal Profession* 137, at 140-3.

19 Burrage, op. cit., n. 3, at p. 69.

20 Paterson, op. cit., n. 18, at p. 138.

ideological spheres.[21] The commodity was built on the notion of technical skill and inherent uncertainty such that professional education was preparation for the exercise of discretion.[22] With the failure of the five-year articles, the last association with an educational tradition which had helped to secure professional power, was university style education. Universities were also, however, experiencing change. Their use of transmission modes of teaching assumed that learners were an intellectually and socially homogeneous group, an assumption which was manifestly less true as access widened from the late 1960s. The professional bodies colluded with a hidden agenda of traditional legal education, the belief that, by keeping the arts of practice 'secret' until admission, it was possible to maintain the fine balance between technicality and indeterminacy and, thereby, to maintain professional mystique.[23] The rationalization of technical skills not only signalled the failure of this approach, it threatened two fundamental assumptions. First, the idea that professional expertise was found and transmitted only within the body of the profession and, second, the idea that a rigid distinction between academic and professional programmes was inevitable.

Paterson argues that, although the declining fortunes of the domestic legal profession were mirrored in world-wide changes, the profession focused criticism on legal education as a displacement activity.[24] Certainly, the Law Society implemented the vocational stage changes in the face of resistance from practitioners and scepticism from many academics. A number of factors combined to strengthen the Law Society's resolve in the face of this opposition. The rapid pace of change in the workplace had led to an emphasis on adaptability, flexibility, and the capacity for action, a fact which had already impacted on higher education.[25] In common with other traditional institutions in the post-modern liberal state, higher education was increasingly subject to the values of rationality, efficiency, and science.[26] At the heart of the attempt to modernize higher education was recognition that, in order to avoid being sporadic and opportunistic, continuing development had to be self-directed rather than symbolic. Learners were now expected

21 Jamois and Pelloille, op. cit., n. 16. See, also, M.S. Larson, *The Rise of Professionalism: A Sociological Analysis* (1972); C. Harrington, 'Outlining a Theory of Practice' in *Lawyers in a Postmodern World: Translation and Transgression* (1994) eds. M. Cain and C. Harrington; A. Abbott, *The System of Professions: An Essay on the Expert Division of Labour* (1988).

22 Abel, op. cit., n. 16, at p. 8; D. Rueschemeyer, 'Professions Cross-Nationally: From a Profession Centred to a State Centred Approach' (1986) *Am. Bar Foundation Research J.* 415.

23 Abel, id., at p. 8.

24 Paterson, op. cit., n. 18.

25 '. . . the fixed person for the fixed duties, who in older societies was such a godsend, in the future will be a public danger' A.N. Whitehead (1926), quoted in C.O. Houle, *Continuing Learning in the Professions* (1980).

26 A. Abbott, *The System of Professions: An Essay on the Expert Division of Labour* (1988) at 188.

to develop generic skills, to 'learn how to learn' to communicate effectively, and work in teams.[27] The change in climate which made the changes in vocational education possible, therefore, included a changing perception of the functions of higher education. A small but significant lobby in higher education in the United Kingdom, including academic lawyers, were arguing for a more practical curriculum. Other common law jurisdictions had already moved towards vocational legal skills, thus creating a competitive pressure. Changes initiated in law degrees reflected a so-called crisis of confidence in the traditional forms of 'professional knowledge'.[28] They fuelled anxiety regarding mounting criticism of the skills of professionals (including legal professionals) and the desire not to lag behind developments in the training regimes of other common law countries. This created a climate more hospitable to skills. Finally, the skills curriculum was legitimized by the endorsement given to legal and generic skills by the Marre report.[29] In terms of the central actors, however, the adoption of a skills curriculum in the vocational stage was the result of an alliance between a relatively small number of academics and influential modernisers within the profession.

SKILLS AND THE ACADEMY: UNDERGRADUATE LEGAL EDUCATION

The university route into the law occurred almost by accident. In 1756 the Bar granted a two-year exemption from the qualification process for a university degree, in order to attract higher status entrants. The Law Society followed suit in 1821.[30] This meant that graduates needed to serve only two years of articles rather than five, a route to becoming a solicitor which became predominant in the late 1960s. Although the Law Society used public lectures to enhance it standing in the early years after incorporation, the profession had very little confidence in university education as a means of reproducing the profession. Whereas the socratic dialogue and case method had replaced non-interactive lectures in United States law schools, English law schools continued to rely on a didactic tradition of teaching 'black letter' or propositional law.[31] From the 1970s until the present day, higher

27 A. Boon, 'Enterprise in Higher Education: A New Agenda for Institutional Change?' (1990) 24 *Law Teacher* 14. For a discussion of the role of generic and vocational skills, see J. Bell 'General Transferable Skills and the Law Curriculum' (1996) 2(2) *Contemporary Issues in Law* 1.

28 D.A. Schon, *Educating the Reflective Practitioner: Toward a New Design for Teaching and Learning in the Professions* (1987) 17. See, also, D.A. Schon, *The Reflective Practitioner: How Professionals Think in Action* (1983).

29 *A Time for Change: Report of the Committee on the Future of the Legal Profession* (1988) ch. 12 (the Marre report).

30 Burrage, op. cit., n. 3, at p. 52.

31 W. Twining, *Blackstone's Tower: The English Law School* (1994).

education has been under pressure to bring more generic skills into the curriculum and make courses more relevant to the 'world of work'. The recommendations made for higher education in the Dearing report, that disciplines should be contextualized, that students should become familiar with work and encouraged to reflect on that experience and that they should develop key generic and subject specific skills, is a continuation of what has now become a well established theme.[32]

The seeds of change in undergraduate legal education were sown in the 1930s when the American Realists challenged the implicit assumption that the education of lawyers could rest exclusively on the study of decisions in appellate cases. In the United States of America this insight was rapidly linked to the proposition that a fundamental principle of professional training 'is to project the student into situations that resemble as closely as possible the circumstances of their future career'.[33] Clinical education, students working on real cases, was a necessary development in the American system because there was little in the way of formal apprenticeship.[34] Despite the differences between the two systems, English academics also became more conscious of the composite skills of lawyering, for example research, analysis, and rule handling, and of the need to teach them in the context of university legal education. The English clinical movement began to develop in the same period. Like the clinics of law schools in the United States of America, the English movement experimented with live casework based at Citizens' Advice Bureaux (South Bank), legal problems collected from advice bureaux and practitioner contacts (Warwick) and campus based clinics (Kent).[35] Despite the fact that these programmes filled a gap left by vocational education at that time, the rationale for clinic in the United Kingdom was not so much as preparation for practice than the provision of understanding of the legal system and the role of lawyers within it.[36] For the purposes of assessment, however, increasing attention was paid to the skills and competence of students.

In both the United States of America and the United Kingdom the cost of supervision drove most clinical programmes to develop supplements to live casework such as simulations, placements or projects.[37] In the United

32 *Higher Education in the Learning Society: Report of the National Committee* (1997) ch. 9.

33 H.D. Lasswell and M.S. McDougal, 'Legal Education and Public Policy: Professional Training in the Public Interest' (1943) 52 *Yale Law J.* 263, at 290.

34 For an account of the development of clinical legal education in the United States of America, see R. Stevens, *Law School: Legal Education in America from the 1850s to the 1980s* (1983) 214 et seq.

35 M. Jeeves and A. Boon, 'The Common Law in Action Simulation: Reversing the Burden of Proof in Skills Education?' (1990) 24 *Law Teacher* 82; A. Sherr, 'Clinical Legal Education at Warwick and the Skills Movement: Was Clinic a Creature of its Time?' in *Frontiers of Legal Scholarship*, ed. G.P. Wilson (1995) at 116.

36 D.F. Cavers 'Skills and Understanding' (1949) 1 *J. of Legal Education* 395 and Sherr, op. cit., n. 8.

37 Sherr, id.

States this shift was also a result of a desire to neutralize the political efficacy of some of the programmes in favour of academic respectability: 'the siren call of efficiency, neutrality and scientific respectability'.[38] The process of relocating the clinical practicum in the classroom was greatly assisted by the increasing availability of analytical texts for a skills curriculum.[39] Programmes from jurisdictions which had implemented skills programmes at the vocational stage were also very influential, particularly the Professional Legal Training programme in British Columbia.[40] Such programmes were based on theories of interpersonal interaction drawn from the social sciences and an approach to course design, pedagogy, and assessment which was exceptionally well organized. Although the groundwork in terms of experimentation and advocacy was laid by the English clinical movement, that movement was largely displaced by these models of superior technical rationality. On one view the arrival of systematic skills training merely completed the process of isolating skills relevant to the legal curriculum, treating them more directly and supplementing them with more vocationally relevant skills.[41] Nevertheless, the adoption of this methodology at the vocational stage was a critically important juncture in the development of the English skills movement which struggled, thereafter, to accomodate the colonization of the field by the profession. Before, the BVC and LPC clinic offered a way of filling very obvious gaps in professional preparation. The gaps which remained were now less obvious and more contentious.

The problem of ambiguity was exacerbated by the fact that the profession had never attempted to exercise any control over the delivery, as opposed to the content, of undergraduate legal education. It prescribed the curriculum for 'qualifying degrees', the holders of which could progress to the vocational stage. Otherwise jurisdiction over the undergraduate programme was hotly contested with academic law schools in an atmosphere of mutual suspicion. When it announced a new core curriculum for the undergraduate stage, the profession could only state that its objective in doing so was that all those qualifying as lawyers should be able to demonstrate, among other things, an appreciation of the social and other pressures which shape the law, the intellectual and practical skills needed to research and analyse the law and present results orally and in writing, and the ability to reflect on the fundamental social concepts such as justice, liberty, and rights.[42] Nothing in the prescribed curriculum related to the

38 J.P. Tomain and M.E. Solomine, 'Skills Skepticism in the Postclinic World' (1990) 40 *J. of Legal Education* 307, at 315.

39 Sherr, op. cit., n. 8, at p. 117.

40 P.A. Jones 'A Skills-Based Approach to Professional Legal Education – An Exemplary Case' (1989) 22 *Law Teacher* 171.

41 Sherr, op. cit., n. 8, p. 117.

42 'Announcement on Qualifying Law Degrees' issued jointly by the Law Society and the Council of Legal Education, January 1995, at 6 and 5, objectives iii, iv, and v.

achievement of these objectives, which was, and is, largely a matter for individual law schools. This produced anomalies. The Law Society introduced its 1993 changes with a number of recommendations regarding skills in the undergraduate stage. The Law Society resolved to: 'encourage law schools to improve their students' oral and written powers of communication and their skills of initiative, leadership and teamwork, particularly where this can be done in a legal context', develop their students' understanding of the practical application of law and 'ensure that their students proceed to the Final Course with . . . adequate abilities in the skills of legal research and problem solving.'[43]

The LPC standards were preceded by a statement that students were expected to have developed certain foundation skills at the undergraduate stage. These did not figure in the statement of objectives. Surprisingly, many law schools did make a commitment to developing skills. Harris and Jones's 1996 survey of law schools found wide agreement that library research, legal reasoning, and case analysis were necessary components of the undergraduate curriculum. Of seventy-six responding law schools, thirty out of thirty-eight new university law schools also had drafting, interviewing, advocacy, and negotiation as part of their undergraduate degrees, compared with thirteen out of thirty-eight in old university law schools.[44]

A 1994 survey agreed that the incorporation of skills in the curriculum was widespread.[45] Substantial numbers of both new and old universities incorporated skills in their degree course although 'vocational' legal skills such as interviewing and negotiation were more common in the new universities. Substantial numbers of both new and old universities, however, claimed the express incorporation of research, advocacy, and communication in the undergraduate law curriculum.[46] Eight institutions, approximately 10 per cent, ran live-client clinics. These concentrated mainly on areas of welfare law. The authors of the 1994 survey were encouraged by these results suggesting that in all law courses 'the skills component may well be significant' and 'are seen by educators as more than training and properly part of the academic curriculum'.[47] It is not at all clear that this enthusiasm was justified. Respondents probably had difficulty in interpreting the questionnaire. In particular it was not possible to determine the relative volume or assessment weighting given to skills.

It is likely that there is, in fact, widely disparate provision of a skills perspective in law schools. The professional bodies accommodate this fact by recognizing the healthy contribution which diversity makes to the

43 Law Society, op. cit., n. 11, para 4.1 and para. 5.1.

44 Harris and Jones, op. cit., n. 9, at pp. 49-50.

45 R. Grimes et al., 'Legal Skills and Clinical Legal Education: A Survey of Undergraduate Law School Practice' (1996) 30 *The Law Teacher* 44.

46 id., at p. 50.

47 Grimes, op. cit., n. 45, at p. 66.

development of legal education. In fact, any attempt to adopt a more prescriptive approach would undermine the investment the profession has made in the partnership model in recent years. The partnership model posits that the development of professional skills is undertaken as a partnership between practitioners and academics in a spirit of mutual respect and support; academics offering the theoretical framework and practitioners the introduction to skills.[48] Despite the improving relationship between the profession and the academy, I will argue that this division of responsibility cannot be effective in delivering an appropriate and responsive legal education. Two consequences of its operation will illustrate a wider range of problems. In introducing the LPC, the Law Society had to embrace skills which, logically, could have been dealt with at the academic stage. An example is client interviewing and advising. Because not all law schools participated in the National Client Interviewing Competition it was felt that the LPC must '. . . introduce students to basic information about the interaction between lawyers and client and lawyer and lawyer in such situations as interviewing'.[49] Similarly, the uneven pattern of undergraduate provision meant that the Law Society could have no realistic expectation of the skills graduates would bring to the vocational stage. It could only resolve to 'encourage those law schools which seek to develop students' understanding of the practical application of law'.[50]

Although the professional bodies appear to recognize some of the unintended consequences of their remodelling the vocational stage, they also recognize that the profession needs support from the academy in order to make further progress. There are significant structural barriers. Nathanson, for example, suggests that the isolation of skills in vocational programmes deprives these courses of a theoretical foundation.[51] He therefore calls for the legitimization of a new category of academic, with a 'research-like stance' in relation to the design of instructional materials, possessing equal status with researchers. Nathanson's argument, that the enthusiasm and commitment which students feel for real-life clients can be stimulated where learning activities are 'thoughtfully, creatively and meticulously designed' is contentious.[52] However, even the relatively small steps necessary to achieve a more thorough integration of theory and practice would require considerable collaboration between academic and vocational course teachers and, probably, support from the profession. There are, I suggest, more

48 This is similar to the technocratic model described by Jones (P. Jones, 'We're all Reflective Practitioners Now: Reflections on Professional Education' in *Teaching Lawyers' Skills*, eds. J. Webb and C. Maughan (1996) 291.

49 Law Society, op. cit., n. 11, at paras. 4.1 and 4.2.

50 id., at para. 4.1.

51 S. Nathanson, 'The culture of design' (1996) 3 *International J. of Legal Education* 301, at 308.

52 id.

fundamental problems than the design of materials which we need to address.

A CRITIQUE OF THE MODEL

This critique addresses some of the issues arising in three areas: the rationale for including legal skills in the education of lawyers, the skills selected, and the methodologies employed to develop skills.

1. *Rationale*

The fact that the new vocational curriculum emerged from conflict meant that a number of compromises were struck. Underlying the 1990 changes was a desire to improve professional competence based on the growing numbers of complaints against solicitors, the increased competition from other professions and 'paralegal' staff and recognition that '. . . [the profession is] moving away from traditional general practice into a greater diversity of work'.[53] At the time the training committee was awaiting two pieces of research, commissioned by the Law Society, which it anticipated would inform its decisions.[54] Although it did not wish to prejudge the conclusion of these reports it suggested a 'classification of skills and knowledge used by solicitors' as follows:-

(a) intellectual skills and knowledge (the role of the law degree);
(b) interpersonal skills;
(c) technical legal knowledge and skills.[55]

In the event the research reports did not provide much assistance to the designers of the LPC. Instead, the tried and tested Commonwealth blueprint was imported and supplemented by the standards methodology developed by the Department of Employment.[56] The breadth and integration implied by the wide statements of skills was therefore lost and the skills curriculum became a selection of the exemplars. Worse, the LPC retained a vast amount of examinable substantive law, and marginalized 'transactions' as a vehicle for integrating the application of skills and knowledge. Even so, providers of the course, and students, complained of over-assessment. In 1996 the Law Society announced a substantial increase in a core substantive subject, business law and practice, added accounts as a 'pervasive area', and removed negotiation from the list of prescribed skills.[57]

53 Law Society, op. cit., n. 11, at para. 13 and 2.3(a).
54 A. Sherr, *Solicitors and their Skills* (1991); K. Economides and G. Smallcombe, *Preparatory Skills Training for Trainee Solicitors* (1991).
55 Law Society, op. cit., n. 11, at para. 3.2.
56 J. Macfarlane, 'Master Skills for Undergraduates' (1988) 13 *New Law J.* 534.
57 *Legal Practice Course Review Group Report* (October 1996) para. 3.6.

The changes were said to be based on a number of research reports which showed that negotiation was the least important skill for trainees and that there was a need to emphasize practical legal research and drafting. In fact they were precipitated by large corporate commercial firms and reflected increasing degrees of specialization and increasing diversity in practice cultures.[58] Some firms imagined that they had a 'house style' on skills issues and were more concerned about substantive material related to commercial law. Large firms also had considerable leverage because, by 1992, they employed 70 per cent of trainees.[59] Many had also appointed full-time directors of education and training, had gained experience of running in-house PSC and CPD programmes and were confident that they could provide customized LPCs.[60] Although the increase in business law and practice may have brought about a short-term respite, it signalled a reversal of the policy of incrementally expanding skills. This interlude supports my thesis: that historic forces still shape legal education and this renders any rational foundation vulnerable to powerful interests.

2. *Content*

The selection of skills for the vocational stage responded to different concerns. Interviewing and advising addressed the problem of complaints about client communication.[61] The inclusion of practical legal research, despite the fact that research is a central skill for the undergraduate stage, reflected concern expressed by law firms regarding the skills of trainees. The inclusion of advocacy was a practical manifestation of the desire to penetrate the *de facto* monopoly of the market by barristers. Even accepting these diverse motives as valid, there are areas of activity with equal or more pressing claims to inclusion. An obvious example is Alternative Dispute Resolution (ADR). The removal of negotiation from the assessment requirements of the vocational stage suggests the further marginalization of consensual dispute resolution in favour of adversarial dispute resolution, as represented by advocacy. This is surprising given that negotiation is apparently more central to most solicitors' work than advocacy. It also cuts

58 See: 'Teething Troubles' *The Lawyer*, 7 May 1996; 'LPC Review: LPC's End-of-Term Assessment' *The Lawyer*, 21 January 1997; 'Testing Times for the LPC' *The Lawyer*, 20 May 1997; G. Chambers and S. Harwood, *Solicitors in England and Wales: Practice Organisation and Perceptions, First Report* (1990).

59 Sherr, op. cit., n. 8.

60 E.H. Greenebaum, 'Development of Law Firm Training Programs: Coping With a Turbulent Environment' (1996) 3 *International J. of the Legal Profession* 315; 'Tailor-Made for Controversy' *The Lawyer*, 20 May 1997.

61 '. . . the great majority of complaints against solicitors and claims on the indemnity fund relate not to inadequate legal knowledge but to failings in the ability to communicate clearly with clients and to organise solicitors' practices efficiently'(Law Society, op. cit., n. 11, at para. 2.3(a)).

across the grain of proposed reform of the profession's jurisdiction, as manifest in Lord Woolf's proposals for civil justice. Although there may well be a need for lawyers to colonize ADR the assumption that their passage will be easy is not justified.[62] There are already signs that parties may opt for the knowledge and skills of disciplines other than law in arbitration, and, as the National Consumer Council has observed, a 'mediator without legal knowledge is definitely preferable to a lawyer who is deficient in mediation skills'.[63] The need to modify the adversarial traits of lawyers, and to accommodate a vision of lawyers as 'healers of human conflict', is no small project.[64] Legal education is the place to begin.

3. *Methodology*

Although methods for delivering skills are extremely diverse, the skills curriculum often represents a continuum. At the poles we find 'atomistic' and 'holistic' approaches.[65] We now have a curriculum at the professional stage built around instruction and performance. Of the available pedagogic choices the missing element is enquiry. This is an omission which the vocational stage is ill-equipped to remedy. The obvious pressures towards atomistic approaches at the vocational stage are the need for accreditation of competent performance combined with time pressures.[66] Less obviously, atomism is a superficial response to the demand for rigour and reflects a fondness for positivist and authoritarian traditions. The essence of atomism is the breaking down of 'tasks' into 'behaviours' which can be presented as standardized outcomes. Even in more enlightened programmes, the curriculum is dominated by a cycle of demonstration and rehearsal whereby performance and assessment is monitored against checklists.[67]

There is no agreed definition of holism. It has been associated with learning theory, with broad rather than narrow framing of goals and, less flatteringly, with unclear teaching and learning objectives.[68] Nor is there a clear example of the operation of a holistic agenda, although some structures, such as the integrated degree offered at Northumbria University,

62 C. Ervine, *Settling Consumer Disputes: A Review of Alternative Dispute Resolution* (1993).

63 J. Flood and A. Caiger 'Lawyers and Arbitration: The Juridification of Construction Disputes' (1992) 56 *Modern Law Rev.* 412, at 414.

64 W. Burger, 'Isn't There a Better Way?' (1982) 68 *Am. Bar Association J.* 274.

65 A. Boon, 'Skills In The Initial Stage Of Higher Education: Theory And Practice For Transformations' in Webb and Maughan, op. cit., n. 48, p. 99.

66 Committee of Inquiry into Equal Opportunities on the Bar Vocational Course, *Equal Opportunities at the Inns of Court School of Law* (1994) 67; H. Brayne, 'LPC Skills Assessments: A Year's Experience' (1994) 28 *Law Teacher* 227.

67 D. Cruikshank, 'Where "Show" Works Better Than Tell' (1994) 28 *Law Teacher* 13.

68 J. Macfarlane, 'The Legal Skills Movement Ten Years On: Triumph or Compromise' (1997) 24 *J. of Law and Society* 440; K. Mackie, 'Lawyers' Skills: Educational Skills' in *Learning Lawyers' Skills*, eds. N. Gold et al. (1989) 840.

offer promising vehicles.[69] I see holism, not just in terms of methods of delivery, but in the context of aims and the educational rhetoric associated with the early skills movement, that is, with activity that demands of learners that they engage in a cycle based on active experimentation, concrete experience, reflective observation, and abstract conceptualization.[70] Holism draws on the literature of education, of socio-legal studies, and of ethics, and draws assessment evidence from clinic, work placements, simulations or performance through mechanisms as diverse as peer review, discussion, learning logs and projects.

The ten years since legal skills became a part of vocational legal education began and draws to a close with the publication of two significant books. In 1989, *Learning Lawyers' Skills* offered an expansive agenda for the development of the skills curriculum but the various contributions tended to reflect the atomistic approach.[71] In 1996, *Teaching Lawyers' Skills* reviewed developments during the period, and reflected some disquiet concerning the results. In her review of the latter book, Macfarlane suggests that the implicit agenda of the skills movement in 1980s, challenging assumptions about what is taught and how it is learned in law schools, is still on the agenda.[72]

The failure of the skills movement in the United Kingdom to harness coherent theories of lawyering was rooted in the need to establish educational justification for an alternative curriculum in the universities. In the climate of that time professional responsibility was perceived to be an irrelevance. The colonization of the area by the profession bridged the gap created by the increasing separation of professional preparation from practice but undermined the legitimacy of skills teaching at the undergraduate stage. The atomistic approach of the vocational courses further prejudiced the academy against the expansion of undergraduate skills. Clinicians were partly responsible for these results because we submerged values in favour of method. In emphasizing the value of 'learning by doing' we prioritized action over inquiry. In preparing students to act like lawyers we prioritized competence over reflection.[73] The problem was not in the intentions of the innovators but in the failure to develop the connections between theory, practice, and values.

I have suggested that the failure of the five-year articles created a moral

69 H. Brayne, 'Law Students As Practitioners: Developing An Undergraduate Clinical Programme At Northumbria University' in Webb and Maughan, op. cit., n. 48, at p. 167.

70 See D.A. Kolb, *Experiential Learning: Experience as the Source of Learning and Development* (1984) and discussion by C. Maughan, 'Learning How To Learn: The Skills Developer's Guide To Experiential Learning' and D. Tribe, 'How Students Learn', both in Webb and Maughan, id.

71 N. Gold, 'Learning Lawyers' Skills: Research, Development And Evaluation – The Future Prospectus' in Gold, op. cit., n. 68, p. 322.

72 Macfarlane, op. cit., n. 68.

73 Sherr, op. cit., n. 8.

as opposed to a cognitive gap in legal education.[74] The rationale for the introduction of the LPC also had an ethical foundation related, as it was, to a perceived discipline problem in the profession. The place of values remains a gap in the present model, particularly because undergraduate legal education is not value neutral.[75] It supports the values of objective enquiry and detached judgement and desensitizes students to value issues. Certain values, engagement in the client's cause, a commitment to service, or a commitment to developing the ethical orientation of the profession are all understated in legal socialization.[76] The often cited aim of legal education, adopted by traditionalists and radicals alike, is to encourage students to 'think like lawyers'. For both camps the emphasis must, perforce, reflect how lawyers do think rather than how they could think. It is perhaps not surprising that new members of the profession are unlikely to regard its collective honour as important.[77] Dominated by the pursuit of technical competence, we have done nothing to cause them to think otherwise.

Technical competence is only one dimension of professional responsibility. The inherent problem of atomism, and hence of the vocational stage, is that the importance of exploring values are denied. In *Learning Lawyers' Skills*, for example, Gold noted that the book reflected not only the desire of contributors to help lawyers to be more skilful and helpful but to 'seek to implement a variety of values inherent in the instructional choices *they* have made and the theory of action which *they* have adopted as the content of *their* skills subject' (my emphasis).[78] Skills training emphasized the instructor's choice of values and therefore gave students no basis for reflective choices about who they are becoming as lawyers or about what lawyers as individuals can or ought to contribute to their profession or to a just and stable society. In fact, atomistic approaches risk rendering the skills curriculum a series of empty technical exercises leading to the replication of existing professional failings.[79]

In order to be supported in deploying skills which support client decision

74 Burrage, op. cit., n. 3.

75 J. Weinstein, 'On the Teaching of Legal Ethics' (1972) 72 *Columbia Law Rev.* 452, and J.F. Sutton and J.S. Dzienkowski, *Cases and Materials on the Professional Responsibility of Lawyers* (1989) at 3.

76 C. Stanley, 'Training for the Hierarchy?: Reflections on the British Experience of Legal Education' (1988) 22 *Law Teacher* 78; A.S. Watson, 'The Quest for Professional Competence: Psychological Aspects of Legal Education (1968) 37 *University of Cincinatti Law Rev.* 91.

77 Burrage, op. cit., n. 3, at p. 72.

78 Gold, op. cit., n. 68.

79 R. J. Condlin, 'The Moral Failure of Clinical Legal Education' in *The Good Lawyer: Lawyers' Roles and Lawyers' Ethics*, ed. D. Luban (1983); R. J. Condlin, 'Clinical Education in the Seventies: An Appraisal of the Decade' (1983) 33 *J. of Legal Education* 604; and J.S. Stark et al., 'The Effect of Student Values on Lawyering Performance: An Empirical Response to Professor Condlin' (1987) 37 *J. of Legal Education* 409.

making, students need a broader rationale than they have at present. Otherwise, there is a substantial risk that skills training will encourage lawyers 'to think cynically of their craft, to regard it as the mastery of the arts of interpersonal manipulations'.[80] The integration of skills and knowledge should assist practitioners in achieving the good of legal professions; achieving justice. The development of virtues consistent with this social good must be a central goal of legal education. They form a foundation for achieving the 'internal goods' intrinsic to a 'practice' which can only be achieved if a person engages with the practice with justice, courage, and honesty.[81] Otherwise practices become merely a way of achieving external goods, such as financial rewards. Skills teaching at the vocational stage ignores or obscures underlying values and focuses on professional conduct issues in order to support a conduct regime which is increasingly regulatory.[82] An alternative is to recognize the sheer diversity of practice, and the irrelevance of deontology to anything but the most basic practice issues. In order to sustain the intrinsic goods of practices, students should be encouraged to subject ethical norms to critical scrutiny and to argue the merits of, for example, prioritizing practice norms or regulatory structures. It will be important to engage their feelings and to have them explore their values. They will be better able to make 'self determined, responsible, self reflective and critical judgements about themselves and their work' if, going in, they have some understanding of how ethics are undermined by stress, competition, authority, and peer and time pressures.[83]

The change to a more performance orientated curriculum presents increased opportunities for the realization, through performance and reflection, of legal study as a truly liberal art.[84] It has been suggested, and seems obvious, that no single methodology can achieve this alone.[85] Learning skills cannot be a meaningful professional exercise devoid of any context but a technical one. The ability to reflect critically on one's self and one's professional role must be a starting point for this. The capacity for reflection is important, and not merely in the sense of developing competence. The provision of humane services to clients can only flow from a humane

80 P.D. Carrington, 'Civil Procedure and Alternative Dispute Resolution' (1981) 34 *J. of Legal Education* 298. See, also, P. Brest, 'The Responsibility of Law Schools: Educating Lawyers as Counsellors and Problem Solvers' (1995) 58 *Law and Contemporary Problems* 6.

81 A. Macintyre, *After Virtue: A Study in Moral Theory* (1981) 187.

82 Tomain and Solomine, op. cit., n. 38, at p. 315.

83 S.G. Kupfer 'Authentic Legal Practices' (1996) 10 *Georgetown J. of Legal Ethics* 33. See, further, D.L. Rhode 'Ethics by the Pervasive Method' (1992) 42 *J. of Legal Education* 31; J. Mixon and R.P. Schuwerk 'The Personal Dimension of Professional Responsibility' (1995) *Law and Contemporary Problems* 87, at 89.

84 I am happy to adopt Llewelyn's broad conception of law as a liberal art, that is, a study embracing three aims: i) technical proficiency; ii) appreciation of the wider social significance of the art; and iii) the drive or quest for the art as both beauty and service (K.N. Llewelyn, *Jurisprudence: Realism in Theory and Practice* (1962) at 380).

85 Rhode, op. cit., n. 83.

education, one which has promoted at least a little self-knowledge. Holism offers a way forward because it can use atomistic approaches in the appropriate place and at the appropriate time. Building a holistic model is, however, a more complex exercise than anything we have attempted so far. We have some promising components. Live clinic, involving legal work for which there is very little extrinsic reward, can convey to students a sense of the ethic of service which is intrinsic to professionalism. Simulation can present problems of complexity, involving issues which may not be encountered in the early years of practice. Higher education is now more sympathetic to novel assessment methods. Finally, we are now developing texts which can support a holist curriculum.[86] But more is needed. The goods of any practice can only be achieved through interaction, what Macintyre suggests requires 'subordinating ourselves within the practice in our relationship to other practitioners'. This relationship is not necessarily deontological but it certainly has foundations in ethics. This is a fact recognized by those seeking a postmodern ethic, who acknowledge that a focus on practical work must be a significant part of their curriculum.[87]

CONCLUSION

It has been said that legal education lacks clarity and focus, that the curriculum tends to reflect the concerns of the time, or more accurately, the problems of yesterday. Skills teaching established its support because of its possibilities: to develop connections between theory and practice, to develop a model of reflective practice or to build an awareness of the lawyer's responsibility for promoting justice.[88] History and politics have conspired to deprive students of the potential that skills offer a solid foundation for legal practice or lifelong learning. What legal education provides is an often incomplete and idiosyncratic foundation for the next stage.[89] Without some intervention the prospects of a more integrated or rational system are remote. This means that a common preparation in skills will remain isolated at the vocational stage.[90] The lack of solid theoretical foundations for skills teaching and the university preoccupation with research, rather than teaching, provides little incentive to change.[91] Academic and vocational course teachers will remain aloof thus proving, if proof is needed, that their concepts of education and research are incompatible. The vital areas between

86 C. Maughan and J. Webb, *Lawyering Skills and the Legal Process* (1995).

87 Kupfer, op. cit., n. 83.

88 Tomain and Solomine, op. cit. , n. 38.

89 id.

90 id., at p. 55; Nathanson, op. cit., n. 51, at p. 313, and Macfarlane, 'Look Before You Leap: Knowledge and Learning in Legal Skills Education' (1993) 20 *J. of Law and Society* 293, at 295 on the American experience.

91 Nathanson, id., at p. 303.

theory, substantive law, and practice will continue to be relatively unexplored.

The profession will continue to be under pressure to further modify its curriculum in favour of sterile substantive 'knowledge'. The emerging division, endorsed by Marre, generic skills, research, and communication at the academic stage, and their application to legal tasks, drafting, and advocacy at the vocational stage, will become more entrenched. This is a defensible strategy, if only because a coherent programme of skills at the undergraduate stage is currently lacking.[92] The underlying purpose, the survival of the academic and professional empires, undermines the potential of legal education to achieve worthwhile objectives. In particular, it leaves no place to enact the rhetoric of 'learning to learn' or 'reflective practice' in relation to some of the key activities of lawyers. The possible intervention of the Lord Chancellor's Advisory Committee on Education and Conduct must be viewed with ambivalence. Although the committee has signalled the importance it places on both skills and ethics in the legal curriculum it has not addressed either the detail or the problem of enacting broad aims. It has proposed 'a more rigorous basic education in common professional values, possibly delivered through a new master's programme in common professional studies' thus, apparently, accepting the constraints of the present structure and the inefficiency of the relationship between its constituent parts.[93] More promisingly, it has several ideas for harnessing the potential of CPD, including through making ethics components compulsory.[94] If, however, the gaps identified in this paper are real gaps, they can only be filled by a holistic approach, in relation to structure, content, and methodology. The vision remains elusive and, as suggested at the outset, could only be realized by an unprecedented level of co-operation between the academy and the profession. The lesson of history is that this will not occur.

92 See A.G. Amsterdam, 'Clinical Legal Education – A 21st Century Perspective' (1984) 34 *J. of Legal Education* 612, suggesting that, for example, critical analysis, planning, and decision-making are essential foundations for practical skills and for doctrinal analysis.

93 Lord Chancellor's Advisory Committee on Legal Education and Conduct (ACLEC), *First Report on Legal Education and Training* (1996) para. 1.1.

94 ACLEC, *Continuing Professional Development for Solicitors and Barristers: A Second Report on Legal Education and Training* (1997) para. 2.33 and see proposals for a small ethics component in barrister CPD in General Council of the Bar, *The New Practitioners' Programme: Information Pack* (1997).